I0613168

Samuel Wood

The plain path to good gardening

or, How to grow vegetables, fruits, & flowers successfully

Samuel Wood

The plain path to good gardening
or, How to grow vegetables, fruits, & flowers successfully

ISBN/EAN: 9783337374266

Printed in Europe, USA, Canada, Australia, Japan

Cover: Foto ©Lupo / pixelio.de

More available books at **www.hansebooks.com**

THE PLAIN PATH

TO

GOOD GARDENING;

OR,

HOW TO GROW VEGETABLES, FRUITS, & FLOWERS

SUCCESSFULLY.

BY SAMUEL WOOD,

(LATE GARDENER TO SIR B. P. WREY, BART.,)

AUTHOR OF "GARDENING FOR THE COTTAGE."

LONDON :

G. T. GOODWIN, 8, PATERNOSTER ROW.

LONDON:
PRINTED BY J. AND W. RIDER,
BARTHOLOMEW CLOSE.

PREFACE.

THE favourable reception of my work, "Gardening for the Cottage," both by the press and the general public, as well as the want of a sufficiently comprehensive book on gardening that will meet every necessity, has induced me to undertake the present work.

My former book was commended for its plain and pointed remarks, a principle I have sought to maintain even more fully, and far more comprehensively, in the present work, in which, I flatter myself, will be found all that constitutes "Good Gardening"—the easiest, surest, and best method of attaining entire success,—knowledge acquired as the result of thirty years' experience, under every variety of circumstances, and not always in the same climate.

I may further add that I believe I have given valuable information, never before published, in reference to digging, sowing, and testing seeds ; the use of camphor, sulphur, sweet nitre, soot, and guano ; the construction of the Dutch and Italian gardens, the wilderness, &c. ;—thus, by an extended range of subjects, combined with a thorough practical treatment of them, I indulge the hope that my work will fully realize what I have sought to make it, and all that is desired by its readers.

I trust there will also be found in this volume all that is calculated to promote pleasure in the charming art of Gardening, all that is useful to the Florist, the Market and the Landscape Gardener, the Cottager, the Competitor for Prizes, and the Lady who wishes to be "her own Gardener."

S. W.

April, 1871.

CONTENTS.

DIAGRAMS.

THE PLAIN PATH

TO

GOOD GARDENING.

THE KITCHEN-GARDEN.—Its Management.

THE quality as well as the quantity of vegetables to be had from a given space devoted to this purpose depends principally upon the management of the land. It is true there are some soils that will not produce like others, still the management is everything, unless in a very unfavourable locality. If the soil is light and poor, dressings with mud, tender loam, and some sandy clay, added to rotten dung, will materially improve it: if of a stiff and livery loam, on a cold clayey subsoil, add good heavy dressings of leaf-mould, fibrous peat, cinder-ash, and chalk; and dig deep, and trench up whilst unoccupied. For particular crops, such as carrots, early potatoes, and peas, the land should be specially prepared by additional and suitable dressing; but in my opinion the digging in of weeds and refuse vegetable matter, such as is left on the ground from the preceding crop is an error, inasmuch as by so doing a host of enemies in embryo are deposited beneath the surface, to rise like an army at some future time; for where do the parents of the wire-worm and the numerous other enemies of the gardener deposit their eggs but on the crops? and from thence they

B

proceed to hybernate in the ground as soon as convenient, unless they happen to be favoured by the gardener turning them into the soil with the refuse of the crop. I would recommend that the land be carefully cleared of all weeds and the refuse of the last crop, and be well dressed with *quicklime;* the ground either ridged or rough dug, and left till wanted for another crop ; then it should be manured, if necessary, with manure suited to the purpose, turned again, and the crop put in.

Where kitchen-gardens are small, as is generally the case with villas and cottages, some additional tact is necessary on the part of the gardener. This department is generally committed to a jobbing man, who may be a very indifferent hand, or if a good hand, is so badly paid that justice cannot be done. It must be a very small plot of land indeed for any man to do justice either to himself or the garden within the limits of a day or a week, and yet the proprietor cannot see that it will pay him to give more time and money to the garden. This is the chief reason why it does not pay, for the day's wages are too low, if the man is a good gardener, to admit of his doing by the land as he would, from the fact that he must attend six or seven such places within the week to make anything like a living.

A jobbing gardener, above all men, should be a good gardener, and such a man should have the liberty to attend to his gardens whenever necessary, and not be limited to a certain day ; and a clear understanding should be agreed upon as to the requirements of the employer, or it should be made plain as to what is desirable and expected, and thus the gardener will be able to comply with the requirements conditionally.

A plot of land containing one quarter of an acre altogether is large enough for the most dexterous man living to do justice to for three shillings per week. There is much difference in gardening; still there is one, and only one rule for good gardening, viz., "perfection of everything." This, however, can only be understood by observation, and I venture to say that this alone will prove satisfactory, and enlist its admirers, while a want of this perfection will result in disappointment.   Therefore two things above all others are the essentials for a good garden, viz., a proficient hand and liberal means.   There is one error commonly committed in regard to *villa gardens*, viz., a wish to grow a "little of everything," which generally means not growing anything well.   *This* is not the way to perfection, as more room is required than can be well afforded for "everything."   Perfection in gardening can only be obtained by a proportionate variety of well-assorted articles to match the scale of the place.   For instance, if there are but twenty square rods of kitchen-garden, it is folly to attempt to supply a small villa family with every variety of herb and vegetable from such a garden; and it would be a better economy of time and expense to limit these small spaces to a few of the earliest and best sorts, as they are of more value, and hard to be obtained; such as a good portion of the very best early potatoes, celery, lettuce, a good bed of herbs, a few early cabbages, and a few early turnips.   The potatoes are the principal, and will afford an opportunity of a successional crop of early winter stuff, such as Brussels sprouts, coleworts for Christmas, and Savoy or kale, early and good.   Nothing but the choicest sorts should be cultivated on these small plots, and these should be first-class, as they are no more trouble, and a very little more expense, than growing indifferent and bad sorts.   Often the land is good, but the crop is not of the best possible quality, nor is it put in early enough.   Just so in reference to the flower-garden.   There is no plausible excuse for deficiency, whether there is glass or no glass; since there is an abundance of things to suit means and tastes. Where there is no glass to preserve tender bedding plants, annuals and perennials can be substituted with equal satisfaction and less trouble and expense. Among annuals there are the *Aster, Ten-week Stock, Nemophila, Larkspur, Schizanthus,* &c.; but lists of these, as well as the perennials adapted for all localities, will be found in another part of this book.

DIGGING.—How to do it.

I FEEL under a necessity to say a little under this head, as I have never seen my particular way of digging published, and I have seen it very little practised. By simply using the heel instead of the toe, or the middle of the foot, when driving the spade into the soil, it will accomplish the work much easier, saving the strain on the foot, and saving the shoes also. And if a man has a tip on the heel of his shoe, so much the better. And every time he lifts the spade to take a fresh spit he should raise himself upright, and hold the spade by the left hand, so as to give it force, striking the ground nearly vertically, having a good open trench. The hardest ground will freely give way with one drive of the heel of the foot. Thin spits should be taken at a time; and once a man gets used to this way of digging, he will become expert, and feel the benefit of it every way; for the heel, be it remembered, has to bear more weight than any part of the human frame, and is in a direct line with the leg, which gives it due strength. I was trained to this way of digging, and have never used any other way since. My old master was a most extraordinary man at digging. Let every master teach this way of digging to his pupils; for it is more economical of time, and less tiring.

Ground should be dug evenly, and full-spade deep,—not six or seven inches deep, as ground is dug in Devonshire;

but it should be dug ten or twelve inches deep every time it has to be cropped. The spade, each time it is used, should be thoroughly cleaned, and wiped perfectly dry with some old hay or an old dry cloth, and hung up ; for it is quite as necessary to keep the spade, as it is a scythe, in good working order.

HOEING.—When and how to do it.

I shall speak of this in reference to earthing up crops under " The Potato ;"—general hoeing should be done carefully and constantly, but never in wet weather, for then few weeds fail to seed ; nevertheless let hoeing be done in time,—

> " For one year's seeding
> Brings seven years' weeding."

Besides taking the nutriment out of the soil which the crop should have, every inch of weed is destructive of so much of its virtue, and in conjunction with the crop acts like two crops ; therefore ply the hoe freely as soon as weeds appear above ground, whether the land is cropped or not. Do not draw the hoe too deeply into the soil, for then some weeds only become partly buried with sufficient earth to nourish their growth and seeding, especially some of the grasses, chickweed, &c. In hoeing it is important to draw the hoe just under the roots of the weeds, and to hoe every inch of the surface, if the land is foul, but do not hoe six inches and leave three inches untouched, with simply some earth drawn over it, as this is easily and frequently done by mistake.

Cast-steel hoes are the best for light land and among crops. Use short, square, and long-necked hoes for earthing up, the half-moon short-necked for drilling, and for stiff and beaten, old-cropped land, a good, heavy, short-necked, steel-faced bean-hoe, as it is called by farmers. To handle a hoe well choose a straight and inflexible stick four feet long ;

and of a size a trifle larger than the ring of the hoe ; drive
the handle into the hoe, set it up on the end of the handle,
and draw the edge of the hoe by one corner on the wall,
or a door, making a mark; keep the handle in the same
place on the ground, and try the other corner of the hoe; if
this come exactly in the same mark the hoe is handled
correctly, if not, re-adjust it, otherwise it will not wear equally.
The hoe should be kept flat ; that is, the whole edge, and
not the corners only, of the hoe should be made to do the
work.

RAKING, AND HOW TO DO IT.

A COARSE rake may be made to do the work of two
degrees of coarseness of the teeth, by simply holding the
handle higher or lower ; by holding it moderately low, and
using the rake briskly; giving it sharp strokes, it will also
do the work of a fine tool.   Few persons can rake well ;
they use tools too fine.   In general, nail-teethed tools are
better than flat ones.

MARKET GARDENING.

THREE things are necessary for a market gardener, viz.,
good ability, *good land*, and a *broad scale ;* then, with these
advantages, if he have any regard for his reputation and his
customers, he should produce the best of everything.   As
a caution to purchasers, I would say, prefer to deal with such
a person rather than with every salesman ; but this perhaps
I need scarcely say, since there are so few who prefer
quantity to quality.   A man who thoroughly knows his
business wants no precaution or advice as to what are the
best sorts of vegetables to grow, or when to grow them ;
but there are too many embarking in this undertaking,
speedily founder for want of one or two, or all three of

these essentials to success. Now if a man is ever so clever, and has not good land and sufficient of it, he will fail in his object; whereas good ability, and room enough for its exercise, will materially alter the case. I have seen some miserable mistakes arising from these deficiencies. It requires a man of good tact, who knows how to sow and what to grow, to be successful as a professional market gardener. If a man have at least two or three acres of land, then, with good management, he may have a supply adequate to his demand.

There is nothing easier, or more profitable, than cropping land on a broad scale; those, therefore, who intend embarking in this line should select three or more acres of good friable land, not too low or very elevated, nor with a gravelly, or cold, stiff, clayey subsoil; for the first causes some disappointment in certain crops, such as cabbage, root crops, strawberries, &c. ; and the last-named will prove late, and very precarious during early spring for brocoli, lettuce, peas, and potatoes at all times; whilst anything and everything will flourish on a tender sandy loam for the subsoil. It is not of so much consequence as to *where* a market garden is as it is to know what the soil is. Distance from the market is but a mere trifle in comparison to the most suitable soil and situation. A very low situation is far worse than a very high one. An elevated garden may suffer from drought during summer, but a low one will suffer most during a time when vegetables of all sorts are more valuable. on account of time ; and this will generally happen during the early spring months. It often happens in a low locality, notwithstanding such a spot is sheltered, that after a hard frost during February and March, as soon as a thaw commences, and a little before a quarter of brocoli should be ready for use, the whole drop their heads; this arises from a vaporous atmosphere. See article, "Effects of Frost," &c.

A slight inclination to the south is most desirable for a garden, and good free drainage is also very important.

It is not necessary for a market gardener to grow everything, but it is to his advantage to do so; although, too often, few things are grown well, on account of the general pressure of such a business, and the frequent narrow and limited scale of land. It would be easier and far better to grow but few articles on a limited space, than divide the land among too many varieties. If a man have but one acre, let him grow a large proportion of things most in demand,—such as rhubarb, sea-kale, early potatoes, radishes, onions, peas, and cabbages; and it would be even better to confine himself to one or two only of these for such a small space of land. Early potatoes come off in due time for cabbage coleworts, which pay exceedingly well. A half-acre of the frame potatoes planted in December, ready for use in May and June, can be succeeded by something like 40,000 cabbage coleworts, to be ready for sale at £1 per 1,000, by the following December. Thus two valuable crops would be realized from the same half-acre or acre within the twelve months at a really good paying profit, and for which there is also a ready sale. A good proportion of early peas also pays, on account of the accommodation it affords for a successional crop of brocoli, celery, turnips, or cabbages. The drift of good market gardening is to manage the land so as to get two crops clear off within the year. Although good digging and change of crops will effect a great deal, still adequate manuring to meet the draw upon the land will be indispensable. Thus, the manure for potatoes will suffice for the coleworts or turnips as well. Peas will succeed late potatoes without manure, and be all the better for it; carrots succeed celery, and when celery succeeds early and medium peas, it is a rest for the land, and puts it in good order for onions, brocoli (Walcheren), or cauliflower, the following spring. The land may thus be kept constantly at work, and not be distressed. A market gardener should study well every subject, and cultivate none but those things that are good, and will answer his purpose to a nicety. There is no difficulty about this, except it be too many sorts in each class to select from. I have made some remarks in this work on this under each article. In cropping a market garden it is of considerable advantage, both in time and to the crop, to run the beds and rows of the respective kinds completely through the quarter or the whole width of the ground, for there is a dead loss of time when it is necessary too frequently to tack about to remove the line, or make other alterations.

THE CULTIVATION OF RHUBARB.

IT is true the sort has something to do with the size, but those who will follow the few simple instructions here given will find that the treatment more than the sort has to be considered. No matter what the kind of rhubarb is you grow, it must receive due regard as to soil and subsequent requirements, or your wonderful "giant rhubarb" will soon become a "dwarf." The age of the roots is not of so much consequence; old stools may be taken up, divided carefully with the spade, and re-planted; but first select a spot where no hedges nor shrubbery trees can intrude upon the land in which the plants are to grow. Let the ground be dug eighteen or twenty inches deep, and well dressed with strong rotten manure turned in. Plant good sound crowns, letting them in with the spade, during October and November, just covering the crown; lay two or three inches of long litter from the stable over the whole, to remain until spring. As soon as you observe the crowns to be breaking, take three ounces of soot and six ounces of guano, and fill a four-gallon waterpot with water, mixing in it the soot and guano. Stir it well for a few minutes ; then saturate the ground with the liquid twice or thrice during the growing season. Although this feeding applies more properly to established plants every season at this particular time, yet it will not overdo the plants during the first season, as there is nothing suits rhubarb so well as this mixture.

After the plants have been four or five seasons on the same spot, they should be taken up, divided, and re-planted. Two or three-year-old stools are excellent for forcing. Where they grow with warm dung and leaves they should be covered up, so as to exclude all light ; or the plants may be taken up and placed in the dark in the forcing-house, merely throwing some leaf-mould, sand, or old tan over the roots to prevent them from drying too fast. Keep the roots moist by frequent applications of tepid water. To get early rhubarb—say at Christmas—the roots must be set to work in October or beginning of November. There are no better sorts suited for forcing than Mitchell's Prince Albert, and the Giantic for late growth, although no other will be really required, as the Albert, by a weekly watering with the liquid manure, continues to produce abundantly throughout the season. I have grown stalks of this sort from eighteen to twenty-four inches long, and of equal size with what are called larger sorts, and of fine quality, crisp and juicy. Those that have not the means of purchasing forcing-pots can cover them with boxes, butter-tubs, chimney-pots, &c.

THE CULTIVATION OF ASPARAGUS.

SOME additional trouble and expense attend the construction of asparagus beds, but in the long run I believe this vegetable really pays better than any other, from the fact that when once the plantation is well made, it will last so many more years than anything else of the useful class, and with much less trouble and expense. One square rod of ground will take about 160 plants to plant it, at a cost of 2s. 6d., 3s. 9d. or so per 100; dung and sand (river or sea sand is best) at a cost of £1 will prepare a soil for the production of 700 to 1,000 heads per annum, worth 2s. 6d. per 100, or an average of say £1 a 1,000; and continue at this rate, if well attended to, for twenty years, an amount of success greater than that of any other vegetable. For the first and second seasons after planting, the beds may be sown with onion seed: the first season a full crop may be allowed on the beds; the second year half a crop, and the third and following seasons a thin crop of summer lettuce may be had off the beds, so that these summer crops actually pay the rent, and for the trouble the land incurs year by year; the asparagus is, therefore, really very valuable. The plants should be planted during the months of March and April, just as they are starting, in rows of three, fifteen inches asunder, and ten or twelve inches in the row; the two outside rows should have about eight inches clear from the row to the edge of the bed, and a pathway of eighteen inches on each side, for the convenience of coming at the bed to cut the young shoots, &c. Two or three-year-old plants are the best to use for these plantations. The land should be trenched eighteen inches deep, the whole width of the bed and pathways, or alleys, as they are termed; and well dressed, as stated, turning and mixing the dung and sand well with the soil. Let the bed lay for a week or two after it is so trenched. On a fine day put the line down the middle of the bed, and with a narrow spade shovel a trench out by the line, preserving a straight edge next to the line. This trench should be the width of the spade, with an even, loose bottom, four inches deep. Place the plants on this bottom, spreading the roots and keeping the crowns as close to the line as convenient, drawing some fine earth with the hand to each plant, to fix it in its position. When the whole row is planted, fill the trench up with the earth that was taken out, shift the line fifteen inches nearer the side, and proceed as before. When the three rows are planted, rake the surface with a coarse garden rake, and sow the onion seed all over, as though there were no asparagus planted, and cut the sides of the bed neatly down by the line. The onion seed may be sown in drills of two between the rows of plants, *i. e.*, four drills in all. The roots of the plants should be trimmed before they are planted, in order to remove any bruised and fractured parts. After the second season manure-water may be given to the beds two or three times during the cutting season, commencing as soon as the first heads show themselves. This liquid manure may consist of two ounces of guano to one gallon of water. Salt is reckoned a fine manure for asparagus, at about three or four ounces per gallon of water; so are nitrate of soda and nitrate of potash (saltpetre), at the rate of four ounces to three gallons of water. The benefit is at once most evident, and the action very rapid, when thus applied in a pure liquid and consistent state to the receiving organs of the plant.

Earlier asparagus may be obtained by setting cold frames over the beds, and by planting beds within raised four-inch brickwork. Let the beds be well prepared, the brickwork raised two feet above the level, and the bed raised inside up to the top of the walls, and the plants planted thereon in two rows eight inches from the sides, ten inches from row to row, and eight inches from plant to plant, which will be twenty-six inches for the whole width of the bed. Add eight inches to this for the brickwork; thus a shallow frame thirty-four inches from back to front will be full wide enough set upon the brickwork. These frames should be seven inches deep in front, and eleven inches at the back;

the brickwork may be thickly pigeon-holed for the free access of heat by linings of hot dung and leaves. By this means forced asparagus may be produced at a trifling expense, while the plants may be saved year by year.

The greatest drawback to forcing asparagus is the expense and also the sacrifice of the roots ; but by this method early asparagus may be grown and the plants preserved. The frames must be covered all along till the young stuff shows above ground ; then admit light to give colour, water with tepid manure-water. After two or three cuttings from each crown let the heat die off; give air, and ultimately take the frames off, and let the bed have the same chance as the other beds. Do not, however, cut from these forced beds after the heat has ceased, but feed them once or twice during the early summer with weak liquid manure. Sow the seed in drills one foot or fifteen inches asunder, about as thick as marrow peas are sown for plants. Five or six years old plants are about the age for taking up to place in the forcing-pit, frame, or house. This should be done in December, January, February, and March, placing them over a tank, bed of tan, or some leaves and dung, first placing some two or three inches of earth, bedding the plants close together in some fine sandy soil, and covering the whole with three or four inches of fine light earth and water. The crowns should not be buried more than three or four inches deep. The bleached part is unsuitable for the table : obtain as much for colour as possible from the crown. 65° or 70° are enough for forcing. Apply some salt water to them once or twice ; two ounces to one gallon of water will give flavour and strength to the crowns.

THE CULTIVATION OF THE CABBAGE.

THE cabbage is one of those good common vegetables that may be said to be such an essential of a garden that one without cabbage some time during the season would be like a house without a door. The cabbage is as useful as it is accommodating at all seasons and circumstances ; for while there are sorts that require a field to develop them fully, there are others that suit a smaller space ; and these, too, happen to be of the best quality. I know well that the generality of gardeners aim at additional bulk in cabbage-growing. This is a matter of little importance when we consider that the best quality is of far greater importance and of still greater value than quantity in anything. Cabbage-growing has an interest in the minds of tens of thousands of all men, whether gardeners or not. I would advise no one to aim at great things without good quality, and by no means attempt to save seed without the greatest precaution in obviating the degeneracy or contamination of the new seed. Seeds should always be obtained from reliable seedsmen. Packets of all these small seeds can now-a-days be had through the Post Office from any distance. Do not get the seed of those who give long lists of non-descript sorts, but of old-established seedsmen, who enumerate the well-assorted descriptive few, warranted ; and select the sorts that will answer the particular purpose. If you want coarse, large cabbage for cattle, sow the Flat-poll, Drumhead, or Purple Drumhead in August of the preceding year you require them ; and plant them out in deep, good land in May, 2½ or 3 feet by 1 foot 6 inches asunder. If you wish large, late cabbages for domestic use, sow in the month of August, plant out in October ; and for this purpose use the Battersea, Paignton, and Enfield Market. The Paignton is a remarkably sweet and heavy cabbage,

though very late ; but I believe it will attain to an extraordinary weight on rich, heavy soil.   For very early
and good serviceable cabbages sow Barnes's Early, Incomparable, and   the   London   Market   in   July   and
August.   On the 20th of July sow either of these to plant
out the 20th of September.   These will stand and come in
by the end of April and beginning of May, especially
Barnes's Early.   This is a dwarf, but good-sized, reliable,
early variety.   The King of Cabbages is also a good
second early sort, and matches the London Market, and
will succeed the Barnes's.   For a still further succession,
sow the same or similar sorts on the 20th of August,
to plant out the end of October.   To succeed this last
sowing, plant out from the same sowing in March, and sow
some of the Sugar-loaf, Nonpareil, and Atkins's Matchless.
Either of these is an exceedingly good, handsome, and
sweet summer cabbage.   The Matchless is remarkably so,
and a piece of this true sort planted on some good land
presents an unusual appearance for cabbage of a dwarf
stature and a dark green colour, and all of one character
or growth.   This cabbage will allow of being planted
much closer together than most others.   Fifteen inches by
one foot apart will be ample room for them.   Its colour
makes it most desirable, and is one that is much wanting in
ordinary cabbages.   It is a very excellent sort for small
gardens, from its compact character, dwarf habit, good
quality, and colour, and answers most admirably for cabbage
coleworts.   This and the Rosette colewort, or any of the
small dwarf kinds, are highly recommended for this useful
purpose.   This is undoubtedly one of the most useful
branches of cabbage-growing.   Nothing pays better or is
more useful to all classes.

Sow either of the above from the 12th to the 20th of
June; the 10th or 12th in the northern counties, and the

20th to the 30th in the warmer counties of the south and
west.   As soon as they are fit to plant out, which will be
about the middle of August or a little before, prepare some
of the early potato or pea ground by adding a moderate
dressing of dung.   If the land is poor, fork it over, make
it moderately fine, and put the plants in rows one foot by
nine inches apart,—that will be about 350 per square rod,
and fetch about 10s.   What can pay better than this?   This
crop is on the land a short time only, and the coleworts are
fit for use from November till after Christmas; in other
words, they are all fit to clear off by the end of November;
that is, the whole time occupied by the crop is not more
than twelve or fourteen weeks; and these coleworts are far
better than savoy, kale, &c., and do not impoverish the
land half so much.

I have said a great deal about these coleworts or young
cabbages, from the fact that I know them to be most useful,
and seldom seen; they are the very things that our market
gardeners should grow largely for winter work; the seed
may be had of wholesale houses at a large discount.   A
constant succession of cabbages may be kept up all the year
round by means of these coleworts, and sowing Barnes's
Early 20th July, and the Enfield Market, King of Cabbages,
and the Paignton on the 20th of August; and the old Nonpareil, or Atkins's Matchless on the 20th of March.   The
July sowing comes in in April, the August sowings in June
and July, and the Paignton at the end of June to August;
and those from the March sowing will immediately succeed
the Paignton, and continue to give good cabbages during
the autumn; and so from these four sowings good cabbages
may always be had.   Three things are absolutely necessary
for growing good heavy cabbages, viz., a good sort, good
ground, and abundant moisture.   It is astonishing the
difference that good land and abundant moisture make in

cabbages. There are some localities that will not grow this vegetable fit to eat; these are high and dry, gravelly, or slaty places; the cabbage delights in a deep, friable loam, with a good drainage, well dressed with any strong manure, and a weekly watering with liquid manure from the time they are half grown until full grown (see article on "The Best Application of Manure "). This manure may consist of one ounce of guano to one gallon of water, or of any of the artificial manures or cesspool drainings.

A good charactered cabbage should possess a comparatively small stem, and be not above four or five inches clear on the leg, and will turn in (heart) freely of itself in due time without any tying. It should have the outer leaves neither too long nor pointed, but somewhat round and concave towards the tip; and these leaves should be symmetrical, neither spreading too far out from the heart nor closing too soon.

When you plant cabbages, plant them (if possible) as soon as they are full of tender fibre, and be careful to make the hole sufficiently deep to admit of the root going straight down, and close tight, driving the point of the dibber towards the bottom of the plant two or three times. Plant when the land is half dry, and in showery weather if convenient. If you wish to save either cabbage, brocoli, or kale seed, and there is anything of the class anywhere near likely to be in flower at the same time, cover the whole head of flower with coarse green gauze, to keep bees away. This must be done before a single bud opens.

THE BROCOLI in Pots.

Sow some seed of the Walcheren, and when large enough plant one in an eight-inch pot, or three in a twelve-inch pot. This should be done from a sowing in August,—or for heads during the winter, as early as in July. Let the pots be filled with rich dung and loam, and made pretty firm, using a moderate drainage ; fill the pots quite full ; plant the plants well, and water them ; encourage them as much as possible by setting the pots in the most sunny place you have. Keep the plants outside as long as you can, and give them weekly waterings with half an ounce of guano to one gallon of water, or some of the artificial manures recommended, but take the precaution not to use any of them too soon ; nor too strong, as it is best to err on the safe side,—" weak and often " is the rule.   As soon as cold frosty nights set in, remove the pots to your cold frame or house ; thus cauli-flower heads may be had during the cold winter months by all who have glass, even in London ; and by constantly feeding them with the above liquid manure, they will attain a size equal to those grown in the open ground, and at a time when their value will be an item worth some considera-tion.   Or they may be grown to their full size first, and then lifted from the open ground and potted.   But this is not so good as growing them in the pots from their infancy, as they receive a check which renders the application of liquid manure almost useless.

THE BROCOLI in the Open Ground.

A CONSTANT succession of brocoli may be had by sowing the Walcheren in March and April, to come in in June and July following ; and some of the Alma cauliflower in May, to come in in August and September.   Sow also some of Grange's autumn white brocoli in the middle of April to come in in the months of October and November ; the Walcheren in July to come in during the winter as described for pots, &c.   To succeed these some of the hardy sorts must be sown in March and April, viz., Penzance, which comes in in February, the Frogmore Protecting and Incom-parable, which come in in March and April, and the Dwarf

Russian, which comes in the last of all, in May and June ; and this brocoli should be cultivated by all gardeners, both amateur and professional, from the fact that the constitution of this variety will bear more severe weather than all others. So that those who grow a stock of this will be sure of brocoli, while those who depend entirely upon the less hardy may be disappointed. It is very small and close-growing, and therefore requires less room than most others. By sowing the Alma cauliflower about the 20th August, for plants to stand through the winter for planting out in the following March, it will immediately follow in use the Russian brocoli. Thus, by selecting two cauliflowers,—the Walcheren and Alma, and four, or even three brocolis, viz., the Penzance, Frogmore Protecting, or Incomparable, and the Russian brocoli and cauliflowers, a continued supply may be had every week throughout the year. Thus two sowings of the Walcheren, two of the Alma,—one in May and one in August, and one sowing of Grange's for late autumn, and one of the Penzance, Protecting, or Incomparable in March, will form a complete succession.

For the growth of good cauliflowers, rich and deep land, and one or two thoroughly good soakings with liquid manure, are essential conditions before they commence heading. Plant two feet by one foot six inches asunder. It is an excellent plan to sow the seed of choice sorts in pots, especially if your seed is more than a year old, for which it will be none the worse if it has been well kept. See the article on " How to Preserve Seed."

THE POTATO.—Its Cultivation.

SINCE 1845 a great deal has been said in reference to this universal favourite as to the causes and cure of the disease affecting this vegetable, more or less, ever since. Some say frost and wet are the chief causes ; this cannot be, for there was nothing new about the early wet or frost in that year, neither has there been before. Others say it is from atmospheric influences ; from other sources, such as the combination of acids, from artificial means, by the introduction of manures, &c. ; but I do not think any of these have hit upon exactly the right thing, for then certain steps might be taken to avoid the calamity. The actual cause of the disease is most difficult to discover, for there is little doubt that second causes have been and are still the origin of this scourge. If we were to have a severe frost at midsummer, so as to cut off all tender herbage, we should attribute the serious results to the sudden low temperature ; and so in the culture of the potato we have to study the conditions by which this malady may be partially obviated or decreased. Bad culture will promote this evil ; but some will say, how is it that in certain localities, and in parti-cular soils, this disease is less fatal than in others ? Let those who would obtain crops of good potatoes use proper means. There are such a vast number of sorts grown that it has become quite difficult to know how to choose, for each has some peculiar quality for its recommendation ; and then there are circumstances which very much alter cases. But what I now propose is to point out the good qualities, and warn my readers against growing bad qualities. The potato is well known to be of the genus *Solanum*, or night-shade. *Solanum tuberosum* is the origin of all potatoes. The *Solanums* are well known to be narcotic; that is, pos-sessing a property calculated to produce stupor, and if some of the varieties of *Solanum* were eaten they would prove fatal ; but we are not to argue, because possibly the origin of the whole class is a deadly poison, that all the varieties are also poisonous. Still it is a fact that the more inferior the potato, the more likely it is to possess more of the poisonous element. As I have said in my " Gardening for the Cottage,"* there are some sorts grown that are not fit for pigs, much less are they fit for bread-making, and for human food. No more expense, or trouble, or room, is required for growing the best than the worst sorts of potatoes ; but it is the same with the potato as it is with most things, that " the largest are the most inferior." The great, ugly, coarse Cornish Apple potato will grow larger, perhaps, than most others under the same circumstances, and the size is the only commendable quality belonging to it ; for if there is one potato partaking more of the poisonous property of the nightshade than another, it is this, —although it is true the flavour of the potato is greatly improved by cultivation ; but no method will produce an equally good quality of this and other inferior sorts to that of the Early Frame, Fluke, and Ash-leaved Kidneys. There are other good varieties, perhaps as good as these ; but for earliness and superior quality I have never met with any like the first-named, and the Fluke to succeed it. The growing of early sorts is the means of escaping the disease. The early and second early sorts are quite as good for keeping if kept in a cool, dry, and airy house. It is the very worst thing possible for keeping potatoes to clump them together in a cellar. The temperature of a cellar is equal to forcing the root, and so is clumping them ; and it is not at all a likely way to preserve the potatoes well or long. Let the potatoes be moderately dry, and then choose a shed, or cool airy room ; throwing as a protection against frost some clean straw over them, proportionate to the inclemency of the weather. By this means any of the early potatoes may be kept firm much later than they could be otherwise. I would recommend the True Early Frame for a first crop, whether for the frame or open ground ; and as many prefer kidneys for beauty, Myatt's

* Ridgway, London, 1s.

Prolific Ash-leaf Kidney are equal in earliness, though not so high-flavoured. The Fluke, and the old Red Lapstone, will secure a good name for any potato-grower, for sale or otherwise, and the quality of these sorts will command any amount of sale, at fifty per cent. higher price than most others. There is a large saving by growing these qualities; the cook will prefer such to any others, from the fact that there are no deep eyes to pick out. They will look well on the table, and whoever the grower may be, he will be praised. The Early Frame, Myatt's Prolific Ash-leaf, and the Fluke, find a ready sale for domestic purposes,—so also does the seed, so long as it can be warranted. Good seed can only be obtained by growing a few sorts, and changing the ground for the crop. The best market should be selected for laying in a stock of these seed potatoes. I used to get mine of seedsmen in Scotland who grew them expressly, and I suppose most of the retail seedsmen do the same. A really good potato of fine quality is neither too dry nor too white. Wheeler's Milky White is said to be good, and whiter than all others; I have always found that the straw-coloured are the best flavoured, although the Fluke is a shade lighter, and of a peculiar silky soft grain, with a most agreeable sweetness, not too dry nor too moist. The Frame is of a higher flavour, possessing a nutty richness, and in my experience not to be found in any other. It is also highly prized. I have said a great deal about these two or three potatoes, but I have no other motive for doing this than to recommend what is good, and nothing but good, for the real benefit of all parties; and I feel that I do no injustice by censuring what is good for nothing. I, for one, would like to see two-thirds at least of the list of potatoes struck out and abandoned; for good potato-cooking is one of the most uncertain things of culinary operation by those who have to purchase every two or three days or so, and this difficulty would be obviated by all market gardeners growing two or three sorts only.

Four things are necessary for the production of good crops of the best potatoes; viz., plant moderate, whole seeds (sets); plant early on fresh land, or that which is manured with leaf-mould, or some decomposed, light, mild manure; plant also on the highest ground you have; use no artificial manures, and take the tubers up as soon as the stems turn yellow.

Planting potatoes should be done with care; the land should be dressed all over with a good coat of the leaf-mould, fibrous peat, fresh loam, &c., before it is dug; and it is good policy to dig enough for a row, and then plant by a line. With a thick-ended hand-dibber dig and plant thus till the piece is planted; plant five or six inches deep, one foot six inches from row to row for the Fluke and the Lapstone, &c., by one foot in the row, and fifteen inches by eight or nine inches for the Ash-leaved Kidney and the Frame. The two last-named sorts are compact growers, and especially suited to small gardens, and for growing in pots, frames, &c.; for this reason I recommend them to all.

Potato-forcing is very simple. Make a bed of leaves in November two feet high; pack the bed well together while the leaves are wet, making it firm by treading, &c.; then set the frame on, and cover the whole surface of the bed inside the frame with six or seven inches of decomposed leaves, loam, or peat, moderately fine. Make this level, and plant whole sets, fifteen inches by eight asunder, of the size of a small hen's egg, previously taking a thin slice off the crown of the set, just so as to cut out the super-abundant eyes or buds; then chop in the holes, make the surface even with a rake, and sow some of Wood's Early Frame Radish. Over the bed chop, or heel in the seed, as the gardeners term it, with the rake, as this, when done

properly, is better than raking. After the seed is sown take
a nail-toothed rake, and slightly and regularly chop the
surface all over with the rake, but not too heavily, as it is
down far enough below the surface. (See " Sowing Seeds.")
When this is done the lights may be put on, admitting
air, and cover up during cold nights as soon as the seed is
up; water, when necessary, with slightly tepid water, and
these potatoes will be fit for table during April. Some sets
of either the Ash-leaved or Frame may be put into five or
six inch pots, and set in a warm pit or house about the
middle of December; and as soon as weather permits may
be planted out at the foot of a south wall, or plunged
(turning them out of the pot) in a cold frame, say about
March, and well covered at night. These will succeed
those planted in the first frame, or some may be grown
all together in nine-inch pots, in a warm house, and kept
near the glass. Some of the same sort may be planted on
a warm border in the middle of December; also in March,
and again in June. By this means a constant succession of
new potatoes may be kept up. As soon as the crops are
five or six inches above ground earth them up with a broad,
heavy hoe. Where land is heavy, the ground between the
rows should be first chopped over with the potato hoe, which
is a scarce but a most useful tool, and will be found to
answer other purposes than that of a potato hoe, and is of
the shape here given. The blade of the potato hoe should

be about three inches wide at top, and seven inches long
from the shoulder to the point of the blade, which should

be of steel, flat in front and circular at the back; the neck also should be stout, with a long socket for the handle, which should be about four feet long and moderately stout. The blade should be set so as to draw into the ground by pulling toward the operator without much pressure. It should not be made heavy, but strong. This tool will loosen the ground between the rows, without danger of injuring the fibre, and is better than anything else I have ever seen for this purpose.

In earthing potatoes up, stride the row and go backwards, doing one side at a time; this will be found the easiest and neatest way of doing it.

THE BEST WAY TO GROW THE PEA.

THERE is no economy in highly manuring the land for peas. There is nothing suits pea-growing better than potato-ground. This is strong enough, for ground that has been highly dressed drives the peas to haulm, and beyond what they would naturally do on suitable land. There is a nick of time when a crop of peas may be the better for manure. This time is when the pods are formed, and not before. The application of this manure must be in a liquid form, given at the rate of one ounce to one gallon of water if guano or the horticultural manure be used. Give this once or twice during the fruiting by a thorough soaking about the row; all peas will be materially improved by such waterings, which will push the crop along astonishingly, and fill the pods with extra large peas, and marrow peas will branch additionally and bear extra crops. The best way to cultivate the pea is to sow the seed in pots or boxes, and set them in a cold frame, house, or under hand-lights, or sow them on a warm border, and cover them with hand-lights. Sow thick, and cover them one inch with fine earth; give air, and let them remain here till March; then take them up with a trowel in patches, and transplant them to the lines cut out for the purpose on some finely prepared ground. Cut the trench out with the spade, deep enough to let the roots of the peas straight down. Cut the trench by line as for box edging; take the peas up and to the trench a few clumps at a time, and spread them open to form a moderate row; draw the earth to them with the hand, and finally fill the trench neatly up, a little above the original ground-mark, watering if the weather be dry. These will soon strike root afresh, and will commence flowering, and, of course, podding, much nearer the ground than they will do if sown there. Stick them as soon as convenient.

One quart of seed treated this way will go farther than three pints sown on the spot, in consequence of the destruction from slugs, mice, and other accidental causes. This plan of growing the pea is far more economical and certain than sowing direct on the spot for fruiting, especially on heavy soils. The same treatment may be followed with broad beans, scarlet runners, and dwarf beans. New seed should be used for early sowings; but peas and beans are none the worse for being a year old for sowing during March, April, and May. (See " How to choose Seed.")

THE PARSNIP.

THE parsnip is a most useful, certain, and nutritious vegetable. I long to see every poor man well stocked with a good large bed of this vegetable, and one pig in the sty, and one in the pickle-pot. What can be nicer for him and his family? The parsnip should be sown either in the autumn or early spring. Sow in drills ten inches or one foot apart. Let the ground be dug deep, and of the heaviest to be found, for the parsnip likes moisture rather than drought in the subsoil, though the drainage should be good. It is true the parsnip will grow in any soil, but the largest and best are grown on rich, deep, and stiff land. The quality of the parsnip varies in proportion to the nature of the soil on which it is grown. I have noticed a marked difference in this respect: a parsnip that is grown on a light sandy soil contains considerable less fatty richness than one grown on a suitable soil, as I have described. The land should be well manured during the previous season, similarly to that used for potatoes, celery, &c.; but this want may be supplied by feeding the crop in due time with liquid manure, which may consist of not more than one ounce of guano to one gallon of water, or any of the artificial manures suitable, and given as directed elsewhere; only remember that whatever is used for this root and the like must be given in quantity adequate to the wants of the crop; for instance, the parsnip makes considerably more progress downward than upward. Thus the tap-root is the chief reservoir and the channel of the root, and is far in advance of leaf and lateral roots, otherwise the root never comes to perfection; hence whatever nutriment is necessary for extra large roots must be made to reach below the tap-root. Two thorough good waterings with the above liquid manure should be given during the season; the first of these when the root is as large as the finger, and the second about a month after. Top dressings for this crop are of little or no use. Thin the crop out to four or six inches in the row, and never take this root up till wanted; or rather, not till December. The parsnip is all the better for remaining in the ground till February; but for market purposes, and where it is expedient from other causes to take them up before Christmas, trim them neatly and pack them in half-dry sand in layers, crowns outward, in a sort of stack or against a wall. This affords an easy means of readily distinguishing the size of root you want, and of pulling them out without delay or trouble. They should be packed in an outhouse, shed, tool-house, or cellar. I consider the cultivation of this useful vegetable a necessary item in the gardening lists for every day.

There is one cause (though perhaps this not the right one) why so small a proportion of this root is cultivated, viz., that few people comparatively like it, though I believe this to arise solely from its being so seldom used, cause and effect thus acting and reacting on each other. There are at least three reasons for growing it largely, viz., certainty of crop, sure demand, and paying as well or better than any similar vegetable crop, for one square rod will produce something like 750 roots, weighing ¾ lb. each average, that would be worth at the least one halfpenny each, so that the produce of the rod would be worth something like £1 7s., and its cost only a trifle.

THE CULTIVATION OF THE TURNIP.

This is very simple; still there are certain things to be practised to produce the best quality. The prevailing opinion now-a-days is that a large turnip is everything, consequently a turnip crop is over-dressed; that is, manured too much.

Seldom or ever do we find an over-large turnip so good in quality as a medium or small one. In the attempt to grow large turnips the principal thing to be considered is overlooked. Large turnips are not to be compared to small and medium-sized ones of the same sort bulk for bulk. Large ones contain considerably more air and water than the smaller ones, and are comparatively tasteless. A turnip of superior quality is solid, crisp, free from fibre in the flesh, smooth in the mouth, of fine texture, and sugary. To grow the turnip well and free from the attacks of the "fly," choose, say, either the American Strap-leaf, one highly recommended and early, the Early Dutch, a good medium turnip, or the Orange Jelly; but I should recommend either of the first two for the garden. Having made your selection, get enough flour of sulphur to form a dry coating for the seed to be sown at once by putting the seed into a basin containing the sulphur; and, after shaking it well together, let it stand for three or four days previously to sowing; then sow as usual; and, having the land in a medium fine state, proceed to either tread or roll the seed in; then slightly rake the surface with a coarse rake, or, if the land is light and the weather dry, it may be left unraked after the seed is sown. When the seedlings have four or six leaves, and are therefore in a fit state, hoe them. Nothing is better for turnips than good hoeing, and they should be set out eight or nine inches asunder. The land should be good, but not too strong for growing good sweet turnips. Sow the first crop at the end of April or the beginning ot May on land that was cropped the last season with late potatoes, using no manure for such land. If manure must be used—that is, if the land is poor—use old manure or burn some weed and earth to dress the land with, as turnips are remarkably fond of this as a dressing; in lieu of which, if needful, use mild manure of some sorts, such as road sweepings, and a small quantity of bone manure and wood ashes; but be careful in applying these artificial manures to the turnip crop, as they are productive of large and pithy turnips.

A second sowing may be made from the end of May to the middle of June, and a final one for the winter use at the middle of July, as there is no dependence on later sown crops.

The steeping of the seed in the dry flour of sulphur will be found effectual in preventing the "Turnip Fly," and is quite a sovereign remedy. For other remedies see in another part of the work "The Gardener's Enemies, and how to Destroy them."

THE CARROT.

SOME people fancy that the carrot is not a wholesome root. I can scarcely say how this conclusion is arrived at, unless it be from want of good cooking, for the carrot decidedly wants more of this than any other vegetable known. To cook a carrot requires no other care than well boiling from three to four hours with some meat if possible; but, unless it is beef, the carrots must be the first in the boiler, when I am persuaded no bad effects will arise from eating carrots. On the contrary, the carrot, consisting as it does of a large amount of saccharine juices, will prove nutritious, cooling, and of easy digestion. On the other hand, if half cooked it will, with weak persons, produce indigestion. The treatment of this root is very different from that of the parsnip; the carrot should not be sown till April or May, and then on recently and well-pulverized soil. It is fond of deep and good sandy ground: where the land is shallow, it should be dug deep, and some pit-sand turned in, if not naturally of a sandy nature. The soil should be good, but not made so by recent manuring. Select some portion of the garden that has been well manured for a crop of potatoes, onions, celery, or peas during the last season. Sow in drills nine inches apart. Rub the seed between the hands till it separates, and can be sown freely. Some recommend mixing dry cinder-ash or sand with the seed, and then rubbing it between the hands before sowing it. But this is not necessary, for the seed will part freely by rubbing it well without such additions, and sow equally well. Let the land be fine, and the drills not more than half an inch deep. The hand-drill will be found useful for this: but in lieu of it, the best thing to use for drilling in small seeds is a four-foot stick the size of a small rake handle. Cut it with the pruning-saw in the middle, halve it, as it is called, $\frac{3}{4}$ of an inch in the grain-way of the stick, then cut at right

angles at the $\frac{3}{4}$-inch mark one-half off. This leaves a
shoulder. The other tenant-like half must be slightly
thinned to form a very thick-ended wedge. Strain the line
tight, and set the shoulder of the drill-stick (which should
have a small nail stump driven into the shoulder, just far
enough from the drill to allow of the line slipping through)
on the line pressing it, and going backwards, being careful
not to push the line out of the straight. Form the drill all
alike and of one depth, according to the nature and requirements of the seed, which must be sown moderately thin if
in April or May; but if in March or earlier, thicker. Cover
the seed with the back of the rake instead of the teeth; no
other dressing will be safe or needful. Sow on a fine day,
and when the surface of the ground is half dry.

Thin the carrots out as soon as they are four or five
inches high, leaving the crop five inches apart in the
row. As soon as the carrots are as large as the finger,
give liquid manure as recommended for the parsnip. This
will push them along wonderfully, and extra large carrots
will be the result; but be careful not to give these feedings
too strong nor too early, for then it would probably be productive of straggling carrots,—forked, as they are called.
Carrots may be sown on warm borders in cold frames; or
on slight heat in shallow frames for early produce to be
drawn young.

THE LETTUCE.

A NICE well-grown, crisp lettuce, fresh cut, some mustard
nine or ten days old, some cress, a little vinegar, and a
little sugar well mixed make one of the nicest and most
refreshing luxuries possible during the heat of a summer
day. Lettuce is one of the most inexpensive things grown
in the garden; two 2d. or 3d. packets of two sorts—
viz., the Alma Cos, and the Drumhead Cabbage—are suffi-

cient. Sow the first of these on the 20th of July and 20th of August ; the last sowing will come into use in early spring. The former will come first if they do not run to seed ; the August sowing will stand, and produce good lettuce. This sowing will form two batches for succession ; thus, plant from this sowing during September or beginning of October, and then again draw from the seed-bed in March, and plant out. Then sow some of the Drumhead during March, and again in May. Thus you will have lettuce during the principal part of the year, but those who want good lettuce during the winter months should sow some of the Stanstead Winter Cabbage and Hammersmith Hardy Green in the middle of August, and plant out at the foot of a south wall on a warm border or in cold frames as soon as the seedlings are large enough, and got to maturity, before the cold nights come on. These and the autumn-sown Cos varieties may be transplanted ; but the Drumhead Summer Cabbage varieties are best sown where they are to remain, and left fifteen or eighteen inches apart by thinning out. The Cos lettuce should be planted fifteen inches by ten or twelve apart ; the Stanstead and Hammersmith may be planted six inches by nine or ten apart.

The land for lettuce-growing must be of a moderately tender nature, and rich. It is important with some sorts, especially the summer sowings, that the plants be transplanted before the roots get carrot-rooted—that is, as soon as they can be handled ; for if left in the seed-bed till the root loses its first stage of fibre, they are more apt to run to seed, especially the Summer Cabbage kinds. It is, however, far the best plan to let the Drumhead and most of the spring-sown lettuce remain on the ground where they are sown. I have found that a thin crop left on the asparagus beds, a few among onions, a drill sown between beans or peas, and thinned out, answers well for summer-sown crops.

It is thought by some that by thrusting a knife through the top-root of a lettuce about to start to seed is a preventive; but this is an error, for the plant will be already too far gone to be recovered, and it is more for want of an adequate supply of nutriment that it runs to seed so young; and by depriving the plant of this strong feeder, "the tap-root," a certain way is provided for causing it to run to seed before its time. There is no remedy for this tendency among spring-planted and spring-sown lettuce but the one above, viz., plant them as early as convenient from the seed-bed, and let them remain where sown. Do not sow too early; it is better to err on the safe side (if at all). For the production of extra large lettuce a timely supply of liquid manure is necessary. This may consist of half an ounce of guano to one gallon of water, given once a fortnight from the time the lettuces are well grown and begin to show signs of turning in; besides which lettuces must be supplied with an abundance of clean water. If lettuce is required through the winter, a large stock of the two cabbage kinds before-named should be planted, and some of them must be removed to cold frames when full grown, lifting them with plenty of earth about the roots with a trowel, and planting them as close as will just admit of the air passing freely between each plant. This must be done if the weather is likely to be severe; if not, they may be planted closer, fed, and got to maturity early, and have portable cold frames set over them.

ENDIVE.

ONLY in the months of July and August is it really safe to sow endive; during these months a sufficient quantity of the green-curled should be sown for the demand. One ounce of seed will produce more plants than nine out of ten families will require. Sow the seed thinly and on moderately light land, covering it slightly; and as soon as the plants show six or eight leaves, transplant them to a rich and light border, which should have been well manured. Plant from twelve to eighteen inches apart, and supply with abundance of water during dry weather; and also with waterings of liquid manure (as recommended for lettuce) when full-grown, which will be about the end of October or November. Then on some perfectly dry day, when the plants are also quite dry, take some strips of bast and tie them up three inches from the top moderately tight, to prevent much water entering the heart, and to blanch them completely. As soon as signs of sharp frost are observed remove them carefully (with a good ball of earth) to some cold glass, as recommended for lettuce, giving abundance of air at every suitable opportunity, and covering the lights during frosty nights. Endive may be sown during April, May, or June, but these soon run to seed.

LAND CRESS.

THIS useful salad is an admirable substitute for mustard in salads, epecially during the winter. Sow thinly one ounce of this seed in August on a good south border ; this will provide salad cress enough for a very large family, and is a very warm and agreeable element in the salad. It is very hardy, no weather affecting it to any degree of damage.

MUSTARD AND CRESS, COMMON,

Must be sown once a week during the year for constant succession. Sow on the top of the soil in pans, boxes, pots, or in the open ground, according to the time of year, the pots, &c., being used during the winter, and placed in the house or elsewhere for warmth.

THE RADISH

May be sown every month from about the middle of December till May, preferring Wood's Early Frame for a first sowing, the Scarlet Short-top for a second, the Long Salmon for a third, the turnip varieties for the summer sowings, and the Olive-shaped for autumn. The land for radish-growing must be light and well dressed with some decayed manure, such as old hotbed manure or decomposed leaf-mould. The radish to be good must be grown quickly, and be well supplied with water during spring and summer; the early sowings must be protected with glass, dry hay, or straw, and uncovered during the day, drying the litter and covering up every evening at four o'clock. Glass protection is the safest, for radishes suffer from long continuance of the coverings during severe and protracted frost after they are above ground, and now that glass is so cheap, and most men are mechanical enough to make the sashes and frames and do the glazing for this purpose, there is no reason why it should not be used; every gardener especially should be able to do such things for himself; such knowledge is almost a necessary part of his training. A planting of the Early Frame Potato, or the Prolific Ash-leaved Kidney (Myatt's) may be made as directed (see the article on the Potato), and some of Wood's Early Frame Radish sown over the surface of the bed, or some drills of Early Horn Carrot may be made on a similar bed with rows of radishes between them about the same time and during January and February. Radish pods while green are good for pickling, but radish seed never pays to grow on a small scale, as it would occupy a moderately large piece of land to produce five shillings' worth of seed, and the seed can be had (wholesale) at from 1s. 6d. to 2s. per quart.

PARSLEY.

ALTHOUGH this is no uncommon herb, and most people know how to sow it, yet very few know how to grow it, and it often happens that good seed gets condemned simply on this account. It is important that the seed should be more than one year old. Now parsley seed is possessed of more vital power than any other small seed of its class, in proof of which I will adduce the following fact :—At a gentleman's seat where I had the pruning and training of the vines and wall-trees, I saw several square poles of lucerne which had stood for seven years, which is the usual time for this plant to remain on the land after sowing; the year before it was put in the land had been sown with parsley, but as it did not come up within the usual time, viz., five or six weeks, the land was re-dug, and the said lucerne sown, which after being on the ground the time mentioned, had in turn been dug up, and the earth of course again turned over. It lay fallow for some time, when to every one's surprise there came up a fine crop of splendid parsley, after having lain for seven years in the ground ! Do not, therefore, despair should your parsley seed not appear above ground within two months, but the chief thing to prevent this is not to bury it deep, for this was no doubt the cause why it did not vegetate in the case referred to. It should be sown once in February for a supply in case the old plants should all run to seed, but if a good sowing of the Winter Garnishing (Myatt's) is made in the beginning of June, and thinned out to one foot asunder, very little inconvenience will be experienced from scarcity, as probably very few plants of this sowing will run to seed during the first season, especially if the seed is sown on a west border, and the land is on a cool subsoil, and good. In parsley growing it is necessary to provide for casualties, parsley being wanted both in winter and summer. To this end sow a few dozen pots (8-inch) with some of the before-named kind, or take some of the young plants up from the bed, and pot them during September, removing them to a cold frame, and feeding them with liquid manure (as for lettuce and endive, &c.)

once a week. The soil for pot sowings should be good
maiden loam and rotten dung ; in cases where there is no
glass some furze may be laid over the bed to protect it, and
a bass mat laid over this.

BEETROOT.

CONSIDERABLE advantage will be derived from cultivating
beetroot year by year ; for it is a well-known fact that this
root contains a large amount of sugar, and is rich and fat-
tening in a great degree. It is very good when boiled, but
it must be remembered that no part of the root (beyond the
mere thready fibre) must be cut off previously to cooking ;
neither must the tops be cut off, but merely broken off with
the hand ; the leaves snapping off readily at the base of the
footstalk. Carefully wash the root, and boil for two hours ;
then trim and peel it, &c. But apart from growing beetroot
for table purposes it is most nutritious for cows and pigs,
and every man who keeps these animals should grow four
or five square poles of this root,—*beet*, not mangel-wurzel,
for there is a vast difference between the two in quality.
Some of this boiled with meal added will quickly make
excellent pork. The time of sowing should be from the
middle of April to the middle of May ; sow in a seedbed
and transplant ; but sowing in drills fifteen inches apart,
where they are to remain till maturity, is the best way.
The land should be well dug twice before sowing the seed,
to render it free from heavy clods below ; make the surface
moderately fine, and sow the seed not more than half an
inch deep, covering with the back of the rake, drawing the
fine soil over the seed. When the seedlings are large enough
to handle, thin them out to six or eight inches apart, and
when the roots are half grown give liquid manure, or lay
some guano over the rows, during showery weather. What
is called the Silver Beet is grown for the sake of the midribs,

and is used as seakale, but it is a poor substitute, and very little grown.

SPINACH.

THIS is, no doubt, one of the most wholesome vegetables grown, and no garden should be without a bed of it, both in winter and summer. A dish of this two or three times a week will regulate the system. There are several sorts recommended, but none is better, or so good even, as the round-seeded for summer, and the prickly for winter use. The former should be sown every two weeks from February till August, and the prickly mostly from the middle or so of August, on a warm border, well dunged, and the plants thinned out to six inches apart. It may be necessary to sow a month earlier in some of the northern counties, and on cold or late soils. The ground need not be very fine for receiving the seed, which will run down between the nodules of earth, being merely knocked over with the back of the rake, and slightly coarse-raked; this applies to broadcast sowing, but if sown in drills the seed should be buried from half an inch to one inch deep, a watering or two with liquid manure as before given, or some other favourite artificial manure, will greatly improve it.

PRIZE GROWING.—CELERY.

THIS is one of the most useful vegetables known, especially for those of a fastidious palate. Celery is good in every way, and has, as is well known, a most agreeable nutty astringency, and every one with a garden should have a row of celery for use in winter. It is not only most wholesome, but easy to grow. Get half an ounce of Incomparable White, or Nonsuch Red, or the Mammoth Red (the latter is the largest sort grown, and solid, but the Nonsuch is the best flavoured). Sow the seed on the ground in a warm spot, in March; let the ground be good, and of a fine light nature. Make the surface fine, and sow the seed thinly upon it, covering it very lightly, and placing a hand-glass over it, but shading the seed from the full influence of the sun by laying some moss over it under the light, sufficient to prevent the surface from becoming dry. This method is nearly equal to sowing the seed on heat, for the heat created inside the hand light cannot escape (the glass being kept close till the seed is up), and penetrating the soil on which the seed is sown, it retains that heat during the night, thus fairly substituting the hotbed. Where, however, there are frames at work, or artificial heat of any kind, the seed may be sown in shallow pans, or wide-mouthed pots, using rich light soil, and set on or in such heat with advantage. The soil in the pans should be made moderately firm, and watered with a fine rose water-pot previously to sowing the seed, then sift some light soil over the seed with a very fine-meshed sieve, and shade as before. When the seedlings are large enough to handle, prick them out three or four inches apart on good ground; shade and keep them moist. When they are three or four inches high, plant them out in rows, six or seven inches apart; the rows must be four feet apart, to admit of earthing up. There is no better plan of growing celery than in single rows; these rows should be formed by first digging out a trench one foot wide, and of the desired length, in some open part of the garden; put the line down, strain it tight, and mark one side with the spade, then move the line one foot from this, and proceed to open the trench, driving the spade down on each side of the trench perpendicularly. Dig the earth clean out ten or twelve inches deep, turning one half out on one side and the other half on the other, thus forming two ridges. Strike the sides next the trench with the spade to prevent the earth falling back into it, and to give it a neat appearance; then fill the hollow with good rotten dung, previously breaking the soil up at the bottom five or six inches in depth; turn the manure into the bottom of the trench by digging thin spits, and turning some three or four inches of fine earth up, in which the plants are to be planted, with a thick-ended dibber, or a trowel. Before inserting the plants, examine them, and remove any small side shoots that may be found at the base of the principal stems; put the plants in firmly, but not more than one inch above the base of the stems; give a thorough soaking with water, and, if the sun is hot and the weather dry, shade them with pea-haulm for a few days; encourage them as much as possible, but do not earth up till nearly full grown; dig and break the earth well with the spade a week or so before on each side of the trench, and provide abundance of pulverized soil for the purpose. Having cleared the plants of all side shoots, stride the row, and draw some fine earth with one hand while you hold the stems quite close together with the other, and thus proceed from one end of the row to the other.

When the earthing has reached above the ground level, a basement must be formed for the embankment with the spade. Having dug the soil well beneath, lay some earth for the base; let this be one foot from the row and well packed, to prevent it from afterwards crumbling down, then lay on more fine soil, proceeding with the hand as at first, and so on till the row has been completely embanked, striking the sides of the embankment with the back of the spade to prevent it crumbling down in frost and wet weather, and to prevent the wet from getting into the trench. Do not on any account earth the celery up in wet weather, nor much above the heart-leaves at a time, and be careful never to let any earth run into the heart of the plants, for this will cripple the growth, and spoil its appearance for the table. It may, ultimately, be earthed up to within five or six inches of the top, leaving the top of the ridge moderately open, to admit of sufficient air to prevent decay. Thorough good soakings with the liquid manure, as directed for lettuce, &c., given once a week, from the time the plants have attained ten or twelve inches in height to the time of maturity, and a free use of clean water must be given at all times. Sowings should be made at three different times in the season for successional crops, viz., one in February, one in March, and one in April. The seed is generally about sixpence per ounce.

PRIZE GROWING.—THE ONION, LEEK, AND SHALLOT.

WHEN I say "prize growing," I mean the production of large and sound articles; these two qualifications are absolutely essential—the former takes the prize, and the latter is indispensable to the preservation of the onion and shallot. Prizes should not always be given for mere size; but this is a real merit in the onion, shallot, and leek. To attain this desideratum

THE ONION

Should be sown in the previous autumn. Select any of the current sorts you please, but if extraordinary size is desired, either the Globe Tripoli or White Lisbon should be chosen, and the seed should be sown moderately thick, on fairly good ground, on a southern border during the third week in August, and when frost sets in sift some cinder-ash over the young onions to the depth of half an inch; let it remain thus till March or the beginning of April, then plant them out into beds of good rich soil, eight inches from row to row, and five inches apart in the row.

The young onions must be carefully raised with a fork, so as to preserve as much of the roots as possible, they will not carry any earth, but this is of no consequence; the preservation of the fibre is the chief thing. Let the ground intended for growing these onions be well dunged, or dressed with the strongest manure you can get. Mark out the beds during December or January, then empty the cesspool and water-closet, and lay it on the surface (previously rough digging the land), in a good heavy dressing; let it lay till the beginning of March, and then dig the ground deeply all over, turning the manure in and well mixing it with the soil. I have advised in "Gardening for the Cottage," that this manure should be mixed with some earth before being laid on the intended bed, but this is the same in effect, as it is applied much earlier, and consequently has time for pulverization; upon the whole, I am of opinion that the direct application of the contents of the cesspool or water-closet is best, for then, although the land receives the whole it becomes reduced to a safe medium and divested of its destructive properties by long exposure and by combination with so many more times its bulk of earth, so that there is no danger of over-dressing. Let the ground lay rough-dug for a fortnight, then lay on some old pulverized manure and sand on the top of the bed (scrapings that have been laid up for a few weeks with the horse-droppings in it are as good as anything for this top-dressing), chop this in mixing it with the soil, rake down, and plant the onions by the line, trim the long roots off, and plant with a thick-ended hand-dibber, letting the roots straight down, for if any of them turn up it will be much against the onions doing well; let the base of the young bulb be from half an inch to one inch below the surface, just sufficient to keep the young plant upright; close the earth firmly about the roots, striking the dibber towards the bottom of the root without bruising it, and let the whole of the blade remain on. When the entire bed is planted, give a thorough good soaking with a large rose water-pot to settle the soil about the plants, unless the weather is showery, which is best.

When the onions are half grown, or have formed good-sized bulbs, give them a moderate watering with two or three ounces of guano to one gallon of water ; give it so as to make sure that it reaches down to the lower feeders, and continue such waterings for a few times till the bulbs are half or three-fourths grown, and no longer, for if continued beyond this it has a tendency to induce them to grow after they are ripe.   Onions should only be watered very moderately, that is, really as little as possible, and if the weather prove very dry, the beds should be kept dusty by hoeing.

The White Spanish and Deptford will answer equally well under this treatment, they will attain additional size, and come on as early as we get the French imported onions. Spring sown Spanish, Deptford, Brown Globe, Strasburg, &c., will be greatly improved by treating them in the same way as regards soil and feeding. Sow in March for general crops, and the Silver-Skin in May, thickly, for pickling, on moderate ground, but give no liquid manure at all to this last sort; the Silver-Skin pays remarkably well to grow for the purpose named, and is the only kind well suited for it, possessing as it does a beautiful silvery white skin.

THE SHALLOT.

THIS should be planted in lines about March, and in precisely the same soil, and at the same distance apart as directed for the onion. The soil should, however, be drawn up into ridges with the hoe before planting the bulbs, on the top of these ridges plant the shallots by line five or six inches apart, merely press three-fourths of the bulb into the soil below the surface, and so leave them.

No filling up round the bulb or watering will be required till the new bulbs are half grown, then give them some liquid manure as directed for the onion. As soon as the shallots begin to swell, the earth may be drawn away from the young bulbs to admit of the sun and air reaching them as much as possible, as this will help to ripen the new parts, for this is the secret of keeping shallots. When the blade begins to turn yellow take them up, and hang them in an open shed, roots and all, till they are thoroughly dry, then trim and put them in some open, airy place for future use. Shallots are very useful in the kitchen, but are generally very dear.

THE LEEK.

Is a most useful and savoury vegetable, and makes a very profitable and nutritious dish. The quality of the leek depends more upon the cultivation than the sort, still there are the London Flag and the Musselborough, worth particularizing; this last is of fine flavour, and will grow large. For this the leek must be sown in March, thinly, on good land, in an open space; and when six or seven inches high should be raised with a fork, the roots trimmed, and planted in rows.

The leek will bear very high cultivation, the land cannot well be too rich, therefore, if extra large and fine leeks are desired, dig out a trench precisely the same as for celery, and fill it with dung within three or four inches of the top of the trench; cover this with three or four inches of earth, in which plant the leeks six inches apart, letting the plants down an inch or two above the *axis*, that is, from where the roots start, so that the stem may be two inches in the ground. As soon as the newly planted leeks have fairly taken root, cut the tops off if they have not been shortened previously to planting; when they are grown as thick as the hoe handle, chafe some of the earth that was turned out of the trench down to them on each side with the spade, filling up five or six inches, and repeat this after a while; by this treatment, and watering once or twice with two ounces of guano to one gallon of water, and by earthing up, very fine leeks indeed may be produced. Those who do not care to take this trouble may chose a good open space, dung the ground well, dig it in deep, draw deep drills with a heavy hoe, and plant the leeks therein six inches apart in the row, and twelve inches from row to row; water three or four times during the season with the guano and water, and by earthing up as space will admit, sufficiently fine leeks will be produced. One ounce of seed, at sixpence, will produce enough leeks for an ordinary family. Sow this quantity of seed on not less than twenty-seven square feet of good ground as a seed-bed.

THE MUSHROOM.

THE mushroom is highly prized by all who know anything of it. There is but one kind purely good and wholesome. The nature of the mushroom is like that of all fungi, viz., more or less good and pure in proportion to the nature of the soil on which it grows; thus, the pure *Agaricus campestris* (pure mushroom) becomes poisonous when grown near hedgerows, rotten wood, &c.; therefore every precaution should be taken, both in preparing the spawn and also the material used for the beds. There is a kind found in the pastures nearly resembling the true variety, which, indeed, I believe to be the same, from the fact that it is always found on less good ground and frequently near trees, hedgerows, woods, &c.; while further in the same field you will find the true sort, and seldom the spurious; from this I have drawn my conclusion, as well as from the positive inclination of all fungi to become less good in proportion to subterranean and atmospheric influences.

To grow the mushroom well, study nature, and no one can miss his object. A high and a dry atmosphere with a poor soil is a sure way to produce insipid and half-poisonous mushrooms. None can be grown so rich and good as those found in our pastures during the cool months of October and November, when the night temperature does not exceed 35°, or even 30° Fahrenheit above ground, and perhaps 40° or 45° of heat below. The chief thing is to cause activity in the spawn while in its embryo state; a healthy fibre must be produced before abundant and good mushrooms can be expected. The mushroom is said to be propagated by seed. If this is the case, how is it that the spark of spawn put into a lump of earth one foot square runs completely through the whole, so as to produce the so-called plants all over this lump? To produce mushrooms certain steps are necessary : first, select from the stable (where the horses are, hay, and corn-fed) two bushels of horse-droppings (fresh), with a portion of short litter, one bushel of cow-dung, and one bushel of fibrous maiden loam. Mix these all together, adding as much water as will enable you to tread and form this compound into a very stout pug or mortar by chopping, treading, &c. When well mixed, so as to hold well together, get a brick-mould of the common building-brick size, or make one, and form this compound into bricks just the same as brick-makers proceed, using some sand to prevent the pug sticking to the mould. Press the pug well into the mould, and form a number of well-made and solid bricks. Set them up to dry, protect them from rains, and when half dry or so, apply sufficient spawn to each brick to impregnate the whole. This is best done by making a hole on each side of every brick two inches from the end, with a dibber nearly through the brick; then take a lump of spawn and fill the two holes, and paste some pug over each hole to keep the bit of spawn in. Set the bricks up again, and let them dry for a day more; then pack them moderately close together, and cover the whole heap with sufficient hot dung to diffuse a nice moderate heat through the little stack of new bricks. This fermenting of the new bricks must not be high; a sweet and moderate heat for two or three days is all that is required to cause the spawn to run through them, which may be known by the appearance of a white, thready fibre throughout the new brick on breaking one in two. As soon as this is seen remove the dung, and let the bricks thoroughly dry, and store away for future use in any dry shed, tool-house, or loft where no damp can affect them. These bricks of spawn will keep good for years, and be all the better for age if kept dry; so that, where mushrooms are in continual use, and the demand for them large, a sufficient quantity may be made to last for years.

To grow the mushroom is an easy matter to any who have a cellar, stable, or shed to devote to this purpose. In the summer it may be grown from May to November in the open air on beds covered with fern, hay, or mats to screen them from harsh winds and excessive rains. These beds are best made at a sharp angle in the shape of a span or lean-to under a north wall for the summer, all that is required for them being a sufficient body of well-sweetened stable dung which has been turned over a few times to let the rank steam pass off. After a week from the last turning of the dung the bed may be made in the same way as that for the melon or cucumber; that is, bedding it well and beating it firm with the fork, raising the back about two feet, so as to form a sharp descent to the front, which should be about one foot high, the whole being about four feet wide ; or the bed may be ridge-shaped at very sharp angles, thus forming two sides instead of one, four or five feet wide at the base.

When the strong heat of the bed has subsided to 65° or 70° (which can be ascertained by plunging a thermometer into it over night, or by thrusting sticks into it, and handling them immediately they are withdrawn : a practical man will tell the heat required), then spawn the bed. This is done by making holes nine or ten inches apart all over the surface and three inches deep with a thick-ended hand-dibber, and pressing a lump of spawn into each hole ; then cover the surface of the bed with an inch of good, half-dry maiden loam or garden soil of a moderately fine texture, and beat it well with the back of the spade to make it firm. Cover the bed with dry hay, fern, or straw four or five inches thick, which will facilitate the spawning. If the mushrooms appear within five or six weeks from this time, well and good ; if not, examine the bed and see if the spawning has gone on all right ; and if it has run well and the bed is dry, give some tepid water (a little above blood-heat) to the bed here and there without the rose on the water-pot, so as to soak the bed to a moderate extent, and cover up again to prevent a sudden chill. This covering may be removed occasionally, and left off altogether when midsummer comes. The bed will produce abundantly for two or three months from the time it once begins ; so that, after one bed has borne fruit a week or two, another bed should be made to keep up a succession. Mushrooms may be grown on shelves in the cellar, or in boxes and pots placed in the stoke-hole, tool-house, and mushroom-house, or in frames, or any convenient dark place where a moderate temperature exists ; filling such shelves, boxes, or pots with pure horse-droppings and a little fibrous maiden loam, beating this compost down hard and spawning at once as soon as the heat commences, observing the same regulations as before mentioned as to heat. As soon as spawning has taken place from 40° to 50° of heat will be enough to maintain. Frequent waterings are not needed, but keep up a moist atmosphere by frequent syringes of everything except the bed and its coverings. Mice and woodlice are the only enemies to contend with, and these must be caught by traps (see " Enemies of the Garden ").

SEAKALE.—THE BEST WAY TO FORCE IT.

SEAKALE will force in any way, but I have only found one really good way of doing it. This vegetable will bear any amount of heat, but it is of the utmost importance not to force it too high, for on this depends its quality. It will be found on trial that the seakale forced above 55° or 60° will be wanting in crispy flavour ; if the heat be below 50° the quality will be improved. Nothing is better for kale than leaves raked up during November ; while wet, they yield a most even and congenial heat for seakale-forcing, and retain the heat. If seakale is wanted before it can have many leaves (as leaves are not often to be had in such abundance till too late for the first batch of seakale), well mix a third of stable dung with the leaves. From the time the fermenting material is put over the pots, it will take fully six weeks to produce good seakale, fit for table. It is far better to use moderate-sized pots than large ones, and to plant seakale roots in single rows instead of the old ugly triangle fashion. Let the plants be placed in single file, two feet by fifteen inches asunder. There is no necessity to plant four feet by three feet apart ; it is a great loss of land, time, and material. Every season, as soon as the cutting is over, remove all the old heating stuff, trim the plants, and well dress the ground between the rows and the plants with good dung and sand (sea sand if it can be had), and dig it in a good spade deep, and let it lay all summer. The plants will then have something to feed upon, and become strong against the following autumn. Only three crowns to each plant should be allowed to remain; the rest should be cut away during the summer. The full development of the three will thus be promoted, and fine, robust kale, if any, will be the result. Give weakly plants a soaking with one ounce of guano to one gallon of water once or twice during the summer, as good stout and well-developed crowns must be the chief object of the summer treatment. Cut away all seed-stems (unless seed is wanted) as soon as they appear, and encourage one crown on the said plant to develop itself. The old stools are apt to spread from the original in the course of a year or two; but this should be prevented, as far as possible, by cutting in and inducing the two or three crowns to maintain a compactness consistent with the size of the pots used for covering them.

A constant succession of kale may be had from Christmas till April or May by covering some with pots every five or six weeks from the beginning of November, or earlier if wanted earlier. Seakale is not worth a straw if allowed to grow above six inches long, for not more than this is eatable. If forced by any other means, such as in boxes or pots, and by taking five or six year old stuff up from the ground, trim and pack them close together in these boxes by bedding them in sand, and placing such boxes or pots in the house or pit, or under the tank; and, of course, exclude from the light wherever they are put. It must be kept moist and frequently syringed to prevent too dry an atmosphere about it, for this ruins both the flavour and the crispness of the kale; and for this reason forcing it where it grows is by far the best plan.

Kale should be cooked as soon as possible after cutting; but when it cannot be cooked immediately, it should be set on end in water in which a handful of salt has been thrown.

Sow seakale seed in drills like sowing kidney beans, nine inches or one foot apart, in March or April.

———

PRIZE GROWING.—THE MELON.

IT used to be thought rather a feat to grow the melon at all ; to grow it early almost an impossibility, and quite out of the reach of the majority of gardeners. Many years ago I thought I could grow melons with less than the usual means, and achieved quite a success. I had an old and very ordinary frame. I made a moderate hotbed, but it could scarcely be called a hotbed, for the fermenting quality of the dung was nearly exhausted before I used it. However, I made the bed, and as soon as it was ready I inserted the plants, and covering them at night, they progressed satis- factorily, and as fine fruit was cut as could be wished for, without any additional heat ; and I have proved that the melon can be grown well with less than the means generally thought necessary. To grow it successfully and very early will certainly require additional heat, but there is more in the management of the thing than in any inherent difficulty.

The melon is far less difficult to grow well than the cucumber. There is an easy "royal road" to produce this fruit ; four things are only necessary to produce it good, viz., light of the best possible degree, an even temperature, not very high, abundance of water while the fruit is coming to maturity, and constant thinning out, to prevent confusion o the vines, as the leaves should never be turned and left the under side uppermost,—while, to obtain extra large fruit, feeding with liquid manure once a week must be resorted to : this may consist of two ounces of guano to one gallon

of water.   Extraordinary melons of the " Golden Perfection,"
"Orion," and the "Beechwood," will be produced thus.
The Golden Perfection is one of the very best, if not the best,
and is both handsome and equal to a pine-apple in richness.
In growing melons, the aim should not be so much a high
temperature as the essential of a bright light, which is
obtainable to a greater degree by bringing the plants up to
the glass, and using lights with large glass, kept as clean as
possible, the sashes under which the melons are grown
thoroughly washed inside and out previously to the insertion
of the plants in the bed, or before the bed is made ; freely
water during the development of the fruit, but not after the
fruit begins to change, as watering will cause the fruit to
burst when full grown ; and keep the vines as thin as consistent with a full crop of fruit.   Cover up an hour before
sunset with double mats and dry hay : if very early, lay the
hay three inches thick, and then your double mats on the
glass, and uncover as soon as the sun reaches the glass in
the morning.

In watering melons care is required not to let the water
fall on the neck of the plant, which is the principal stem,
where the whole of the vines spring from : preserve this
sound, and all must go on well.   As soon as the leaders are
laid out, stop them, and they will throw out laterals, on
which come the fruit.   Allow each of these laterals to bear
one or two fruit, and as soon as they are fairly set, stop them,
two joints above the fruit : allow no more vine to occupy
the surface of the bed ; by this means earlier and finer fruit
will be obtained, and the whole crop of fruit will be more
under command.   After the plants are fairly established they
will not during the day require more shading.   The melon
is a native of a hot and clear atmosphere.   When the foot-
stalk of the fruit is observed to be cracking at the union with
the fruit, it is ready to cut, but not before.

If red spider appear on the vines, as they will at times during the ripening of the fruit, lay a little flour of brimstone on some quicklime put into a seed-pan, set it inside the frame in the evening, and close and cover up. The *red spider* is often troublesome at this stage of the melon, but the *thrip* is far worse than the spider, and more difficult to destroy, as it appears at all stages, and more especially during the swelling of the fruit. You may easily see when this pest is attacking the vines by the curling of the edges and the spotted and sickly appearance of the leaves. A practised eye will instantly discover when either of these destroyers have made their appearance, and when they have there must be no delay : cautiously fuming must be resorted to, laying small quantities at a time of flour of brimstone on some quicklime ; but as a preventive is better than a cure, lay some brimstone on the bottom of a flower-pot turned upside down, to raise it up near the glass ; let it remain in the frame, and this will give off its fumes so imperceptibly, and yet so effectually, as to clear the vine of the thrip and red spider, and not injure the tender leaf. Do not stop till these enemies are in possession of the frame, otherwise they will require stronger remedies. See " The Gardener's Enemies, and how to Destroy them," in another part of the work. The melon is best struck from cuttings for very early work, as these plants are less liable to make wood, and more likely to produce fruit, and at the same time more hardy. Select two or three buds or eyes from the top of the short-pointed young stuff. Strike them in a moderate heat during September. Plants from seed should be raised on a lively heat in January for very early, in February and March for second early, and in April and May for late crops. Special means will be required to ripen the fruit in January and February ; this is done by a small pipe running round the pit or house, on the surface or above the surface of the bed on which the plants are growing. Melons may be conveniently grown during the summer months in large pots or boxes filled with maiden loam and dung, kept close and fed with manure water, in an ordinary little greenhouse, such as are frequently found connected with small villas. Those of a hardy nature, such as "Turner's Scarlet Gem," should be selected. Care is required in saving seed, and one sort only should be saved in a season. The "setting" of the fruit is of some importance, and must never be omitted if wanted to produce vital seed; but apart from this I believe it has its uses, as most probably the pollen gives additional energy to the fruit, and helps to develop it, as it has been proved that fruit that has not been "set" has nearly all fallen just at the point of swelling off, while that which has been operated upon has remained and developed itself: this applies to cucumbers also. The setting should be done an hour or two after the sun has risen upon the fruit, and when dry. The difference between the male and female blossom is easily known. Strip the petals from the former, and twirl the anthers of this gently in the stigma of the latter, observing that each is fully developed; this is discovered by the one leaving itself upon the finger, while the stigma gapes and is fully expanded. Melon seed may be kept three or four years in impervious tin boxes, such as are used for coffee; and they are all the better for age. By adopting the method I have described I have grown melons up to twelve pounds or more, and of a fatty richness seldom to be met with.

POTHERBS IN GENERAL.

THERE are many of these of little use, and many that are necessaries to all. Let us imitate the French in this one particular at least, for they will make a most savoury dish, consisting principally of herbs. I know not if it can be proved that the wit and liveliness of the French and Irish can all be attributed to their food, but it is a fact that herbs exercise an important influence on the body. No one can do without herbs such as thyme, mint, marjoram, savory, sage, rosemary, carraway, basil, fennel, horehound, tansy, balm, dill, chives, coriander, rue, and parsley. Every one with a garden should have half a dozen roots of each of these, especially the thyme, mint, marjoram, sage, chives, and a good proportion of parsley, from which to pick or cut the small quantity required to flavour the soup or broth, which will be materially improved by the addition of a sprig of one or more of the above-mentioned herbs. Most of these can be obtained from seed ; a threepenny packet of each will produce sufficient stock for a dozen gardens of the ordinary size. The seed of these herbs is very fine gene- rally speaking, and must be sown on soil of a fine and good quality, with the surface made smooth and even : sow the seeds thinly, barely covering with fine sandy soil. Basil requires heat to raise its seedlings, and is afterwards planted out. Herbs should be cut for drying when in flower, and dried out of the sun in an open shed, loft, or room. Those used for drinks only, such as horehound, rosemary, tansy, balm, mint, dill, and carraway (the seed only of the last two), should be preserved in paper bags, and the others tied up in bunches and suspended from nails in some dry room free from dust. Any man may do exceedingly well by growing herbs alone for the trade and market ; those who have never tried it would be surprised at the amount of profit arising from an acre of well-cultivated herbs during one season. Herbs are fond of light land.

THE CUCUMBER.

WHAT has been said here in reference to melon-growing may be repeated, with one or two exceptions, for the cucumber; viz., a constant supply of water; but no water, or very little indeed, must be given to melons whilst ripening. The cucumber is best struck from cuttings for winter work. Strike the two topmost joints of the young wood, select those that are short-jointed; fill a five or six-inch pot with one-half maiden loam, and one-half rotten dung; insert three cuttings in each pot halfway up the cutting, close the soil moderately, water well, and set the pot on a lively heat; shade from the mid-day sun for a week or so; stop each as soon as it shows signs of growing. The cuttings should be struck in August and September, and finally put out into their winter quarters as soon as thoroughly established in the pots. The most effectual and economical is a low span-roof pit or a lean-to, as circumstances best admit of; if the latter it should face the south or thereabout, if the former it should run about north and south. Thus such a house will get a portion of the sun on both sides once during the day, which is of infinite importance in growing cucumbers for the winter. But of the two I prefer the lean-to roof at angles of not less than 45° or 50° for winter work; such an angle will answer admirably for melon-growing for summer, and growing grapes in pots after the winter cucumbers are over, which would probably be in April or May. This pit may be nine feet wide, and of any length required, up to sixty or seventy feet; this angle will give a roof of ten or twelve feet of glass, and is large enough for winter growings. There should be some ventilators at the highest point, and openings in front near the ground. One of these within six or eight feet nine inches square, or a little less, in the front wall, with close shutters, to be opened and closed at will. The roof should be fitted with permanent rafters, and the glass well puttied in; the floor should be sunk two feet below the ground level; this will admit of head-room, while the roof will be conveniently near the ground, say two feet; thus there will be four feet clear inside the pit in front. One advantage of this low frontage is that it easily admits of being covered with mats during severe frosts, a matter of immense importance at this season of the year.*

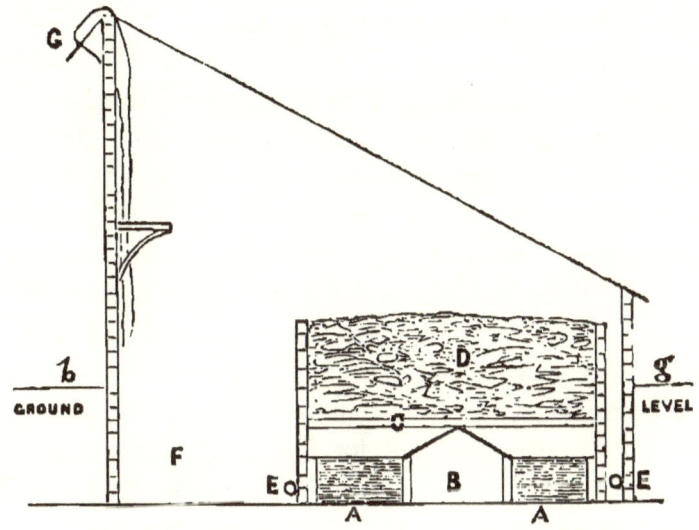

Fig. 1.—END SECTION OF CUCUMBER PIT.

REFERENCE TO DIAGRAM.—A A, Tank, flow and return; B, Chamber in which rhubarb may be forced; C, Floor on which the bed rests; D, the bed of earth; E E, Flow and Return-pipe for surface heat; F, the Pathway; G g, Ventilators, the one at the top of the pit has two cords, one to open the shutter with and the other to close it.

There is nothing so economical and so effectual as the *tank* for heating these pits; this tank should be made with

* December and January.

yellow deal, three-inch stuff; for the sides, and $1\frac{1}{2}$-inch for the bottom, in the shape of two rough troughs, well nailed together, each eighteen inches wide and seven inches deep; the bottom must be nailed on crossways; these troughs must be lined either with zinc or galvanized iron, and rendered watertight, and each will run the whole length of the pit; one for the flow of the water from the boiler, and the other for the return to the boiler. The flow should be nearest the front of the pit, and the return farthest from it; and both these must be enclosed in four-inch brickwork, carried up $2\frac{1}{2}$ feet above the top of the higher edge of the side of the tank, at the least.

It has been said before that the flow of the hot water should be nearest the front of the house or pit; this being the coldest part, there must be a space between the front wall of the pit and that of the wall which encloses the tank for the free escape of the heat from the pipe to the interior of the pit where the plants are growing, as is seen in the diagram. The floor (on which the earth rests in which the plants grow), may be of two-inch slates, three feet long, and any convenient width, from one to two feet, two feet being about the most convenient for handling; these must rest on a bearer in the middle, running the whole length of the pit over the chamber between the tanks; this bearer must rest on brick pillars, and be $4\frac{1}{2}$ inches by three inches, set edgeways, and may be of oak or yellow deal well tarred, or it may be of slate of the same cantling; the floor slates meeting here and resting upon a ledge of bricks left for the purpose in the walls enclosing the tank. They should be cut in close, and fit nicely, but need not be cemented, but merely mortared round the sides next the walls to keep out steam, which must be guarded against at all times. This tank, floor, &c., will last for many years; its cost is not much when compared to its effect and economy; and it will be easily seen that there is seven or eight times as much water in this tank as there can possibly be in as many pipes* of the ordinary dimensions. The ordinary saddle boiler is as good as anything that can be used for heating the water. This must be made of dimensions according to the length of tank to be heated; one eighteen inches long and two inches deep, that is, holding two inches of water, will heat a tank of the dimensions named (thirty feet long), and would cost about thirty shillings; one two feet long and three inches deep will heat a pit, containing a tank sixty or seventy feet long with a very little fuel. Welsh coal is about the best thing for a steady and regular heat, and for economy, but a little domestic coal will be of good service if at any time the temperature should fall too low through extreme cold or the lowering of the fire, as well as for lighting it at any time. The culm, or Welsh coal, will retain its heat longer than any other fuel I know of, for if the fire is cleared well at the bottom, and the furnace well filled with moderate-sized coal, packed in at eight o'clock at night, and a moderate draught be allowed, a good fire will be found in the morning at seven or eight o'clock, and no loss of necessary heat; in very severe frost backing up the fire at ten o'clock, and giving a little more draught, with the addition of dry hay and mats outside, will be desirable, and is of more importance for winter-growing cucumbers than a greater fire heat with no outside covering, which should consist of three inches of old hay on the glass, and the mats over all, using dry hay every time—I press this particularly, for wet hay will do more harm than good.

Do not fill the pit over the tank with all the soil necessary at the time of inserting the plants, but add it by degrees; first form hillocks in the middle, of three or four bushels each, and when they are of the temperature of the

* The double set being necessary to keep up the heat.

house insert the plants on the top, training them to sticks to conduct the leaders to the roof, and training the vines on galvanized iron or zinc wire strained on the roof six or eight inches apart for this purpose. The soil to be used for the bed in which the plants are to grow should be kept in an outhouse, tool-house, or shed, for if allowed to remain exposed to the cold and drenching rains of this time of the year, and then taken into the house, it will cause a probable chill to the plants by a sudden lowering of the temperature. It may consist of such as directed for striking the cuttings in, but in no case sifted, but merely chopped moderately with the spade; this loam should be such as can be had from a fertile common or old pasture, the top spit should be had, turf and all, and be laid up so for twelve months. Should this not be done, merely pare the sward off, using the remainder with the dung, chopped and well mixed.

The vines must not be trained too near the glass—one foot is near enough for cucumbers—therefore the wires must be let down, or rather be fixed at this distance from the glass, iron eyelets or wires with two holes to fix them to the rafters by nails, and one hole at the lower end for the wires to run through. Stopping and thinning must be resorted to, and a sharp look-out kept for thrip—for which see "Enemies of the Garden, and How to Destroy them." When the vines show signs of weakness, give them weekly waterings of one ounce of guano to one gallon of water. Always use tepid water, and take the same precaution as in the case of melons to prevent the progress of thrip, red spider, &c., although this latter will seldom if ever trouble the cucumber, though the former probably will. Place some lumps of camphor in muslin bags along the front of the house, suspending them over the front pipe, which have a beneficial influence on the house where plants are growing, by imparting constant and almost imperceptible fumes highly dis-

agreeable to insect life ; also lay some lumps of lime in pans
and set them here and there along the coping of the pit,
and lay half an ounce of flour of brimstone on each lump.
As the lime absorbs the vapour from the house it will
gradually slacken and cause the brimstone to give off gentle
fumes, such as will not be felt by the tender leaf. This will
prove an effectual remedy against the cucumber's enemies,
the thrip and louse, and may be practised constantly without any difficulty or danger, so long as neither too much
lime nor brimstone is used at a time ; three or four good-
sized lumps of lime placed at intervals of ten, twelve, or
fifteen feet, with the quantity of sulphur before named, will
be found sufficient at one time. All these pans must be
removed before syringing the vines. Charcoal in moderate-
sized pieces should also be laid pretty thickly on the surface
of the bed, whether in frames, houses, or pits, to fertilize the
air (see " Charcoal "). If the plants are to be raised from
seed for winter work, it should be done in August and
September on a lively heat, and the plants potted off into
six-inch pots, to get them strong and woody before they
are finally planted into the bed ; this should be done at all
times, both in cucumber and melon growing.

There are two or three other methods of growing the
cucumber, viz., the hotbed made with dung and leaves, and
the dead tank and pipe ; but the first-named kind of pit and
system can scarcely be excelled, from its adaptation to
other purposes, and is most suitable for market gardeners
and where large quantities of fruit are wanted. When the
surface heat is not required the circulation of the water
should be stopped in the pipes by the stopcock provided
for the purpose near the boiler. Air must be admitted
cautiously during the mild days of the winter months. This
is best done by opening the shutters only at the top of the
house, and on hot sunny days in spring open the little

shutters in front, but be careful of draughts of cold air. This tank system will never burn the feeders of the plants, the principal cause of the failure so often complained of.

Do not look for two impossibilities in growing early cucumbers, viz., great length and great quantity ; a cucumber fifteen or eighteen inches long is quite large enough ; all the size obtained above this is at the expense of number. Cucumbers can be grown in large pots and trained to sticks, but these will require additional feeding.

THE GRAPE-VINE.—Indoors, Outdoors, and in Pots.

Climate is the most important thing for successful grape-growing. Some sorts certainly appear more hardy than others, but even these are greatly improved by a generous climate. Take the Common Sweetwater, for instance, and introduce it into the hothouse, and you would fancy it was another variety; and the Black Hamburgh planted against the most favourable outdoor wall, would so produce as to create a doubt of its kind, the berry being so poor, notwithstanding the goodness of the soil. This is the nature of the grape ; therefore in selecting sorts for any particular purpose (whether, that is, for hothouse, greenhouse, or outdoors), study the natural constitution of the kind.

When very early fruit is wanted, some of the early and hardy sorts should be selected for either pot-culture, or that of the permanent vinery, such as the early and prolific Sweetwater, Black Cluster and Black Frontignans, the Black and the Golden Hamburgh, the Chaptal, the Muscat of Alexandria, and the Cannon Hall Muscat. These will form a stock for successional crops for any establishment, whether private or for market. The first three are the hardiest and earliest grapes grown, and will bear most abundantly, ripening their fruit out of doors in ordinary seasons, but being planted on the vine border, or placed in a house devoted entirely to them, and subjected to high temperature and equal treatment, they will give additionally fine fruit, and come on before any others; they also answer admirably for pot-culture, of which more presently. The two Hamburghs and the Chaptal are very generally known and esteemed; alike adapted for the common greenhouse and hothouse as well as for pot-culture, and come in intermediately, following closely on the above, while the last two named are of superior merit, and come in immediately after the Hamburghs, under the same circumstances; thus, for forcing, the Sweetwater, &c., will come in in May or June, according to the time you commence forcing, the Hamburghs in July and August, and the Muscat of Alexandria and the Cannon Hall Muscat are grapes that will come late under similar circumstances; so that, in a good dry house, these will last good nearly up to Christmas. Four conditions are necessary to be observed for success in grape-growing, viz., a good sound dry vine-border, good bright light, a sharp pitch of angle (55° or 60°), and an elevated and pure atmosphere; with these four essentials you cannot fail. The first is attained by digging out the original subsoil (if it is cold clay) to the depth of, say, three feet, and filling in with good turfy loam and sand, mixing in a good portion of old dung and bones, with good underground drains to draw off all superfluous water. It is great folly to deluge the roots' of the vine with stagnated liquid manure, or to apply it too closely to the stem and glut the feeders with rich fatty matter. No wonder we often see comparatively young vines dwindle away under such circumstances. It is only necessary to examine the roots of a vine (on a border that has been heavily dressed with nothing but dung, and had

carrion, blood, &c., introduced into it a few feet from the
stem, (the border being perhaps ten or twelve feet wide) to
see the bad effect of such treatment; these vines were
planted at the usual depth from the surface originally, some
ten or fifteen years ago, and by the addition of the dressings
every year, the border has risen eighteen or twenty inches,
thus the roots are buried for the greater part of three
feet; consequently, the root, for perhaps the whole width
of this border, will be nothing more than unhealthy avenues,
laden and oppressed, covered with a bark like old decayed
cork, of an unusual thickness, a provision of nature to ward
off the influence of an overdose of detrimental matter.
By-the-bye, there is no use for either good or bad matter
here, for there is not a feeder in the whole width of border;
they are gone beyond the limits of this border twenty or
thirty feet, in search of something suitable for food near the
surface; there you will find the feeders (called spongioles)
in abundance, four or five inches under the surface, and
perhaps only two or three inches below.   Now if these
feeders chance to find a good supply of food, the vines will
continue to do well, if not, a failure must ensue, and a poor
crop and mildew will be the result.   Vines will live and
bear well to a very old age under favourable circumstances.
In making a vine-border, do not aim so much at depth of
soil as at surface room, and never apply undecomposed
matter, such as horseflesh, blood, &c.; this is enough to kill
an oak, and is of no service whatever put anywhere near the
stem.   Let the soil be made good with a suitable compound
about two feet over the surface for a space of twenty to
thirty feet from, and under the house; set the front wall of
the house on arches; the floor should be laid on brickwork,
in a sort of drain fashion, the spaces filled with good loam,
such as the top-spit of an old pasture; plant the young
vines as shallow as possible, immediately on a good cartload

of old mortar, loam, and bones, and cover the roots with the sandy loam. Grape-vines are very fond of sand; this induces a healthy fibre and a thin bark, and hard and well-ripened root and wood. The second condition necessary to good success is a "good light" in the house; this is attained by the sharp angle of roof, large squares of glass, and good ventilation. Flat roofs are very conducive to impurity of atmosphere; the sharp angle has the opposite effect, in consequence of the elevation, which produces a draught of air from within the house, causes rapid circulation, and preserves purity. This will require an equal supply of heat, as, unless counteracting means are adopted, the sharp angle will require more heat at the fountain than one less sharp to keep the house of the same temperature, and this can be best done by an air-drain. According to the diagram here given, this drain consumes the condensed air, renders it light by rarefaction—in which state it flies over the higher parts of the house,—when it is immediately drawn down by the air-drain, and thus actually answers the twofold purpose of diffusing an equal healthy heat and ventilation throughout the house; for by the constant motion of this circulated air, air is, so to speak, actually created; thus the vines and plants in such a house will naturally be more healthy and robust than they would have been in the absence of such means; and this is a thing of immense importance in early forcing, when little or no external air can be admitted.

A A A A, exterior walls. B, flow and return pipes. C, elevated brickwork over the boiler, over which is a 6-inch iron tank, covered in by a slate slab D. D, air-drain and grating, discharging the air into the tank over the boiler. E, the air escaping from the tank into the house. F, tank, which supplies the boiler with water. G, furnace and ash-pit. H, doorway. The brickwork over the boiler must be raised

sufficiently above the floor of the house to give a good
draught to the drain ; three feet high and three feet square

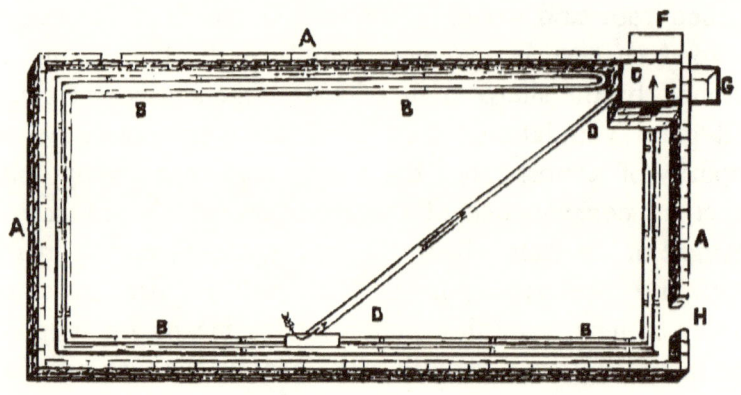

GROUND-PLAN OF HOTHOUSE.

will be found enough : two inches clear must be left over
the water and the covering for the free circulation of air.
The grating must be about the middle of the house in the
pathway, and the drain must be perfectly airtight, except at
the grating ; by this principle the air of the house is supplied with the necessary moisture in due proportion, and if
at any time a perfectly dry atmosphere is required, there is
nothing to do but to let the water over the boiler out of the
tank.   One opening, with shutters, within five feet along
the front wall close to the ground should be left, and an
opening completely along the top of the highest point of the
house should be provided with tight shutters nine inches
wide, with pulley cords to open and shut them at will.

This house, I think, will be found one of safety, and as
useful and economical as possible.   One of the vines should
be planted within three feet along the front of the house, and
each vine should not be allowed more than two canes,
trained up the roof eighteen inches asunder, on wires nine
inches from the glass, both summer and winter.

PRUNING THE VINE

Is a matter of nice importance, but not at all difficult to
do. The chief thing is first to obtain a short-jointed, sound
long rod; this will thè first season produce two bunches
of fruit at each eye (except four or five nearest the stem),
from the bottom to the top of the rod. As soon as the
bunches appear, snap the laterals off the second joint
above the fruit; one bunch of fruit is enough on each of
these. As soon as they are as large as a pea, thin out carefully with a pair of pointed scissors, and tie the shoulder
of the bunch out. Keep all young wood from advancing,
and lay out the stuff nicely right and left, and when the
fruit begins to swell, raise the temperature, and syringe
freely with tepid water. Should the red spider make its
appearance, use the *brimstone water* and quicklime and
sulphur, and apply it once a week in small quantities as a
preventive to either mildew or spider; no air, or very little
beyond what is created by the action of the air-drain, will
be required till the fruit begins to colour; do not thin the
leaves with a view to colouring the fruit; let them remain
one leaf thick above the fruit, and no more. The fruit will
ripen best under about one leaf thick for a shade. Three
or four years' spurring for winter pruning is about the most
economical and safe, and as fruitful as any method that
can be adopted for the vine, during the first season of the
cane. After the fruit is off, early in November, cut the last
year's wood off to one eye; see that this bud is prominent
and firm; allow but one piece of young wood to proceed
from this the ensuing season, as sometimes two will issue
from the spur—not from one bud, but from the bud left for
the purpose, and one from the base of the spur. Rub the
weakest off as soon as observed : the following autumn, cut
close back to a prominent eye; the next summer, leave a

strong bud at the base of the original, to provide a long rod to take the place of one which has been fruiting the last two or three seasons; one of these may be dispensed with every two seasons, and a new one supplied from the base. The vines will do this very well without being exhausted or overdrawing the root, as will be the case when worked exclusively upon the long rod and no spurs. See that the wood is well ripened. This is best done by keeping the vines clear of every bit of lateral wood, tendril, and leaf, beyond what the fruit is growing upon, the rod advancing for the ensuing season, with the leaf necessary for base shade, and giving abundance of air as soon as the fruit is ripe. When the month of November comes, prune the vines, as late pruning causes bleeding. Whitewash the whole of the house with fresh lime, mixing the wash with soft soap water; when dry, give the house a moderate fuming with flour of brimstone and lime, and shut it close for a night or so; this will destroy every insect, and its larva. Never lay the vines outside the house to harden them, with the view to making them earlier or productive. After the vines have been sharply forced, they should be allowed the following season to bear only a moderate late crop.

THE VINE IN POTS

Has some advantages of its own; the same house can be used every season for very early and very late crops, thus one half the house can be filled with vines for an early crop, and by-and-bye, say two months after, the other half can be filled with some of the same sorts, or any other for a late crop, or the same house may be wholly filled and forced every season, provided there are two sets of vines in pots, for early or late crops. These vines should be raised from eyes, and grown in 11-inch pots for fruiting, using loam, dung, and bone dust, and should be trained to a stick three feet high; fruit them on spurs, and feed them while fruiting with one ounce of guano to one gallon of water weekly, top-dressing with loam and dung once a year, in November or December, and plunge the pots in cinder ash during rest. The other essentials to good success are the same as we have said in reference to the house vines. The first and second sorts named, and the late varieties only, are best adapted for pot-culture.

THE VINE OUTDOORS.

Is a most useful and interesting branch of horticulture, especially since the price of glass enables every one to utilize it for the production of good grapes. This is very different from what it used to be; our forefathers had to depend upon the season, but now we can buy a square foot of good glass for twopence or threepence, and convert that foot into an article both economical, convenient, and useful, especially to the outdoor grape-grower. As said before the principal thing for the production of good grapes is the most suitable climate; more depends upon the adaptation of the climate to the nature of the grape than anything else, for it is a fact that if everything else agrees and this be wanting, no grapes can be grown; while, on the other hand, a crop of some kind is certain, if only a suitable atmosphere is secured. This can be proved by introducing a single rod of a vine into a house of an elevated temperature in March, and it will soon be seen what the heat will do; the limb inside the house will produce fruit and ripen it well, while those outside will not probably ripen at all, although growing on the same root. Just so in respect to ripening single bunches of grapes on a vine outdoors on a wall or otherwise. What has been said in reference to soil, situation, pruning, training, for the indoor vine, both in summer and winter may be applied to the

vine outdoors. All grape-vines should be trained serpentine or zigzag fashion, rather than straight, perpendicular,
or even straight up the roof of the forcing-house, for it is
evident both in theory and practice, that this serpentine
form has a very beneficial influence, as the natural tendency
of the sap to run to the extremity of the vine is thus checked,
and a more equal distribution leads to more equal growth
and crop.

As drawers and a protection, the glasses used for ripening
single bunches of fruit are simple and cheap, and as effective as larger glasses. Grape-growing requires for the
bunches (not the roots) the higher atmosphere, and the

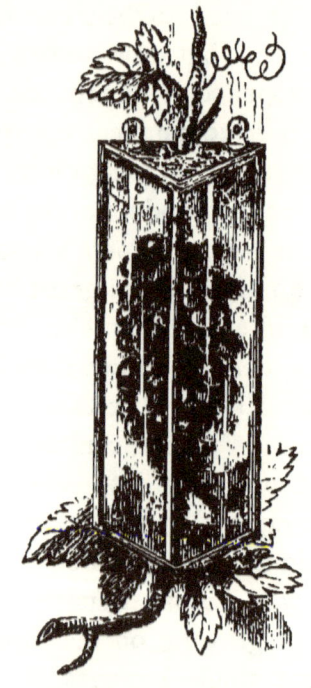

GRAPE-GLASS.

same precautions are therefore required for single bunches
as for large quantities. The diagram of a grape-glass here

given shows the construction adapted for the purpose I have described.

The two ends are blank, with a small opening for the vine, having two pieces of zinc with holes in them to suspend the glass on the wall, and a small staple at the bottom for a string or a piece of copper wire to secure it to the wall below ; the whole frame may be made with zinc, and glazed with two squares six inches by eight inches each. This is large enough to cover the largest sized bunch, and this made of the best glass will not cost more than threepence ; or the glazing and frame complete about a shilling each. The glass may be put over the bunches as soon as they are of full size. The effect of the glass upon the bunch in producing flavour and increasing the size of the berry is astonishing. The glasses may be made of larger sizes, to adapt them for use as hand lights to protect cauliflower plants during winter, and for various other purposes.

The sorts of grapes for the open wall depend in some degree upon the climate ; for instance, the Black Hamburgh would thrive in the south of England, whilst the Dutch Sweetwater, Black Cluster, a very early and hardy grape, would be more suitable for the north ; but there are none better than the early White Sweetwater for table or wine-making. The best way of propagating the vine is either by eyes or cuttings ; eyes on solid and well-ripened wood of about an inch or an inch and a half long, preserving the bud in the middle, and planted like beans in a pot or in a heated bed : cuttings six or eight inches long, of the last year's wood, of a well-ripened and short-jointed sort, should be selected and planted halfway into the soil.

STONE FRUIT.—Its Management.

ALL stone fruits are particularly partial to a gravelly and sandy soil; not very deep, especially in the case of plums and cherries. And when the soil is of a cold, clayey nature, it is of very little use to plant either, unless the subsoil can be rendered gravelly and porous. Introduce abundance of sand, with small stones in it, before the plums and cherries are planted; and when they begin to make wood, and the fruit drops off before it is stoned; in November, take the plant up and replant it, reserving as much of the roots as possible; plant it well, and probably in the ensuing season a full crop of fruit will be produced. In some parts of the country we can rarely go into a garden and see in the season a full crop of fruit on every plum and cherry tree, whilst in other parts abundant crops of both are annually produced. Always plant as shallow as possible consistent with safety.

THE PEACH AND NECTARINE.

WHEN peach and nectarine trees produce more wood than can be easily removed without severe pruning, either take them up and re-plant them, or lay all the young wood you possibly can; for it is altogether useless after the wood is made either to rub the buds out or cut the stuff off. When a tree is given to make more wood than usual, it will bear more fruit. When a tree is weak and makes puny stuff, dis-bud it, and do not allow such a plant to bear so much till it has recovered itself. Peach, nectarine, and apricot trees will bear abundantly in maiden loam and sand without dung, which, in fact, is very little good to them; for when planted on very rich borders they will make abundance of growth instead of fruit. As the benefit intended by the dressing is partially lost, being either washed away before the time or absorbed by additional growth, and that just at the time the fruit requires additional nourishment there is less of it; hence there is frequently a failure of nearly the whole crop of apricots. Plant the trees only in maiden loam and sand; give no manure to them till they are in full bloom, and then thoroughly soak the border on which the apricot grows with one ounce of guano to one gallon of water; and this may be done once a week until the fruit is swelling off, or is about the size of a walnut. In giving the liquid manure, see that the ground is well soaked, so that the manure may reach down to the feeders of the plant; otherwise the tree derives no benefit from such waterings. At the very critical time of the stoning of the fruit of plums, cherries, apricots, and even peaches, liquid manure dressings will be found most beneficial; far more so than heavy dressings of dung during the spring or autumn; for it is evident that the principal reason why stone-fruit falls off at this time is because the plant cannot supply nourishment equal to the demand; and this liquid food is applied just in the condition and in such necessary proportion as trees thus progressing require; but without this liquid manure the evaporation at this time of the year, and the scattered fragments of nutriment found by the slow progress of the feeders in search of it, the fruit entirely fails.

ON TRAINING.

In the case of the peach and nectarine, if the wall is high enough, an immense saving of wall, and a larger number of fruit can be obtained from the same space in superficial feet by planting one dwarf and one standard, and by training the standards chiefly downward, and the dwarfs fan-shaped.

Peaches and nectarines should be completely unnailed from November till January, and the walls syringed with sulphur-water, and then pruned and nailed in. In training, let the chief leaders be nailed in first, dividing them about equally; then lay in the second leaders, and thirdly the laterals, always pointing each clear of the preceding one; ever remembering to lay in a good proportion of young stuff at the base. Always let the shred be on the pulling side, to prevent the nail pressing against the wood, as that will cause canker or gum.

THE GOOSEBERRY

Does exceedingly well as espaliers round the borders of small gardens, and in this way they even thrive better; each plant should be placed about four feet apart, and may be trained on wooden or iron sticks, set neatly eight or ten inches asunder and two or two and a half feet high. The same plan will also suit currants. Whenever plantations of gooseberries are to be formed, use two or three-year old plants: older plants should never be used, as they seldom if ever do so well. A gooseberry tree over the age of five or six years, unless it has been shifted every two seasons, should never be removed, and if it is, the fruit will be small. The gooseberry is particularly fond of well-drained, rich, and friable soil, and it does not object to partial shade where there are quarters of the garden devoted solely to its cultivation. The land should be rough-dug during November with a three-pronged potato fork, and a heavy dressing of the contents of the common sewer and cesspool should be taken during the frosts of December to the ground of the gooseberry trees, and spread over the surface, and all the winter, and in March, after the pruning is done and the cuttings raked up, the surface may be slightly pricked over or merely chopped with a heavy hoe. This system of top-dressing gooseberries is very beneficial. Gooseberries should not be pruned until the end of February or March. If the plants require thinning, leave as much as possible of the last season's wood; do not stump or spur them in, but cut out the old limbs entirely, still preserving an open symmetrical bush, merely taking off the tops of the long flexible shoots.

THE BLACK CURRANT.

THE treatment of the black currant, with one exception, is like that of the gooseberry; it is improved by strong land well-dressed annually, and should be pruned in a similar way. The black currant and gooseberry bear their fruit on the last season's wood. The black currant tree will bear transplanting to an indefinite age.

RED AND WHITE CURRANT

TREES will bear removing to a new place at a greater age than the gooseberry: yet it is no great advantage to transplant them after they have stood on one spot six or eight years. The treatment of these fruits is altogether different from that of the gooseberry and black currant. In forming good permanent plants of these, secure clean six-inch stems, then out of these provide five or six principal branches, standing well out, and one for the centre ; these should not be stopped till of the desired length to form the permanent bush; then cut the top off, and the next season these will give laterals, in the following autumn and always after these must be cut in to a bud or so. These plants bear their fruit on the old wood, therefore cut all the new wood away, except what is wanted to fill up any vacancies, as these will do remarkably well as espaliers.

THE MANAGEMENT OF THE RASPBERRY.

THIS may be called a biennial, for it takes one season to form the stuff to bear the fruit, and then dies. The necessary requirement, therefore, to maintain a constant succession of this is good land. The raspberry is very impatient of removal. When a plantation is to be made, render the soil open and porous (if not naturally so), by introducing a good portion of sand and dung, digging deep; select canes for this purpose that have moderate canes and good spawny fibrous bottoms, and plant in September or October, four feet by three; do not bury the root too deep, three or four inches under the surface will be deep enough. Every autumn cut away the canes that have borne fruit, and reduce the new ones to four or five to each stove; tie them neatly to the stake, well dress the land, and fork it up with a three-pronged fork, leaving it moderately rough. Remove all stray suckers. Old stools are never worth transplanting.

THE APPLE.—Its Management.

The pyramidal-fashioned apple tree has many new charms, like every new-fashioned thing; but in my opinion the old-fashioned espalier will be found the more economical of the two for either large or small gardens, from the fact that the pyramidal plant is found a difficult thing to maintain within the limits of either beauty or economy; and as it is culti-vated and sent out by the growers of it for sale, and for three or four years after it is permanently planted, the beauty of symmetry is lost, and ultimately the plant will become cumbersome, and of greater disadvantage to the small garden than the standard, unless taken up and replanted every two or three years; but the espalier can be kept within the limits of reason, economy, and use, forming a most desirable protection and screen for summer and winter, as well as affording more than an equal proportion of fruit. Choose prolific sorts, such as Hawthornden, Keswick Codlin, and one called in the west of England Bough Hill, a very good early and free-bearing sort, espe-cially adapted for either espalier or pyramids. These three are very early sauce apples. The White and Red Jun-eating, the Quarrendan; for early table use the King of the Pippins, Newtown Pippin, Ribston Pippin, and the Russets, will form a complete successional variety from the earliest to the nearly latest, and of the best for use and quality. Nothing among apples can, I think, supersede the last three, either for flavour or beauty; especially the King of the Pippins and the Newtown Pippin. The apple tree should be planted shallow, on moderately good soil, as it does far better on a free than on a cold, stiff soil; especially the Hawthornden. For a well-formed espalier let the stem be eight or ten inches clear from the surface of the ground, and containing five or six leaders on each side, which should be laid in straight and horizontal. The leaders should not be shortened, till they have extended to the desired length to form the full plant; and a sufficiency of leaders should be neatly laid in from the centre to form the proper height (say five or six feet), and tied fast with rope yarn. As soon as laterals are produced on the leaders, either thumb and finger, or prune them as soon as they are an inch or so long, or cut off (to one bud) during winter. If handsome pyramidal or dwarf plants are desired, the summer wood should be instantly nipped off. The same may be said of pears; these do not so well as espaliers, but do remarkably well on west and east walls, but wherever they grow, frequent removing and root-pruning will be requisite to prevent them descending into the cold clay or dead subsoil, which will prove unproductive of fruit.

THE FIG.—ITS MANAGEMENT.

THE fig, like the grape-vine, requires a full southern aspect, and bears its fruit upon the same season's wood, hence the treatment will be plain; viz., obtain the necessary young stuff as early as possible, and as much of it as is required for a full crop; and as soon as the last young fig appears on each piece of fruit-bearing wood, pinch the top

of it off immediately above the fruit, as this is the only sure
way of hastening the perfection of the fruit ; and if this
stopping is carefully attended to, and the plant planted in
the warmest part of the garden, on the wall, and on a
border consisting of sandy loam, old lime rubbish, and well
drained, the fruit will ripen the same season it is produced.
In the middle and northern counties, the wood should be
nailed in close to the wall ; but in the south the fig does
well even as standards, will bear abundantly, and ripen the
fruit any way.

As soon as the full crop has fairly developed itself, and
the size of a filbert, commence the weekly applications of
liquid manure recommended in this work for stone-fruit
till the fruit is full grown. By pinching off the tops of the
young wood as described, I have seen an amazing crop of
fruit ripened on a single plant the same season ; and adding
to this the timely feedings extraordinarily fine figs may be
had in the autumn, which is far better than taking the
trouble to preserve the green and half grown crop through
the winter. Still, as there is a hazard in cold counties, the
winter crop may be protected by dry hay and mats during the
cold weather. The fig has two crops upon the plant in the
same season, but never ripens more than one in the year,
except under glass or in the south.

THE TRUE TEST FOR SEEDS, &c.

It is of the utmost importance to every one to know
how to buy seeds as well as how to sell them. Now I do
not mean to infer either that no man can be trusted to sell
good seeds to his customers, or that some seeds are any
the worse for being above one year old, for some particular
cases and seasons,—but since seeds are usually sold to
purchasers as new and sound, I do think it will be useful
for all to learn that there is a true sign whereby to know

old from new, vital from non-vital, or less so, as well as to
form a correct opinion as to the character of the seed.   It
will be very useful in purchasing new flower seeds from
non-descriptive catalogues.   When you want new seed-peas,
put one from the stock into your mouth, and bite it ; if it
is very hard it is more than one year old, if the teeth enter
it with moderate ease it is new seed.   Old broad beans are
always of a light brown, new ones very pale brown,
approaching to dead white.   The green Windsor, &c., must
be tested in the same way as peas ; and so also must
kidney beans.   New carrot seed always has a green shade
on it ; old seed loses this, and is of a dead, pale brown, and
less fragrant.   New parsnip has a shade of green, which
it loses if more than one year old.   Onion seed is more
difficult to prove than most other seeds, but if you take a
single seed at a time, and carefully bite it, you will find that
old seed has a tough dry skin with a very white and harsh
kernel, while new seed has a more tender, moist skin,
and the kernel possesses a greater degree of moisture, and
is somewhat oily; the seed may be cut with a penknife
instead of bitten.   Onion seed that has no vitality at all has
no kernel, or one perfectly dry.   Test this by pressing the
seed on a piece of white writing-paper.   If it leaves no
moisture on the paper it is of no use, and has been tampered
with, or has lost its vitality by age.   New cabbage and
brocoli seed possesses a pale green shade in the kernel when
pressed out or cut, and a tinge of green in the brown skin
also ; but old seed loses this in proportion to its age,
becoming of a dull dark brown ; cabbage, brocoli, kales,
&c., will retain their vitality longer than any other seeds,
and will grow well when three years old, or even six years,
if well kept.   Beet seed has a faint tinge of pale green
if new, but is a dull brown if old, and its vitality is very
doubtful if old.   New celery seed has a faint tinge of green,

and is very aromatic, but it loses the green and becomes less fragrant if more than one year old, and is doubtful. Lettuce seed is of a bright silvery grey if new, and the kernel has a green tinge with it, both of which it partially loses with age.   Lettuce seed will grow very well two years old, but above that it is doubtful.   The black-seeded varieties can only be tested by the colour of the kernel, which is the same as in the white-seeded.   Radish seed always has a strong green colour in the kernel up to two or three years old, which changes to a dead, dirty whitish brown if past growing quality ; radish seed will, however, retain its vitality four or five years, although it will not do for early sowing. New spinach seed is of a greenish grey, but old seed is of a dead grey.   Seakale seed is of a pale green inside if new ; this seed is of no use above three years old, and can never be depended on at more than one year old.   Cucumber, melon, and marrow seeds are of a bright creamy white when new, and the kernel of a pure white ; while the outside becomes a dead pale brown, and the kernel a dull cream colour when old.   Either will grow very well up to three or four years old, after that they are doubtful, unless they have been preserved very carefully.

HOW TO PRESERVE SEEDS.

This is of the utmost importance to all, for it depends upon the manner of keeping stocks as to whether they prove more or less vital, even for a few months, especially such as have less power of resistance in themselves.

I need scarcely remind the reader that it is the decomposing elements in the surrounding air that destroy the vitality of seed ; and, consequently, those that contain less oily matter, and have a porous shell or skin to the kernel, are the kinds that perish soonest.   Either seedsmen do not seem to know this, or cannot reconcile themselves to (as it may appear) a more inconvenient method of keeping stocks than the usual wooden drawers; these are of all things the worst unless lined with impervious material, for in due time these seed-drawers become the haunts of insects which drill them full of pin-holes. Now I am convinced it is out of the question for wholesale seedsmen to provide means for the perfect exclusion of the atmosphere; but it is not with these men that the seed becomes deteriorated, for two reasons : first, they are in large and compressed quantities, and they dispose of them within a few short months, and generally clear out year by year; but it is with the small seedsmen where the seed grows old. These men should either keep their stocks in impervious canisters, bags, or bottles, and then what stocks are left over would be good for another season. Tin canisters, such as those used by grocers for coffee and tea, are excellent for such a purpose as the storing of seeds, more convenient than bags or bottles, and quite as handy as drawers. These canisters should be made of the very best tin.

THE SOWING OF SEEDS.

THIS may be classed under four heads, viz., planting seed, deep sowing, shallow sowing, and surface sowing. Under the first comes—

TREE SEEDS.

I MAY name amongst tree seeds, for example, the Walnut, Chestnut, Common Nut, Acorn, Plum and Cherry stones, Hawthorn, Holly, Laurel, and all seeds of trees and shrubs of this degree of strength. These should be buried from two to six inches below the surface of the ground, and may be either planted with a dibber or drilled in, or the soil turned off the necessary depth, the bottom made moderately fine and even, and the seed sown, and then covered with the same soil,—the Walnut and Chestnut five or six inches, the

Common Nut, Acorn, Hawthorn, Holly, &c., three to four inches, and the other sub-class two to three inches.

Under the second head come—Apple, Pear, Asparagus, Seakale, Lupin, Nasturtium, Convolvulus, Iris, Gladiolus, Beans, Peas, &c.; and all seeds of this strength and degree of endurance should be buried from two to three inches below the surface ; otherwise they may never vegetate, especially the tree seeds.

Under the third head come both tree, shrub, flower, and vegetable kinds. For example,—Carrot, Onion, Cabbage, Spinach, Parsnip, Nemophila, Wallflower, Aster, Phlox, Candytuft, Dianthus, Aquilegia, Delphinium, Arbutus, Barberry, Gooseberry, Raspberry, the Fir tribes, and all seeds of this strength and size, or thereabout, which should be buried from half an inch to one inch below the surface.

Under the fourth head come every class and variety of flower, vegetable, tree, and shrub seed. For example, Calceolaria, Campanula, Lobelia, Celery, Thyme, and most potherbs, Turnip, Rhododendron, Azalea, and all fine dust-like seeds, whether tree, vegetable, flower, or shrub.

Frequently the seedsman complains of some seeds not coming up, when the fault is probably that the seeds complained of have either been buried too deep, or not deep enough. It is equally wrong to sow some seeds too shallow as it is to sow fine seeds too deep. Before sowing the seed, the surface of the soil should be made fine and even, and then it should be barely covered with some fine, light, sandy soil ; if on a large scale, such as good broad beds, the surface may be a trifle less fine, and the seed sown evenly over it, then slightly beat the part sown with the back of a spade (about the weight of the spade), and slightly draw the spade towards you every time you strike the surface of the bed of seed. This I find better than raking, or any method for the safe covering of very small seeds ; the fact

is, if the surface is of a consistency equal in fineness to that
of the seed, and therefore fit for its reception, the fine seed
runs into the surface, and then the soil, by the motion of
the spade on the surface, buries the seed quite deep enough
without further trouble. But the surface of the soil must be
dry previously to sowing. All broadcast sowing may be done
this way effectually without raking after, but the surface must
not be too fine nor too coarse before sowing; the one must
be fitted to the other; thus, Spinach seed will require the
surface of the soil considerably coarser than Onion, Onion
coarser than Lettuce, Lettuce coarser than Celery, Celery a
trifle coarser than Rampion, and so on. This is chiefly the
art of sowing, and if observed, almost dispenses with raking
after the seed is in, too much of which is dangerous,
and a waste of time. In cases where it is objectionable to
use the spade to beat in the seed, it may be heeled in,—
that is, chopped in with the rake regularly, instead of working
the rake to and from you; and is especially applicable to
Cabbage, Spinach, and the like. A short-toothed rake should
be used for this operation, and a long-toothed one, not too
fine, for raking off after; the teeth should not be closer than
one and a quarter to one and a half inches apart.

FLOWER SEEDS,

WHICH should be packeted (by retail seedsmen) in a
close-textured paper, and put in close drawers adapted
to the purpose, are, for the most part, so very fine that
they have much less power of resisting the influence of
the air than vegetable seeds; consequently they soon lose
their growing property. Many of our flower seeds come
from hot climates, which is very much against their doing
well in this country, even if they belong to a hardier class.
This fluctuating climate has a worse effect upon seed than
a colder one that is more constant; the seedsman often
gets blamed for what is no fault of his at all. Imported

THE GARDENER'S ENEMIES, and how to Destroy them.

SOME people enumerate more of these than there really are, and some appear to think them fewer. I will endeavour to avoid either extreme, and give every one its due. One of the worst enemies a young gardener has is bad teaching and self-conceit, for this will founder his bark ere he has well set sail. I once knew a professional gardener who used to take his book with him to prune wall trees, and whenever men are taught by unpractical works,—books made only by mere theorists, they discover an ignorance too offensive to be sanctioned by any possessing the least taste for good gardening ; these men are often so puffed up by the little they know, that sound practice is almost contemptible in their eyes. Young men often too lightly estimate the serious nature of good gardening. I have seen young men who have made some sad blunders through this ; they undertake what is too much for them, so, instead of progressing they go back ; their unsound books are far worse than can be conceived by the untaught. Young men who wish to learn gardening well should place themselves under thoroughly good practical men for seven years; in the meanwhile get the best books on the art, and read and work, work and read. Bad books, then, are one of the worst enemies. Well, there are some more beside, but not so bad as they might be to a man who neglects his business. I could never find time to walk about for want of something to do, nor any other purpose but purely business. Well, the enemies of the garden are not a few, but by close application they are not so bad.

THE SLUG AND ITS LARVA

Is perhaps the most general foe, but it is slow and tender too ; all sorts of ways and means have been devised as a preventive and cure for this pest, but as a preventive is better than a cure, never bury old refuse matter in the ground after the crop is off; especially on cabbage ground, celery, turnip, carrot, or potato land. This is frequently the origin of the mischief, and gives rise to numerous enemies. The slug manages to find its way to the refuse matter so buried, and solaces itself on the genial discovery, forms a colony, deposits its eggs, and sends forth its numerous progeny during the next early spring,—or, may be, the next crop, should it be one that is agreeable; if not, the parent and its numerous family have patience, and wait till a crop is put on that suits their taste. And you may often find, on digging up a piece of heavy land, cavities where a whole batch of eggs are deposited. These cavities, in all probability, have been formed by an old turnip, cabbage-stump, leaf, or a stem of old celery. Lime is very effectual in destroying this pest if applied at the right time; let it be half slacked by exposure to the air, and when reduced to a powder sow it over the crop land or lawn while the slugs are visible. This must be frequently repeated, as many slugs are out of the reach of its effects. And after the caustic or burning quality of the lime has been exhausted, which is very soon after its exposure to the open air, rain, &c., it will be useless for the destruction of slugs. Slight sprinklings with barilla will destroy the slugs,—and the crop too if applied too freely; but where there is no crop it may be used with good effect. Salt is an excellent thing for the prevention of slugs; and if a moderately strong solution be applied it will not injure a hardy crop, but will penetrate to a sufficient depth for the destruction of both the slugs and their larvæ. I proved many years ago that salt can be given much stronger to crops for this purpose, or that of manure, than by sowing it (in the dry state) on the surface. Once, in a mistake, I watered some young onions with a concentrated solution of salt, in the form of brine; thinking, after I found it out, that all the crop must perish from the effects of it, but not so ; it never in the least affected the onions for the worse, although I have seen vegetation destroyed by only a moderate application of dry salt. But there is still another thing that will effectually extirpate them, which has but one drawback to its general use, that is "corrosive sublimate ; " this at sixpence per ounce retail is rather dear, it is also poisonous, though not of the nature to affect vegetation, and of course no one would think of either drinking it, or pouring it immediately on anything ready to use for table ; neither should it be used upon tender herbage or plants while under the powerful influence of the sun, but it is best applied on cropped ground during cloudy or shady and damp weather, for two reasons, viz., first because the slugs are nearer or on the surface, and therefore the better effect, and secondly, no bad effects are experienced by the presence of the full rays of the sun. Obtain an ounce of this remedy, put it into a delf quart mug (but in no case put it into pewter, iron, or tin) to dissolve it, fill the mug up with hot water, let it stand till dissolved, then put it into a four or five-gallon water-pot, fill it up with soft cold water, applying a good or a moderate soaking with the rose, according to the object in view, to the spot infested with slugs, grubs, wireworms, woodlice, thrip, &c. ; the wireworm will require it stronger than anything else.

This remedy, if once it come in contact with the vital juices, has a fatal effect upon all animated nature ; not perhaps immediately, as this depends upon the strength of the solution. Let gardeners try it upon worms, grubs, &c. ; they will soon learn, although that has been already stated, the strength required, and that is strong enough for slugs, worms, &c.

The next worst enemy the gardener has is the thrip among cucumbers, melons, plants in frames, greenhouses, and stoves. I have noticed particularly that it is very fond of moist heat, but by narrow watching this pest can be kept back. Should it, however, once get fairly established, it will prove a most tenacious enemy, the eradication of which frequently causes the loss of the plants. It has more the appearance of a disease than of a real animal, for it is evident it can be easily germinated and also easily destroyed. The thrip is always found on the plant at about a certain state of atmosphere and moist heat; too much of either drought or moisture appears to be unsuitable for it, for I have had cuttings of verbenas, &c., in a moist heat in spring which have been suddenly infested with this pest, but as soon as they have been removed to a colder and drier atmosphere, they have disappeared; and I have proved that a constant daily syringing with pure water will not only cure them, but be disagreeable to them as well, as they will not then trouble you. The difficulty is greater by far with early forced plants, cucumbers, melons, &c.; in such cases a keen look-out is principally what is wanted, and a little judgment also merely to observe the first signs of its location, which is discovered by the upper side of the leaf assuming a crippled and sickly form, curling at the edges, and contracting instead of expanding. The leaf quickly indicates the attack of this foe, for it attacks the chief channels of the leaf for the flow of sap, viz., the midribs. Some think that this insect acts with malice, and has some antipathy either against the person or plant, as they seem to think it commits its depredations for mischief alone, by stinging the leaf as it were to death, by piercing its midribs with its proboscis, and infusing its venom to poison the object of its malice, but this is not the case ; the fact is, in proportion to their strength of numbers on the leaf or plant, so is the draw of the vital juices for the support of their existence ; and feeding upon the plant night and day, without intermission, no hope is left for the expansion of the plant, or any parts of it, and the plant ceases to live sooner or later, just in proportion to the numbers of this pest so located. Just so with aphides on roses and peach trees, &c. Now the remedy is simple enough. See " Cucumber and Melon-growing," also " Red Spider."

THE APHIS

Is another troublesome insect to the gardener, and comes in such swarms as to overwhelm him at times; but fortunately this foe is very tender, and soon dislodged. Clean cold water, applied with the force of the syringe, will do this, but not unfrequently they are able to re-ascend the tree ; in lieu therefore of this, put a box of the Gishurst compound, cut up into small pieces, into a tub holding as many gallons of water as there are ounces of the compound : stir it occasionally till dissolved, then let it settle, and when clear syringe the tree or plant with the liquor, drawing it off carefully, so as not to disturb the settlement at the bottom of the tub. In cases of plants in flower this syringing should be omitted, or be done very carefully, to avoid wetting the expanded flowers ; generally this insect attacks roses, wall trees, &c., as soon as the trees have formed two or three inches of young wood, just at the time the young stuff is fairly starting with vigour, and before roses are in bloom ; it is very good policy to give them a dressing with this compound before the roses are in bloom, as it will prove a preventive to their attacking the plant ; but should this pest have made much progress before it is observed, and the plant (supposing it to be a rose in the ground) in bloom, get a fine thin calico bag, made sufficiently large to admit of the head going into it, when the branches are drawn together moderately and tied with a bit of matting ; let this bag have a sufficient depth to admit of the whole head being enveloped without doubling down, and.let it have a slide string to draw close below the head ; then draw the bag gently over the head of the plant, slide it nearly close, and with the fumigating bellows fill the bag with tobacco smoke ; draw the bag slide quite close, let it remain for ten minutes or a quarter of an hour, and then shift it and proceed to another. This and all syringing should, if necessary, be done in the evening, or when there is no prospect of the sun breaking out for some hours. Smoking, &c., should be done when the foliage is perfectly dry ; and syringing, after these applications, with clean water is indispensable for the eradication of all insects, before the sun bears upon the trees.

THE RED SPIDER

Is another enemy the gardener dreads, for he is in some cases a troublesome little pest. I have referred to this under the treatment of the "grape-vine," melon, &c. ; but still I feel it necessary to mention it here. The red spider is a very diminutive little creature, so small that it frequently forms a vast colony before it is observed by an unpractised eye, hence the greater the difficulty to despatch it. The red spider generally appears during a dry atmosphere on vines indoors and outdoors too ; and on melons when they are ripening. A damp atmosphere and frequent syringing are easy preventives, but in cases of ripe fruit this cannot be practised to much extent ; still there must be no delay. The first indications of its presence is a rusty colour of the under side of the leaf, the upper side presenting a sickly green with whity-brown and rusty spots. Plants very soon indicate its appearance by the healthy green dying off a shade or two within a day or so after it has commenced its ravages ; therefore keep a sharp look-out, and at once . apply the remedy of flour of sulphur and the quicklime named in the articles "The Grape-vine" and "Melon." In cases like peaches on walls, apple trees, &c., the "insecticides" can be used freely, and in every instance syringe afterwards with fresh clean water, and the next morning, or soon after, before the sun has much power. This little fellow is very nimble, and runs over the whole territory of a vine and frame with melons in a very short time, but is quickly despatched if taken at the onset.

THE WOODLOUSE (*Oniscus*)

Is a terrible enemy to mushroom-growers, and is trouble-some in frames where melons are ripening; also among flowers in the frames and flower-beds; they eat anything that is tender and to their taste, and are particularly fond of mushrooms in the earliest stage, and as this article must be grown in the dark, it offers better accommodation to its deposition. Young gardeners often wonder how it is that after taking so much trouble in the right direction, they cannot get a crop of mushrooms; an abundance of young mushrooms may have been seen coming up, but few or none have come to perfection; the fact is, that whilst he was asleep, this foe has been at work. As it is one of the most difficult things in gardening to despatch these insects when once fairly colonized about a mushroom-bed, the precaution should be taken not to let them settle thereabouts. As soon, therefore, as a bed is made, get some bamboo of moderate size, and cut it into lengths of one joint, open at the other end, and bait these with nice, mealy, boiled potato and bread crumbs mixed with a little arsenic; they will creep into these traps, abide, and live and die there. Exa-mine these traps every two or three days, empty and re-bait them with fresh bait, and you will have destroyed them before the mushrooms appear, as it is of very little avail to leave this business to be done when the bed is in fruiting. In the melon-bed these traps will be most effective in trapping these night marauders, by merely filling them loosely with dry moss; they may be baited likewise, as an inducement to them to enter for food, for it is certain they do not merely go out by chance in search of food, but that they possess an instinct of knowledge "when and whereabouts" to find something suitable. How great the wisdom and knowledge displayed in the creation of these creatures ! still, as they are so injurious to the garden, we regard it as right to destroy them.

THE SCALE

Is another pest of no ordinary class, and it is amazing with what rapidity these dormant-looking creatures will seize upon their victims. They are to be found upon the Orange tree, Acacia, and various other plants, always apparently in the same place, but it is not so, for they advance slowly but surely ; otherwise they have a very peculiar power of increase, for we find every few days a little further on toward the extremity of the plant a few more added to the number, although never observed to be moving. I am disposed to think that this mysterious insect is something like young dip-chicks (moorhens), which run with the shell on their heads ; for doubtless this plant-enemy, as soon as hatched, and before it can be seen with the naked eye, advances farther on in search of food ; so that one parent will soon form a whole colony, and ultimately overrun the entire plant, and draw so rapidly upon its vitals that the plant pines away and dies in the end. Plants subject to the ravages of this insect should have prompt attention, and be washed with a strong solution of sulphur and soft soap, Gishurst compound, or some of the popular insecticides, and should afterwards also be well syringed with clean water.

THE MEALY BUG (*Coccus*)

Is a disagreeable, partial enemy; and is found most frequently upon plants which grow in warm localities, such as
greenhouses, stoves, and salubrious parts out-door; some
plants are more subject to it than others. As those most
liable are not always the object of its ravages, the principal
thing to observe is to maintain, as far as is consistent with
convenience, a perfectly pure atmosphere, as a preventive
of its attacks, as every insect of this kind appears to gene-
rate and flourish most in an impure atmosphere. It is well
known that an east wind in the spring brings in this way
numerous troubles to the garden. Now I cannot conceive
how any one can imagine that the "aphis," called the
"American blight," is actually wafted from that country to
this, as it not only comes from a contrary direction, but it is
also improbable that either this or any other insect should
be transported such a distance, from the fact of their sudden
appearance in large numbers. It seems to possess a
poisonous quality in its effects upon the vitals of its victim,
for the immediate spot on the plant or tree infested actually
becomes ulcerated, while the remainder of the tree continues
to flourish; particularly in its attacks upon the apple tree.
There are numerous varieties of this insect, but all have a
similar nature, and may be cured by the same means; viz.,
a strong solution of the Gishurst compound on stems and
stout branches, put on them with a new painter's brush.
Other insecticides may be used, such as sulphur and soft
soap and lime mixed to a thin paint, or a strong solution of
"corrosive sublimate" syringed upon them, and washed
again with clean water an hour after. This is a certain and
rapid insecticide, but must be washed well off by the syringe
from the foliage before the sun strikes forcibly upon it,
especially tender stuff, but the mealy bug attacks almost
exclusively the hard wood.

THE TRUE AMERICAN BLIGHT

Is that white unlike-looking insect which appears in spring upon our apple trees, and may be destroyed as aforesaid.

THE GARDEN MITE.

THIS insect is about one of the worst things that can find an entrance into the cucumber frame or house in early spring; and is as bad, or worse than the thrip or red spider, from the fact that it commits its depredations under the most unfavourable circumstances for its destruction, viz., a warm moisture, the discontinuation of which proves fatal to the cucumbers. I have noticed particularly that this insect breeds and flourishes exceedingly over tanks; and the more moisture there is the better it likes it. The chief difficulty in destroying this pest in frames and forcing-houses is the application of a sufficient quantity of the insecticide without injury to the cucumbers; as it has the advantage of the soil of the bed for its protection, and any kind of fuming has but little effect, on account of the vapours rising instead of descending while the insect descends. The only effectual remedy that can be applied to destroy them without injury to cucumber plants, is to sprinkle the surface of the bed over with Scotch snuff, or flour of sulphur; and avoid watering the surface of the bed for a few days after. As a preventive to these and other insects in confined places, use half a pound of camphor, dropping as much spirits of wine upon it as will cause the camphor to crumble into dust, say fifty or sixty drops at first; and if this does not produce the desired effect within half an hour, drop more spirit upon it, and let it stay for a time; and when reduced to a powder sow it broadcast over the surface of the bed. Again, put half an ounce of camphor into an ounce of spirits of wine; which will be half a pound of camphor to one pint of spirit, and enough to dress a large frame, &c. This should be

done with a new paint-brush, painting the inside of the
frame, brickwork, &c. The spirit will evaporate immediately, and the camphor remain to give off its fumes for some
time, and this will not injure anything among plants, so long
as the spirit does not at the time of application drop upon
the leaf. The camphor is a vegetable product, and will not
injure anything but animated nature ; to which it is disagreeable at all times, and mortally destructive in confined places.
Some do not regard this as of any good, but I have used so
much of it that I can vouch for its utility : but, as I have
observed before, the principal thing is to maintain a pure
atmosphere, the absence of which produces this pest. Let
some good pieces of charcoal also be kept in the water
used, and some scattered about on the surface of the bed,
and see to the constant consumption of the contaminated
air by means of the fire, specified under the head " The
Grape-vine Indoors ;" see also the article " Charcoal and
its Uses."

CATERPILLARS.

THERE are several varieties of these, the principal being
the cabbage, gooseberry, and thorn ; but the gooseberry and
cabbage caterpillars are upon the whole the worst enemies
of the garden. Volumes have been written upon these
two, as to the best way to prevent their ravages. This
enemy appears on the gooseberry at a critical time for
destroying it, viz., just as the fruit is about half-grown.
The moth deposits her eggs on the leaf early in spring, and
if looked for under the leaf, numerous mites will be observed, which soon commence work by drilling the leaf
with pin-holes. These destructing attacks make rapid
progress, and soon strip the whole bush of its leaves ; and
exposing the fruit to the full power of the sun deprives the
plant of its lungs, the consequence of which is the pre-

mature death of the tree, and the loss of the present crop
The caterpillar having done all it can, proceeds to hiber-
nate.   It is evident that the moth deposits her eggs on
the gooseberry early in the summer; and a few days after
the eggs are deposited they are hatched on or under the
leaf, and all the moths are developed in spring.   The only
thing that can be used as a preventive is to syringe the
leaves with a solution of the Gishurst compound, or soft
soap and sulphur.   The moth will be cautious in coming
near plants so dressed.   As soon as the pin-holes are observed in the leaf, proceed at once to syringe, as recommended.

THE CABBAGE CATERPILLAR

MAY be prevented by the same means, and washing with
clean water afterwards.   Of course it is scarcely applicable
to full-grown cabbages, nor those with much heart, as the
compound will settle in the interior of the cabbage, and
become disagreeable.

THE ANT (EMMET)

Is more of a friend than an enemy in numbers of instances, though it is true this little busybody will eat a
little fruit, and it will form a colony where it is not convenient for it to remain.   If a nest of these little creatures
is found anywhere else than in a flower-pot, occupied with
a plant, or in a hotbed frame, do not disturb the ants, but
watch their movements.   They will be observed coming home
with what is of no use to the garden; on the contrary, the
industrious little things will be seen carrying an enemy of the
garden, as large as themselves, such as they cannot manage
to carry home whole, they sting to death and feed upon.
Watch them also in the frames of melons, cucumbers, or
other plants, and upon wall-trees, and it will be seen that

they are actually slaying some of your worst enemies in embryo; and where they visit, few things else care to frequent. They may be seen in numbers on pot-plants, where, perhaps, there are numerous thrip, aphides, red spider, or some other pest; and it will be observed that they are engaged in the destruction of these garden wasters. They will also climb to a height beyond the reach of the syringe, and therefore make up for its deficiency. When ants get into a plant-pot, they may be driven out by setting the pot up to the rim in a tub of water for a day or so.

MICE IN THE GARDEN.

These little creatures are at all times decided enemies of the garden, especially during the early spring, but I have remarked upon the way to avoid the mischief they commonly do to early peas under that head; in other cases they may be soon despatched, but it often happens that they do a large amount of damage to plants and crops before they are known to be in the locality. There are two kinds of mice; one is fond of dry corn, &c., and the other is fond of green stuff, and they differ very much in appearance. The house-mouse is whiter than the other, is smoother, and has a long tail; the field-mouse is larger, rougher, and brown, and has a short tail and large ears, and this will sweep off the plants and do many pounds' worth of damage in a house or frame of plants in a single night, by cutting them clean off down to the pot. To prevent these ravages soak some marrow peas in a weak solution of arsenic for twelve hours, or a strong decoction of nux vomica for twenty-four hours, and then lay these peas, fresh from the solution, about your frames, &c.; the mice will readily eat them and disappear. As soon as a crop of peas or beans is sown some of these soaked peas should be laid about the rows, and the future mischief will be avoided, for they seldom attack the sown peas or beans till by lying in the ground they are soft. The soaked peas for bait may be washed once in clean water to cleanse the superfluous poison from the exterior of the peas, as too much of this has a repulsive influence, and may deter them from eating the bait at once. If the poisoned peas are laid under a tile or slate a little elevated at one end by a stone or some earth raised to rest on, so much the better, as they prefer secrecy, and seem to like stealing. This trap answers for both kinds of mice. Rats may be destroyed effectually in the same way. Of the two remedies the arsenic is the better one.

BIRDS INJURIOUS TO THE GARDEN.

THE house-sparrow will eat the young peas when they are an inch or two above ground. This may be prevented by running some two or three lines of shoemaker's hemp over the rows. The tomtit will pick the pea-pods and some fruits, but the gardener should avoid destroying them, for the sake of the good they do by the destruction of vast numbers of caterpillars infesting cabbages, trees, &c. The blackbird is an avaricious enemy among fruit. The best means of prevention is to cover the fruit with nets, baiting a gin with some of their favourite fruit, and setting it near the trees in fruit.

A sparrowhawk or buzzard, or a good cat, is as good as anything that can be kept in a garden to prevent all kinds of birds committing their wonted depredations. The blackbird and jay have a particular antipathy against the cat and the hawk class, and will shun their company. The buzzard or hawk, on a perch that can be shifted from one part of the garden to the other as required to guard the ripe fruit, will be conspicuous, perched up three or four feet from the ground, and will thus act as an alarm.

THE BULLFINCH

Is a most confident and daring enemy of the garden during the early spring months, committing a vast amount of mischief among gooseberry bushes by picking out the buds. Running round the gooseberry ground with a spring rattle such as policemen use is an effectual remedy, for the birds will speedily make their exit from the grounds to some other distant locality. I have observed that as soon as the rattle is sprung it seems to paralyze these bold intruders, so that the effect is wonderful on the little creatures. Gooseberry trees should not be pruned till March, to give the advantage of leaving full-budded wood for fruiting, as the bullfinch will probably thin some particular leaders or parts of a tree in spite of every endeavour to prevent it. (See "Gooseberry.")

THE CHAFFINCH.

THIS bird is tedious on seed-beds, viz., cabbage and spinach, especially cabbage and brocoli, but the mischief is easily prevented by merely sowing the seed, and then cover. ing it up with a net or some coarse old hay, just sufficient to hide the seed, or rather the surface of the ground, and no more. So also with radish seed, of which they are very fond. I never observed that the chaffinch was addicted to any other mischief in the garden. It is a very cautious bird, and will not attempt to come near anything that looks like danger.

There are other birds of a mischievous character, but these are the principal. The chaffinch is very general, so is the house-sparrow, the blackbird, and the bullfinch, but the jay and some other troublesome birds are not so abundant in every locality.

THE GARDENER'S FRIENDS, AND HOW TO USE THEM.

THE friends of the gardener are numerous. The following deserve notice. Long practical experience for a teacher is one of the best friends of the young man, good smart tact and ability, with an orderly discipline stringently enforced in everything,—in time and in material ; economy without being niggardly, and liberality without being prodigal, are also some of the young gardener's best friends. As I have always observed, there is but one way of doing things well, with which every teacher should be conversant, and expect from his pupils undeviating compliance. Young men anxious to attain to eminence should possess a good moral character, be active and orderly, well educated, studious, and constantly increasing their practical acquaintance with their business ; be polite without affectation, and ever ready to learn from those whose age and experience qualify them to instruct others who have not as yet had the same opportunities of advancement in a thorough practical knowledge of their profession, and for want of such qualifications as these I have witnessed sad mistakes. Young gardeners should not read every work on gardening, but study those most practical, short, plain, and to the point.   Pupils should study botany in all its departments, and learn to draw flowers, so as to be able to preserve the character and colour of any favourite ; they will find this not only a pleasing pastime, but a very profitable one.   Perfection in gardening is attainable by a close application of the mind for a moderate time, as a thorough knowledge of gardening is not, as some imagine, acquired by only two or three years' indifferent teaching.   Those intended for gardeners should early manifest their taste, and be apprenticed, say from nine or ten to 12 or 14 years old, or as soon as they can handlea spade or hoe, till twenty-one years of age, and to a man of known ability.

LANDSCAPE GARDENING

MAY be carried out both on a small as well as on a large scale; this kind of garden should resemble nature in a general way, with some modifications. Reduce what you observe in nature in some lovely dale, or park, or forest, to any scale you like; but instead of planting oaks, elms, and ash, substitute some of the birch, holly, acacia, pine, and fir tribe for the most distant objects, and the deodars, arbor vitæ, red cedars, hemlock spruce, junipers, araucarias, Irish yew, lilac, syringas, laburnums, acubas, laurustinus, and Portugal laurels, &c., for the nearer objects, and the rhododendron, azalia, kalmia, Daphne, Andromedas, Berberis, roses, &c., for the foreground. If the scale is sufficient to admit of bold clumps of acacias and birch, with some Pinus and larch firs, with thorns and laburnums on the outsides, so much the better. Good broad openings should be left to form the landscape, and to give distance and effect to the scenery; and here and there a cedar of Lebanon in the distance; a little nearer a Wellingtonia, a *Pinus insignis*, and deodars, in single plants, and at a distance from each other, to admit of the beauty of the landscape being preserved. This principle must be maintained throughout, whether on a large scale or a small one; no hard lines should be observed, nor any abrupt terminations, but one continuous succession of openings and objects; this is the beauty of landscape gardening, and of the landscape too. This principle should be carried out in the flower-garden. A man with a mechanical eye will find more difficulty in laying out the landscape than one with an artistic eye, hence so few well-devised landscapes and ornamental grounds. There is nothing but correct taste to guide in this matter, and unfortunately but little of this is to be found in ordinary gardening. One reason for this is that most men want some certain guide, and this is supplied by mechanical tuition, which is all good enough in the kitchen garden, but completely upsets the beauty of nature in the pleasure-garden and the landscape. The chief reason why so little of the necessary judgment for making a good land-scape gardener is to be found in the want of artistic taste; this is only attained by cultivation and experience. There are many young men capable of high genius in this line, which would develop itself by studious cultivation, and such would feel their independence of mere mechanism. Let the landscape gardener study nature, and improve that if he can. It is waste of time (in my opinion) for any writer to attempt to give a plan of landscape gardening, or a set of rules for it, as these, however good, would not answer for more than one of his readers out of a thousand in all probability. When a bit of land is to be laid out as a landscape or a parterre, a sketch of the original should be made on a card; take this home, and at leisure make what designs appear desirable to enhance the beauty of the place; working always from the dwelling-house—let that be your standpoint—looking to future while you plan for long-lived subjects, as for clumps of trees before named—these will form the chief objects of the scene,—study what they will be ten or twenty years hence; denoting on the paper the differ-ence of each subject in character, colour, and feature, by figures and references; that is, fig. 1 might denote cedar of Lebanon, fig. 2, *Pinus insignis*, fig. 3, a clump of chestnut, firs, acacia, thorns, or laburnums, &c., with letters for each sort; thus letter *a* in the clump, the chestnut, *b*, the acacia, *c*, the laburnum, thorn, and so on.

Then go over the ground with a man, some stout sticks, and the plan, mark down the identical spot for each as denoted on the plan. I have seen some very valuable trees and shrubs obliged to be sacrificed to the woodman's axe for want of taking this precaution, which, having stood fifteen or twenty years, was a serious loss.

The laying out of a home shrubbery and the flower-garden is the same in working, and should be the same in effect, as far as resemblance to nature goes. A superb effect may be given to a well-devised pleasure-ground by planting freely the hemlock spruce, China arbor vitæ, *Juniperus pendula*, and laurustine in prominent places; these form remarkable and beautiful backgrounds to the flower-garden. Small plants should be planted at all times, and those grown in pots that have been lifted every season are preferable. The ground should be trenched or dug deep, and should be of a porous, sandy nature for the fine fir tribe; in cold clayey soils the planting is best deferred till April, unless it can be done in September and October. In porous, sandy, and gravelly soils it can be done any time between October and March, the autumn preferred. (See chapter on "Planting.")

THE FLOWER-GARDEN—its Merits and Defects.

No one need go to Sydenham to see what a perfect flower-garden is. Every flower should be perfectly grown, whether in beds or pots. Symmetry of form, with fulness of flower, are the characteristics of a perfect plant. Some attain to this; but the wisest plan is to provide adequately for these requirements in good time, and this requires calculation long beforehand, and then preparation to carry out the results of this calculation by propagating accordingly, so that the beds or houses may be as complete as possible. But this cannot be attained by the full complement half grown, nor half the required number well grown, which is the cause of so many defective gardens, and is not calculated at all as the necessary number of plants required respectively, or too few calculated upon to form perfect beds; so that by some means the number comes short, and when the beds or the stand have to be filled, the plants must of necessity be put too far asunder to form a perfect object. I do not mean to say a bed is the more perfect because it presents nothing but a mass of yellow, blue, or scarlet, without a due proportion of green, for this in a moderate proportion contributes materially to perfection, but often we see too much leaf and too little flower. But this is not all that constitutes imperfection in flower-beds; it consists chiefly in beds that never make the display that it is intended they should, or are capable of; and if accomplished, it is but a short time before overtaken by the cold, chilly rains of autumn,—and why, in these days of variety, should there be such short-lived flower-gardening? The answer is that there is a want of an abundance of good, well-grown stuff, planting sufficiently close to cover the bed quickly, and using soil to suit each subject. But this will be treated of under its respective head.

The perfection of the flower department is not merely growing a few plants to an extraordinary size, but sufficient of them and variety enough to keep up a constant display in the conservatory and flower-garden for the season; that is, from January till November. Over crowding, either in the conservatory or flower-garden, is as much to be avoided as planting or growing too thinly. The number should be provided of full-grown plants for the house, and the speedy filling of the respective beds early in the season. Soil is very important. Some plants do far better in a poor than in a rich soil; even the scarlet geranium will produce better trusses and more flowers in a moderate soil with pit-sand than in a gross feeding soil; and the *Mesembryanthemum speciosa purpurea*, and others of this class, will not do so

well with anything as with sandy soil, or sand and gravel ;
that is, pit-sand and gravel, and a full sunny place.   With
these advantages, the display of the plants will be beautiful.
This, as far as plants have to do with it, is the way to produce a perfect flower-garden.   There is still another thing too
frequently disregarded, and which materially retards perfection ; that is, overcrowding plants, and beds too large or too
small for the surface on which they grow.   To avoid these
faults, and to do things to a nicety, scale the beds to the
area on which they are to lie ; obtain the length and
breadth of the lawn in feet, draw a line showing the boundary,
then try on paper the sort of bed desirable for taste or
place, on a scale of one eighth, two-eighths, or four-eighths
of an inch to the foot, and it will soon be seen which scale
suits the space best.   The disagreeable, heavy, or poor-
looking beds frequently to be met with will thus be obviated.
Too many beds on a given space are worse than too few.
There should be a certain degree of freedom, a proportionate
relief to each bed.   In constructing or designing beds, all
is easily done with a straight-edge, and a pair of proportionately stout large wood compasses, five feet long.   First
with the straight-edge line the bed out into one-foot squares,
marking each line with a pointed stick so as to be plain
enough to be seen ; then with the compasses draw the bed
designed on the trial-sheet before referred to.   No matter
what the shape of the bed, all may be struck out by the
compasses ; as, by simply setting one of the feet of the
compasses on an angle indicating the points of the squares,
all kinds of figurative beds representing leaves may be as
easily formed as circles, which look very ornamental during
the winter when vacant, and the more so if filled with
different coloured crocuses and other dwarf bulbs to flower
during the early spring.   The perfection of the flower-garden
consists in harmony without mechanism.   Every bed should

have its corresponding one to match, but this has given way
to the natural landscape; and should be carried out, as far
as possible, both on the small and large scale. The defects
of the flower-garden are the opposite of all this, and may be
thus summed up,—beds too large, beds too small and too
many, a want of relief and of mechanism, and a sufficient
display for the season. But these failures can be avoided
by careful study, and not without. Some say they cannot
afford to spend so much time to carry out these arrange-
ments, but there are others who would be charmed to see
something of this sort. I once knew a gardener who took
great delight in flowers, and in making improvements. He
undertook a gentleman's grounds who, it was said, did not
care anything about flowers; certainly it did look like it.
However, the gardener was not prohibited from doing as he
liked, and in the course of time he had the pleasure of
knowing that his employer was exceedingly gratified in seeing
what he had never seen on the spot before, and what was
said by some good judges to be a perfect flower-garden; a
satisfactory proof that a good garden has an irresistible
influence few can altogether resist. I am therefore convinced that the success of gardening depends much upon
the skill and taste of the gardener himself.

HOW TO MAKE THE LAWN, AND HOW TO MANAGE IT.

SOME gardeners and amateurs think to save something
by levelling the space intended for the lawn, and merely
sowing it with some choice grass seed recommended for
the purpose; but I think such persons will find, on calculation, that there is a considerable loss by adopting such a
protracted way of obtaining a really good sward. For it
will certainly take many years for a sown lawn to attain to
one laid with cut turf from a good old tough common.
Having practised this way of making lawns very little, I

cannot say exactly, but certainly it would take at the least ten years for a grass sown lawn to equal the texture of one turf-laid of the first or second season.   There is so much difference in the qualities of lawns, that it is necessary, before a sound judgment can be formed, to make personal observation by a visit to some nobleman's grounds, or where first-class lawns are to be seen kept in the highest order.   The texture of a new Turkey carpet will give the best idea of what is meant by "good sward."   An old, half-dry, common one, that has a flat, moist subsoil; that never suffers from perfect drought; constantly grazed and kept short, where may be found certain spots of far better texture than others: these are the spots from which to select turf for laying new lawns.   The turfs should be cut three feet long and one foot wide, for convenience of handling, as well as for calculation, as they are often cut by number instead of day-work.   They should all be cut one thickness; one inch and a half, or not more than two inches, and each one not more than twelve inches wide and three feet long, and should be rolled up tight, grass side inwards.   A raser, a line, a six-feet measure, and a good turfing-iron are necessary tools.   There are different-shaped turfing-irons; but I have not seen one I like so well as one of the description here represented.

TURFING-IRONS.

No. 1. The turfing-iron, the blade seven inches long and seven inches wide; and the stem, up to the crank, about eight inches long; the crank about six inches rise; stout, but not clumsy; and blade, stem, and crank should all be of good steel, with a fork socket and a short spade handle. This tool should be wiped particularly dry, and greased before it is put away, to prevent rust. No. 2. The raser, a common ash or oak stick, sawed in the end to admit of the point of an old scythe being riveted in, with a drop-point of about two inches for the raser.

Put down the line and strain it tightly, place the raser close to the line, and drive it before you, pressing it down to the ground, taking care not to shift the line out of its straight position. In using the turfing-iron, stand at the side and not at the end of the turf; dig the ground (breaking it fine) regularly over for about six or nine inches, then run a light roller over it afterwards, scarify it over the surface with a coarse rake, raking off all coarse stone, &c., and lay the turf, driving it close at the joints. When the whole is complete run a moderate roll over it regularly one way; then do so by crossing the previous work of the roll; then cut the work of the roll again and so on, and as unevennesses will occur, beat them to a level with a heavy turf-beater and then roll again. Lawns may be laid any time from October till April, rolling frequently after heavy rains. Never sweep lawns with half worn-out brooms, nor with the whalebone or cocoa-nut fibre brooms ; for these injure the heart of the grass by bruising and tearing it. Nothing but a moderate-sized new birch broom, moderately flat, should be used to sweep lawns. The sweeper, to sweep well, should stoop about as much as if he were mowing. Some men stand erect in sweeping a lawn; this soon destroys the broom, and does not do the work so well. Lawns should be swept and rolled once a week all the year round, and should be swept in dry weather during winter ; *i. e.*, choose dry days to do it. In mowing a lawn, practise cutting the grass three-eighths to half an inch above the ground ; this will make the best lawn, and not suffer from drought and hard frost like one that is cut close to the surface, and laid nearly bare. Some mow the lawn every week, but once a ortnight is enough during the season ; early and late in the season there are often white frosts, and the grass will be found quite crispy, but never roll or mow a lawn on such occasions, as it will do material injury to the grass while the frost is on it. When moss grows on lawns it is a sign of poverty ; as soon, therefore, as this is observed manuring must be resorted to ; and this is best done with some mild manure during the winter months, such as lime and earth, rotten dung, &c.

Whatever is put on the lawn should be of a decomposed nature and spread over finely, so as to wash in by the rains completely before the spring. By brushing it about occasionally a well-kept lawn is like a good background to a picture ; a good flower-garden with a poor, shabby lawn, is like a beautiful painting with a background out of harmony.

THE AMERICAN GARDEN.

THIS appellation is generally understood to be American plants, or a compartment where all the plants grown come from America ; but this is not the case. It means all plants that are more partial to peat soil than others, and includes plants from all parts of the world ; but of course the " American garden " includes none but those of a hardy nature, unless the garden is in a warmer climate than ours, or under glass ; but what I mean by the " American Garden " is a plot of sand not entirely devoted to the growth of rhododendrons, of which there are five or six classes, with a great number of varieties, and all beautiful ; many grand and superb. Nothing can exceed in noble beauty, variety, and display a garden of these alone ; but the azalea is included here ; and, if it were not for one defect, this would even surpass the rhododendron ; but its being deciduous militates against it as far as a winter beauty, while the rhododendron is still desirable on account of its grand foliage, which is evergreen—a most desirable feature for a garden of pleasure. An evergreen flowering shrub possesses a twofold advantage over one that is wanting this; the contrast to the cold, wintry-looking, deciduous shrub makes the rhododendron a favourite everywhere. A garden of evergreens without flowers at all has a beauty and a charm of its own. I do not know what can compare to the magnificence of a well-assorted collection of this plant when in flower, planted in well-proportioned beds or clumps, with some well-grown standards as single objects, situated so as to give effect to a well-designed garden. Clumps of bold features are, I think, far before under-sized ones, and have a double advantage over small beds; first, they have more soil suited to their particular nature, as it generally has to be made especially; and secondly, the large clumps combine to produce greater effect. Clumps are best planted in groups of one colour. A bed of one class and one character is better than mixtures, both for boldness of feature and display, as well as to the maintenance of symmetry, for some grow faster than others. The broader the scale, the better for an American garden; in fact, it is impossible for this purpose to have anything like variety and boldness of feature too on anything less than one and a half acre to two acres of land. Grass or gravel may be used for the spaces between the beds; but grass is the most convenient, and perhaps the neatest upon the whole. The grass should be equal to the lawn described; the beds should be marked out the same as for the flower-garden, and be taken out to the depth of at least two feet; that is, if the natural soil is not peat, and should be filled with peat,* first throwing in at the bottom a foot of the turfy peat, and then filling up six or nine inches above the level with chopped peat. If peat

* See Peat.

is scarce, it may be mixed with one-half, or even two-thirds leaf-mould and sand (pit-sand) and some virgin loam, with the turf. American plants will do very well in this : but they will do no good in anything less suitable, for they really prefer peat alone ; and the plants will bear transplanting at a more advanced age as regards the rhododendron, azalea, kalmia, and such as carry a solid, compact ball of earth about their roots ; but on the whole they are best planted young into the quarters where they are to remain.

Dwarf, bushy plants should be chosen, such as will form symmetrical plants, and it requires some judgment to plant these, as all planting does, at a reasonable distance to allow of certain growth, and for the plants to develop themselves without getting crowded. Calculate upon ten years to come, allowing, say, four inches' growth for the year. This will place the plants of eighteen inches high too far asunder. The better way at first is to plant double the number, and then in five or six years' time take every other plant out to leave room for their growth. The kalmia must be planted in pure peat : this plant is of slow growth, but of exquisite beauty. The Andromeda is a very dwarf plant of free flower and great beauty. The Daphnes may be introduced into the garden with advantage, and are among scented flowering shrubs what the ranunculus is among flowers, — the masterpiece. A bed in the American garden of each of *D. mezereum, cneorum*, and *strictum*, will, on a beautiful spring evening when in flower, be an enchanting feature, and the fragrance will be wafted by the gentle breezes of an April and May evening over a considerable area. Nothing can be compared in beauty and fragrance to a bed of well-grown mezereons, and they can be raised by seed or grafted (see " Plants by Seed "), but nice plants may be bought for a shilling or eighteenpence each. The Irish heath, the moor heath, and Ericas of a hardy nature, should each have a bed to themselves; these are all very beautiful dwarf shrubs, and grown in good peat will make very lovely objects of indefinite duration. The Berberis is a most beautiful thing in the garden, especially the Darwinii, Asiatica, and the dulcis, and these shrubs are extraordinary flowerers, that can be kept within bounds by cutting-in. The deutzia also makes an attractive object in the garden, and so does the hydrangea, which will produce blue flowers if it has irony peat to grow in. It produces this colour constantly and without any trouble in the Dartmoor peat, which abounds with mineral matter, such as tin, iron, mundic, &c., &c. Ericas will pine away in this peat, while the hydrangea produces the blue, and flourishes in it. The hydrangea requires abundance of water and cutting back every season to form fine objects; as fine heads of flowers, and the young stuff should be thinned out to give more strength to the remainder.

The pæonia, some magnolias, and lilies of the Japan varieties may also be introduced into the American garden ; these can be planted in the beds of azalea and such plants as lose their leaves, and will flower when the shrubs are out of bloom. To secure an annual crop of flowers from the rhododendrons, as soon as the flowering is over snap the seed-pods or old flower-stalks off, for if these are left on to perfect the seed it will probably prevent them flowering to anything like perfection. In very dry seasons a good soaking of water should be given them once or twice immediately after the blooming is fairly over, to induce the plants to make wood, or no flowers can be expected the ensuing season. The standard rhododendrons should be fed once a year just at the time they are making new wood, or just before they flower, to encourage vigour and to maintain fine specimens. These form, on a well-kept lawn, exceedingly noble objects as flowering shrubs. There should be a distance between the beds and round the standards to admit of two or three ladies walking fairly abreast. The best season for planting is in the spring, just before the flower-buds begin to swell. This applies chiefly to the rhododendrons and azaleas.

THE DUTCH GARDEN.

THIS garden is a spot sufficiently large to grow a collection of bulbous flower-roots, which should be complete. I do not mean to say it is absolutely necessary to grow every variety of bulb in this space to deserve the name, any more than a spot deserves the name of Dutch Garden where there is a bed of tulips, ranunculi, anemones, and so on. A garden of any class is supposed to contain everything really worthy of such a garden. The Dutch garden is the rarest ; every other variety of garden may be seen within a reasonable distance, but where, except in Holland and a few other places, are we to see plots of ground devoted exclusively to the cultivation of bulbous flowers ? And why are we, professors of the love of Flora, so exceedingly backward as to suffer imitations of this section of it to appear in drapers' shops, on our draperies, carpets, in bonnets, and everywhere, and not a single bed of tulips, ranunculus, anemone, or iris, to be found within anything like a reasonable distance ? What can be compared to a spot of ground devoted to the development of these unique, diversified, and gorgeous flowers? Really nothing ; and yet there is nothing to hinder every ten out of twenty having a complete collection of Dutch bulbs growing on their own grounds ; they are comparatively cheap, and a collection may be completed on a medium, large, or small scale, to suit every place.

The growing of Dutch bulbs is not attended with much

trouble after the ground is once adapted to their peculiar nature, which in many instances requires no addition to that of the ordinary soil. Sand in most cases is the principal ingredient in the cultivation of bulbs ; this should be river or good pit sand ; one-half sand, and two-fourths may be leaf-mould and loam or the original soil, well mixed to a good depth. Generally speaking the feeders penetrate to a consider-able depth. This garden should be sheltered from the strong westerly winds by a hedge or wall ; a spot which is sheltered by a distant boundary of the spruce fir and laurustine, bays, common laurel, &c. ; these form a most agreeable protection and background to the whole, but care must be taken that the beds should not be too near to the trees, or shrubs of any kind, for the roots of shrubs and trees will naturally intrude upon the beds, and will travel a consider-able distance in search of nourishment. Firs are very great impoverishers of land, but may be within forty feet without much danger. Shrubs, such as common laurel, laurustine, bay, &c., may be within ten or twelve feet without doing any harm to the beds. But the Dutch garden will be materially improved by being belted with pillar and climbing roses on a rustic or wire fence, with a distant boundary of firs, &c. These roses will form one of the prettiest imaginable objects. (See " The Rosary.")

I cannot regard the Dutch garden in common with gar-dening in general, as such an extraordinary change of nature takes place as cannot be found in any other department of the garden ; such a resurrection indeed of nature's beauty, that I cannot but think that it has addi-tional charms for every lover of the garden, combined as this class of flowers is with the most extraordinary variety of colour, shapes, and changes.

THE TULIP.—Its Cultivation.

I AM convinced that a great deal depends upon a certain management of a flower, whether we obtain a better or worse variety; and also as to whether we help that variety to produce an improved flower by certain steps, or merely give it ordinary treatment for ordinary flowers; but I have thought since I wrote the article on this flower in the "Gardening for the Cottage," that the old Dutch gardeners were something like the old English gardeners, who used to think it quite a feat to produce a cucumber on Christmas day. No doubt, when the tulip was the leading flower, it was appreciated beyond its merits; and then either to enhance its value, or to make it beyond the reach of the many, all was done to mystify the direct path to perfection; nevertheless, there was then, as there is now, something of a royal road to produce the "perfect flower," and it was of more value than it would be now-a-days. The tulip still, however, possesses a value in proportion to its quality, ranging from five pounds to sixpence, or even twopence: this shows a very great disparity in the tulip.

Tulips seem to possess the property of transformation almost beyond conception, hence the undying interest connected with tulip-growing.

Florists divide tulips into classes, and each of these possesses a peculiarity of its own; seedlings are called breeders until they bloom and the flower has two colours in it, then if the markings are good they are called rectified; then there are the permanent classes and their sub-classes, viz., violette, byblomen, roses, bizards, baguettes; this last is of a peculiar nature, possessing the property of producing no two flowers alike. The quality of a tulip, or rather the value of it, depends upon the colour of the ground, which must either be yellow or white, and with regular markings·

of black, lilac, purple, crimson, pink, or scarlet; these colours should be beautifully laid in the petals, in some cases very decided, and in others graduated into the ground ; but always presenting a degree of cleanness on the ground. The beds for growing the tulip should be prepared in the autumn, say September or beginning of October; dig the soil out one spit, and if the subsoil is poor and clayey, turn it out another spit, and fill this in with good old rotten dung and loam and sand, mix a liberal portion of good pit or silver sand and old decomposed cow-dung with the top soil of the bed ; this need not be made too fine, nor sifted, but chopped fine with the spade, picking out any very coarse stuff, stones, &c. ; the bed may be raised six or nine inches above the level, to allow of settling down before planting, which should be done about the middle of November. On a nice dry day draw some drills eight or nine inches asunder, and full two inches deep, with a half-moon hoe ; take the bulbs and press them one by one into the bottom of the drill, giving each a gentle pressure to bring them all to one depth from the surface ; plant them five or six inches from bulb to bulb, and when all are planted, draw the earth over them carefully with the back, not with the teeth of the rake, and when all are carefully covered, lightly rake the bed with a coarse rake ; do not rake it down too fine by any means, for this does, on some soils, material harm, by rendering it in a condition for binding down hard, forming a surface impervious to air and the fertilizing influence of the sun.   Bulbs should be fully two inches from the top of the bulb below the surface, and should be classed by sellers of them into dwarf, half standard, and standard, their height being denoted by figures ; when this is not done they may be classed the first year, and the tallest growers can be planted in the middle of the bed.   Should cold, cutting frost ensue after the bulbs are above ground, some protection should be afforded them, which may consist of furze carefully laid on, spruce fir branches, or Russian mats kept up, if a circular bed, a foot or eighteen inches in the middle by a hoop laid on crutch sticks or kept up (if an oblong square) by a rod, and the mats fastened down with strong pegs at the outside of the bed. Tulips are not at all tender, but the sudden changes of our climate often kill much hardier things than these. Shading during the blooming season is also necessary, and hoops of wood or iron stretching over the whole bed, over which is an awning of thin calico, is as good as anything : and the length of blooming is considerably protracted by this means.

By taking large quantities, tulips may be purchased of most sellers at a considerable reduction from the catalogued prices, but if large quantities of superior sorts are required, it is best to correspond with growers for wholesale purposes, either in this country or Holland.

Krelage & Sons, 146, Kleine Houtweg, Haarlem, are confidential growers of tulips on an extensive scale, having upwards of 2,000 varieties of this beautiful flower under cultivation. Just as the flower-bud of the tulip is about to open, some weak liquid manure may be given to it, as that will materially improve the size and markings of the flower. This manure may consist of sheep-dung, half dry, thrown into a tub at the rate of one peck to eight or ten gallons of water. The bulbs should not be taken up from the ground till the leaf and stalk turn quite a dead yellow; they may then be taken up and dried in an open shed. When the leaves, &c., are quite dried off, trim all clean off, and lay the bulbs for a day in the sun; then place them in dry, cool boxes, or on shelves in some airy, cool, and dry room.

THE RANUNCULUS.—Its Cultivation.

THERE are many species and varieties of this tribe, such as shrubby, perennial, and annual, and aquatic ; but the one here referred to is of the perennial class, and is a hardy exotic, as it comes, or did originally, from another country, but this beautiful variety is the most exquisite and diversified of all. Nothing amongst flowers can well be compared to a large bed of well-grown ranunculuses, because a large collection will naturally contain more variety and become more effective in large masses; but a bed of ranunculuses of any size is exquisite for its diversified beauty, although, as a matter of course, this perfection can only be attained by a careful selection, as the ranunculus varies in quality like the tulip, and requires very similar treatment; as the soil may be the same as for the tulip, except that it may be made finer, and the roots not planted till the middle of February instead of the autumn. The soil for the bed of the ranunculus should be compounded in the autumn; that is, the rotten dung, sand, and the maiden loam, should be put together in the autumn, mixed, and laid up into a heap or ridge, and turned once during the winter, leaving it in a ridge ; a fortnight before planting the roots it should be thrown down, leaving the surface of the bed in a moderately fine state, unless the land is of rather a heavy nature, and the weather prove wet ; then the surface would be better left coarser. The soil should be in a nice working state before planting ; there is no fear of its being too dry at this time of the year, but on a fine day, and when it looks as if it would be fine for a few days to come, proceed to plant the tubers, first raking the surface of the bed with a medium rake to a nice level or even surface, then marking the bed with a straight-edge across it, at intervals of six inches, then with a half-moon hoe draw a slight drill an inch and a half deep on these lines, and plant the tubers four inches asunder in the drill, pressing the tuber into the soil up to the crown, holding the little tuber tight between the thumb and two fingers, pressing the fingers and thumb into the earth with the tuber, leaving the root planted, and so proceed; as soon as all are in, cover up as directed for the tulip, only observing to rake the surface finer; and if it should be wet weather protect the bed with straw mats, or set over the bed thatched hurdles, span-roofed fashion. The ranunculus prefers rather a firm soil; shade the full-blown flowers from the influence of the hot sun, take the roots up when they are ripe, which is indicated by the same sign as that of the tulip, dry and store them away, give liquid manure of the same kind and at the same stage as recommended for the tulip. The best sorts of the ranunculus may be obtained wholesale at about 8s. per 100, if mixed, at 4s. or even 3s. per 100; the second best, and really good, may be bought for 10s. per 1,000. The ranunculus may be raised in abundance from seed. (See " Plants by Seed.")

THE ANEMONE.—Its Cultivation.

THE anemone may be cultivated in the same way as the ranunculus, with one exception. I am convinced that the anemone does better in maiden loam than in anything else with a good proportion of road sand, and no dung; for unless it is of a very old and pulverized nature, dung has a tendency to cause canker, overgrowth, and too much foliage, and not enough flower. Turfy loam that has been laid up for a twelvemonth is the very best soil to produce a crop of flowers and sound roots. The roots are in their best condition for producing the full crop of flowers, and the most perfect when three years old. The same rule is to be observed in planting the roots, except that no drill is required, but simply pressing the root into the soil of the bed, which should be fresh prepared to render it light, three or four inches deep previously to planting (as described for the ranunculus), so as to bury the crown of the bulb an inch or so below the surface, when it should be covered up. The roots may remain in the ground through the winter; it is, however, best to take them up, as by so doing a positive degree of rest is insured, which promotes better flowering. A bed of anemone has a most charming effect when in full flower, and affords an undying interest for the beauties of Flora. If I can measure the interest of others by my own love of what is really good among flowers, I should say a collection of tulips, ranunculus, anemone, and iris possess a charm of their own beyond all other flowers, standing over these beds when in full flower, observing without weariness the variety of colour and beauty of form; but in these lovely productions of the earth our thoughts should certainly be lifted up to Him who has displayed such infinite wisdom and goodness in providing for the enjoyment of His creatures.

The anemone may be raised from seed in abundance, and an excellent speculation it is if the stock is good from which the seed is obtained, viz., good semi-double flowers. (See " Plants from Seed.")

THE IRIS.

THERE are several classes of this most gorgeous and splendid genus, consisting of Moracea, Vieusseuxia, Dietis, and several sub-classes, such as Herbaceous and Bulbous. Of these there are the German, Spanish, and English. No collection of flowers combines so large an amount of diversity of colour with so high a degree of contrast and boldness of feature as this most beautiful plant. There are already many varieties, and new sorts are continually being raised from seed; and still a wide field is open to speculators in this branch—embracing, as this genus does, so numerous a natural order ; in fact, it is the type of a large natural order, to which belong numerous classes of flowers ; and hence a wide field opens itself for research. But, apart from this, the iris presents actual and permanent points of interest, accommodating itself to every circumstance—heavy and light soils, sunny and shady places,— which cannot be said of the tulip, ranunculus, or cultivated anemone ; or, indeed, of few things else.

The treatment of the iris is simple, and the effect most gratifying. Let the soil be dug eighteen inches deep, and mix with it one-third part of sand, one-third peat, and one-third leaf-mould or old dung, well incorporated, during the winter. Plant the bulbs in the month of October seven inches from row to row, and five inches from plant to plant ; or they may be planted six inches every way from bulb to bulb, and four inches deep from the top of the bulb. This is not very easily done, except you plant over the work ; that is, draw a deep drill, plant that, and then draw another drill standing over the one previously drawn and planted. The soil from the last falls on the bed next the planted drill, or they may be cut in with the spade ; that is, put the line down and cut a drill with the spade by it, or use a hand-dibber with a thick end, and press the bulb carefully to the bottom of the hole, and carefully fill in with soil after. The herbaceous varieties may remain two or three years where planted, and these prefer a rather stiff soil, of good quality. All these will be materially improved by one or two waterings with liquid manure (two ounces of guano to one gallon of water), given as soon as the flower-buds are fully developed, and not after.

The species is propagated by division of the root, cuttings of the fleshy roots of the herbaceous sorts, and offsets of the bulbous varieties. New sorts of divers value may be raised freely from seed by taking a little pains to cross the different sorts. (See "Fertilization" and "Plants by Seed.") A good large bed of these forms a most attractive object in the Dutch gardens; and for the little trouble they give and the beauty they display should have a place in every garden. They are very cheap, and may be had in large quantities from 10s. 6d. to £1 per 1,000.

THE GLADIOLUS

MAY be classed in three divisions; viz., early, medium, and late sorts; Blandus, early; Formosissimus, &c., medium; and Gandavensis, late. All the sorts require planting in the autumn or very early spring; naturally the gladioli all flower in the autumn earlier or later, according to the sort and the locality. Considering this peculiar feature of bulbous flowers, their exquisite beauty, and the grandeur and fulness of the flowers and foliage, together with the un-usual duration of both, the gladiolus is pre-eminently suited to all kinds of flower-garden, especially the "Dutch garden." Accompanying the Grand lily Auratum, Giganteum, Rubrum, Belladonna, and Guernsey; the Tigridia, Crinums, and the beautiful autumnal crocus, of all which I shall speak sepa-rately in this article. The gladiolus is scarcely surpassed by the lily tribe in its delicate pencillings, the substance of its flower, and the character of the plant; in which last feature it far excels the lily, and fits it for those small gardens in which the lily is out of place.

The treatment of the gladiolus is simple; they are cheap, and may be had in large quantities, from 3s. to £1 per 100 of growers. It should be planted any time between November and the end of February; from four to six inches deep in good, deep-dug, common garden soil, mixing in some old rotten dung, peat, and pit-sand into the bed several weeks previously to planting. The most con-

venient way of planting these bulbs is to dig them in; that
is, dig eight or nine inches, then cut the trench across the
bed, straight down the required depth of five or six inches.
Make the bottom of the trench fine and level, and plant the
roots five or six inches apart with the crown uppermost;
then turn some fine earth gently on them, and proceed
again as before.

The strongest roots should be planted in a plot by themselves, and those less strong by themselves. They are
multiplied by offsets and seed; by crossing the different
flowers new and splendid varieties will result, probably
worth half a guinea each. It is not absolutely necessary to
remove the gladiolus every season; still I am of opinion
that this flower is benefited by being taken up every season
as soon as the bulbs are matured. Let the offsets be taken
off, and the bulbs stored away like the tulip, and re-planted
in the spring. There is no necessity to re-buy the same
varieties any more than there is in the case of the iris,
tulip, &c.

THE HYACINTH.

CONSIDERING the three peculiar qualities of the hyacinth,
which place it pre-eminently in advance of every species
and variety of bulb, I cannot help wondering why this
plant should be so scarce in our gardens. It accommodates
itself to every variety of garden by its dwarf habit and
profuse flowers, in which are found every shade of colour in
the floral world, and, above all, in its matchless fragrance,
which alone should give it a place in the garden nearest the
dwelling-house; so that the sitting-room window can be
opened on a beautiful May morning, and the sweet odour of
this plant in its beauty be inhaled without the trouble of
going into the conservatory. A bed of hyacinths of various
colours, well grown, surpasses all conception. There is
majesty in the lily as well as strength of colour, peculiarity

of form, and grandeur of scale ; but where is the fragrance as compared with that of the hyacinth? There is exquisite colouring in the ranunculus, anemone, and tulip ; but where is their fragrance? This one property alone places the hyacinth far in advance of them all, and no other bears so large a proportion of flower as does the hyacinth ; for a good, well-grown hyacinth is three parts flower, which can be said of no other.

The treatment of the hyacinth is as simple as that of the tulip. The soil must be composed of good loam, decomposed dung, and a good portion of sharp sand—road or pit, well incorporated by turning it over two or three times previously to planting. Let the bed be dug eighteen inches deep, and well drained. If the loam is of a good quality, that is, free from shallet and rubble, it will retain moisture sufficient to the requirements of the plants. The sand acts as a regulator in all cases where it is employed, and prevents stagnation, yet retaining the due proportion of moisture necessary to the well-being of the plant. This is why bulbs do so exceedingly well in sand. The bulbs should be planted from the month of November till the end of December, the former being preferable ; plant seven inches apart and four inches deep. To do this well the same process of planting must be followed as is given in detail for planting the iris and gladiolus (see page 130).

The hyacinth is propagated by offsets and by seed. If the weather is likely to be severe five or six weeks after planting, some slight protection must be given to the bed, such as fern or furze, &c. It will be necessary to put sticks to support the flower-spikes as they advance in flower, and an awning to shade the bed from the influence of the sun's rays, and for the prolongation of the flowering season. Some liquid manure may be given them when the spike of bloom is nearly full grown, but only once. This must be given so as to reach completely down to the feeders; that is, to the bottom of the bed, or no great benefit can arise from it. This may consist of one ounce of guano to one gallon of water, or the sheep's-dung water recommended for the tulip.

It is not absolutely necessary to take the bulbs up every season. When they are left in the bed for another year, top-dressing must be resorted to, by laying some good rotten dung or two or three inches of half-dry sheep's dung on the top of the bed during January or February, previously forking the bed over carefully; and if the sticks to which the flowers were tied are left in the bed till after the surface is forked over, they will indicate the place of each bulb, and so prevent the fork injuring its crown; still I recommend taking the bulbs up as soon as the leaf turns a dead yellow, drying them like the tulip, and storing away in the same manner year by year. It is pleasant to have hyacinths in early flower in the conservatory, or sitting-room window, grown in glasses, or in moss, &c.; but I think it a pity that such a valuable plant as a hyacinth, that has risen to the value of 2s. 6d. or perhaps 3s. 6d. once within three or four years, should be absolutely sunk and lost the first season; the system is a dead loss of capital. I cannot refrain from making this observation here, for two reasons, viz., the sunk capital and the wearing-out system; for there are few who can or will afford to purchase these very expensive plants annually during life; the pure and innocent love of flowers becomes a burden, and so there is an end to poor hyacinth, although he is "a beautiful boy." Therefore I advise that they should be grown either in pots or in the open ground, for in this way the cultivation of this flower will exert an influence for good, and increasing demand entails no corresponding increase of expense.

THE NARCISSUS.

"Beautiful youth" as it is called; this flower is but rarely seen to the best advantage. Although there is scarcely a deviation (in all the whole tribe) from white and yellow, yet they are desirable as bedding plants, from the fact that they are all possessed of fragrance, and some of them highly so; and on account of the earliness with which they flower. They are of easy culture : any good, deep-dug soil suits them, and almost any situation. A few beds of these in the garden indicate the coming season of Flora's display, they being the first on the list (of any note) to herald the approach of glorious spring, lifting up their conspicuous heads above the foliage. There is one drawback to this plant as a permanent bedder, viz., the length of time that the beds are deficient of flowers; but this may be considerably remedied by planting a gladiolus, or lily, between each bulb, and if these are fed with liquid manure of a mild nature (such as half an ounce of guano to one gallon of water) once or twice during their flowering, they will do well, and neither will suffer from want. The lily, gladiolus, or narcissus, may be planted the same depth, viz., five or six inches.

I cannot think but that a diversity of colour could be introduced into this species, if a little pains were taken to cross them with some opposite colour from some neighbouring species. It belongs to the lilyworts, classically, so that any of the liliaceæ and amaryllidaceæ may be chosen to fertilize them with, or *vice versa*. (See " Hybridization.")

THE LILIUM.

This name, if taken as an indication of the colour of this superb tribe of flowers, is misleading. "Lily" properly means white; hence I suppose the name to have arisen from the fact of the first species discovered having been a white one, probably the old *candidum*.

There are several species and a great variety in this genus. The whole of this tribe of bulbous flowers is magnificent, exquisitely formed, and superbly contrasted in the richest colourings of nature, with the greatest substance of flower; which gives them a durability scarcely to be found in any other similar plant. The flower of a lily cut from the plant may be preserved good in a glass of water longer than any other. The lily is equally adapted for either pot culture or for beds; hence it is remarkably suitable for those who have no garden or greenhouse, so long as they have a yard or window with a share of sun; it is not at all tender, and will flourish equally well out of doors as in.

I have said elsewhere that no one should be without a collection of iris, tulip, ranunculus, anemone, and so on ; but let any one possess a garden of well-assorted lilies alone, and I can imagine such a one saying, " I need no more !" Fancy yourself walking among beds of white, red, purple, orange, lilac, pink, and rose-coloured lilies, of various stature, from one foot up to four feet in height ; and these beautifully shaded and spotted, some with white grounds, and red, pink, or crimson spots ; others with crimson spots on pink and orange grounds, and so on. Surely such a collection would be a sight worth looking at, at once rare, rich, and incomparable ! I recommend these (as well as all other bulbous flowers) to be planted in class beds, that is, a bed of a sort ; the effect is doubly superior to that of mixtures, inasmuch as one detracts from the other in the latter case.

Some may object that a garden filled with lilies would be too expensive in proportion to the end, to which I reply that the first expense is an item of little moment compared with the display obtained and the duration of these bulbs but, apart from all this, the sole outlay would not exceed

that of ordinary flower-gardening.   In the first place, bulbs
of choice sorts may be had of wholesale growers from £1
to £2 10s. per hundred, and even cheaper; but to form a
choice and complete collection of this beautiful flower, at
little expense, I should select, say, one dozen of each
variety, and plant each of these dozens in beds of equal
size, planting them two feet apart.   The first season most
of these beds will produce one dozen offsets, and some of
them 100 young bulbs, by the root, and up the stem near
the ground, especially if some fibrous peat is laid round the
stem in a hillock.   Every joint of the stem will give a young
bulb this way, and so the one dozen may be increased to
100 good flowering bulbs within three years, or less.   The
bed will hold the offsets the second and third year, but after
that time it must be enlarged to hold the 100, and this will
(if required) form a bold bed on a good scale, and be very
effective.

Now suppose I have, say, fifty sorts, and 100 of a sort in
a compartment for each, that would be 5,000 stock plants;
each of these will give give a good strong flowering bulb (as
an offset) once within two seasons, when I should take them
up.   What shall I do with them as an amateur?   Why, sell
them at half-price to the trade, to be sure, and so secure
pleasure with profit.   New sorts may be raised from seed
by hybridizing.   The beds must be well drained, and be
composed of loam, fibrous peat, and leaf-mould, or peat and
leaf-mould added to common garden soil.   The bulbs must
be planted five inches deep, clear from the top of the bulb,
in October or the early part of November.   When the bulbs
are transplanted take them carefully up; take off what
offsets you wish; add some fresh soil, and plant again
immediately, preserving as much of the fleshy root as
possible without injury, and carefully trim off any bruised
parts, and lay the roots nicely out; they may be planted

nine inches apart, and dug in with the spade as recommended for the gladiolus, &c. There is yet another way of propagating the lily, viz., by the scaly parts of the bulb ; a few of the outside ones may be carefully broken off when sorts are scarce, and these may be inserted three-fourths of their depth into pots filled with fine sandy peat of good quality, made firm, watered and plunged in a mild heat, or set in a close cold frame in spring, or under a hand-glass plunged in sawdust, old tan, or cinder ash, and kept moist by frequent sprinklings with water. A dozen of these scales may be inserted in a 6-inch pot; the pot must be well drained ; these will form flowering plants in three years, but not more than three or four should be taken off at a time, as the original bulb is injured in proportion to the number of scales taken off. A very strong and large one might have five or six taken off once within two years.

Liquid manure may be given to lilies once a fortnight from the time the flower stems are one foot above ground, or before they flower, till in bloom, but not after; these waterings may consist of one ounce of guano to one gallon of water, given in a good soaking, or any of the recommended artificial manures; but I have found the guano suit them admirably.

I heartily wish the lovers of the lily would enter upon the cultivation of this flower with spirit, and begin with one, two, or three of a sort, if they cannot afford room or money for more ; and by judicious management, and following the instructions here given, they will soon possess a stock equal to their wishes. The lily is indispensable in the "Dutch Garden," flowering as it does at a time immediately succeeding the ranunculus, tulip, and iris. The Messrs. Kreloge, of Haarlem, Holland, cultivate all the species and varieties.

K

THE CROWN IMPERIAL.

THE crown imperial is a very noble old fritillaria, peculiar and most beautiful in its character. It may be compared to a set of bells mechanically arranged to a great nicety, the flowers being suspended from the upright stem in a most conspicuous manner. In one or two varieties there is a double set of these bells, and so beautifully arranged that the top set barely reaches the lower. These sets of six bells (as I call them) are all of one size and colour in the set, and on a straight, erect, stout stem of about two feet high, or perhaps a little more, according to the strength of soil and the situation. The class is rather limited, and only affords three shades of colour, viz., red, yellow, and dark yellow, which do not much recommend it; but its character is unique, and for this reason, as well as for its early flowering, it is most worthy of a place in the Dutch garden. The bulbs must have deep rich and light soil to grow in, and must be planted in the autumn, five or six inches deep : they may be multiplied by offsets. Strong roots may be had for 6s. per dozen.

FRITILLARIA.

THIS is a very different thing from the Crown Imperial, although that is a Fritillary. The word Fritillary does not convey a description of the Crown Imperial; the genus derived its name from the chequered varieties, probably Nigrus, Meleagris, or Minus, or some of that kind. They are a most beautiful class of dwarf bulbous plants, of one foot and under in height, of a beautiful character, free flowering, and of a graceful habit, forming lovely small beds of brown and purple (not blue), purple and yellow or white, and red. A mixed bed makes a charming object in April and May, for they flower very early, are beautiful in character, and particularly worthy of a place in the " Dutch garden."

Good mixtures may be had in large quantities for about £1 to £1 10s. per 1,000. The Fritillary likes good light ground, with some sand and peat added. Plant the little bulbs about as thick as crocuses are generally planted ; viz., four inches apart, and two inches deep or so. They may remain in the ground for several years together, or may be taken up every season, and kept in sand in a cool place, and planted again in September or October. They are admirably adapted for the fronts of compound flower borders, and the outsides of the beds in the " American garden ;" also for pots, putting three bulbs in a six-inch pot. The Fritillary is allied to the lilies ; and hence offers something of a field for the production of new sorts of either by hybridization. The Messrs. Kreloge, of Haarlem, possess a fine collection.

THE DOG'S TOOTH VIOLET (*Erythronum*)

Is not a violet at all, but more like a miniature lily ; a beautiful early flower, and very dwarf; fit for small beds, requiring good soil, like the last-named species. The class is very limited, containing about seven or eight varieties only ; a major and minor kind, of white, red, lilac, yellow, and rose colour. They are perfectly hardy, flowering, as they do, when there is little else, except Crocuses, &c., in bloom.

THE SCILLA (SQUILL).

A RACE of very hardy, early, and beautiful bulbous flowering plants, of rather extended genera. I know nothing to compare with small beds of this beautiful early and very dwarf flower ; scarcely clear of the surface of the ground in which they grow are conical clusters of flowers, of a size that might be looked for upon some tall, robust stem. The colour is of a lovely, delicate tint ; blue being the prevailing hue of the tribe. Its earliness, its abundance of flower and lively colour, make it well worthy of a place in the garden. They should be planted in September in good soil, three or

Missing Page

THE GUERNSEY LILY.

This is another of those conspicuous flowers that flower in the autumn without leaves; it is a very showy Lily, consisting of scarlet, purple, pink, and red varieties; the flowers are thrown up to a height which renders them more conspicuous than the Colchicum, and the colour of some of the varieties, such as *Venusta coruscea*, is most showy. This genus (proper) is very limited, containing something like six or seven varieties only. The Old Sarniensis is bright red, free-flowering, and a very desirable variety for the "Dutch garden;" forming one of the most conspicuous objects possible; flowering with a fascicle (bunch) of six or eight flowers, on the top of an erect stem, which is stout and rigid. The species is not frost-proof, therefore plant them six or seven inches deep, in good common garden soil, with a good portion of sand and peat added. It will be necessary to protect the bed by a canvas awning, that the leaf may not be cut down by frost before the bulbs are matured in the late autumn. Besides being exceedingly showy in the autumn, in a good-sized bed they are well suited for pots.

BELLADONNA LILIES

Accompany the foregoing in flower and beauty. A lily-like class of delicate hues—shaded pinks and white. They may be treated in the same way as the last, using leaf-mould, sand, and dung with the original soil; both of these should be planted during June, July, and August, and should not be kept long out of the ground.

THE SPARAXIS AND IXIA.

The Sparaxis may be confounded with the genus Ixia, but the former has a jagged sheath, the latter no such serrations. The treatment of both is similar; a nicely prepared bed or border, consisting of leaf-mould, sand, and loam, or the two former added to good common garden soil, will answer well for them; plant them, October or February, four inches apart, and three or four inches deep; if they are planted in the autumn protect the bulbs by covering the bed with ferns, straw, or furze, during severe weather. Drain the bed well by turning in an abundance of good rough peat at the bottom. This is a very desirable class of plants, embracing, as they do, every variety of colour, and flowering from May till August; that is, taking the whole genus. It is a class of bulbs at once sufficiently abounding in colour and successional flowers to form a garden of themselves, plants of a foot high, of free flower, of easy culture, and cheap; they may be had of wholesale growers in quantities of from 100 to 1,000, at about 5s. to 6s. per 100; mixtures, select sorts, at 7s. 6d. to 10s. A couple of soakings with half an ounce of guano to one gallon of water will greatly benefit them, given as soon as the flower-spike has formed the buds, and not after the flowers begin to die off.

THE TIGRIDIA.

This is a very small genus, containing only four or five varieties, and said to be difficult to preserve; it is seldom, indeed, that you can see a plant of this in flower, much less a bed; everything is difficult till known, when it is easy enough to grow this rather extraordinary sort of Iris. Prepare a bed of leaf-mould, peat, and sandy loam, or a good portion of sharp sand added to the original soil, together with the two former, especially the leaf-mould and good drainage, secured for the bed in which they grow. It is best to pot the bulbs,—three in a six-inch pot, filled with peat and leaf-mould; set these pots in a frame, or house, at work, in March or April, or a cold frame if the two former means are wanting; let them remain here till four or five inches above the pots; if they have been subjected to a little heat, harden them off, and then turn the plants out of the pots, ball entire, into the bed, previously prepared as directed, watering to settle the soil about them, then the Tigridia will do well; as soon as the flowering is over, and the leaf fairly dies off to a dead yellow, take them up carefully, with all the root, flower-stem, and leaf about them, and hang them up in a dry, airy room by the flags; let them hang here till wanted again, if secure from frost. I have found this method of preserving the Tigridia to excel every other; they are subject to dry rot, and will not keep if buried in sand ever so dry. A bed of Conchiliflora,—yellow, and Violacea,—violet, each will form most conspicuous and lovely beds in the " Dutch garden " in May and June. Good flowering bulbs may be had for 30s. down to 8s. per 100.

This class may be crossed with any of the Iris tribe, whence we may look for still new varieties. The Tigridia will live, and do very well left in the bed, if planted five or six inches deep, the bed rendered dry, and protected a little during severe weather with cinder ash, sawdust, or tan.

THE PÆONIA.

THIS tribe of bulbous plants throws everything into the shade for character, colour, and magnificence. In the first place, they are hardy and dwarf, and thereby suited to gardens that the dahlia is not; in the second place, they embrace every shade of colour that constitutes choice variety, worthy of a place in the garden of the connoisseur; and thirdly, they possess a grandeur of character entirely wanting in any other hardy flower. Considering all these striking characteristics, viz., magnificence of flower, diversity of colour, hardiness, duration, and dwarfness of habit, it is strange how seldom we find a collection of even a dozen varieties of this desirable plant. There are between two and three hundred species and varieties of this magnificent old-fashioned plant, embracing the greatest possible contrast in colour,—rich crimson and pure white, lilac and red, purple and salmon, yellow and rose, striped and shaded, &c.; and they flower very early, which makes them more desirable still. A bed of each of the most desirable varieties scattered over the surface of the "Dutch garden" will form a feature not easily appreciated, except by those who possess them. They may be had of large growers or of importers of bulbs, for about 6s. to 9s. per dozen choice named sorts. They should be planted where they may remain several years without removing; plant them six or seven inches below the surface in any good ordinary ground of a sandy nature; the beds should be dug deep for all these gross feeders; and where such are best left undisturbed for years together, plant during September, October, and November, eighteen inches apart for strong roots, and a little less for smaller ones. The stems may be cut down in the autumn, or as soon as they die off; and the beds top-dressed with rotten dung, liquid manure being given at the rate of one ounce of guano to one gallon of water. One or two soakings with this, as soon as the flower-buds are formed, will materially assist the development of extra large flowers, as well as prolong the flowering season. As seed is easily procured from this tribe, more beautiful varieties may be obtained by crossing the colours.

THE OXALIS.

NOTHING can exceed the loveliness of a bed of *Violacea florabunda* during a bright summer day. They make exceedingly showy small beds, planted pretty thickly, in equal parts of leaf-mould, peat, and sand. The tender species must be kept dry, or nearly so, in pots in the green-house or dry coal pit, through the winter, and turned out into the beds in May.

THE CROCUS AND SNOWDROP.

Both of these are too well known to require any comment, except that whole beds of a colour are more effective than mixtures; and snowdrops are exceedingly pretty in patches, or continued circles, lines, &c., round other beds, than they are in beds alone. They should both remain undisturbed for several years together, and the grass or leaf should never be either tied up or cut off before it turns yellow.

There are several other bulbous plants that might be added to the "Dutch Garden," such as Alstromeria, Arum, Crinum, Cyclamen, Musceria, Convallaria, Dielytra, Ornithogalum, Tritonia, Winter Aconite, Babiana, &c., &c.; but those I have treated of are the chief, and form a sufficient collection for perfection of feature and successional flower from March to September.

An objection has been raised to the growing of bulbs, on account of the sterility of some of the beds during the summer months. This may be relieved considerably by pricking out some Phlox Drummondii, German Stocks, Asters, Marigold, Schizanthus, Zinnia, Jacobea, *Dianthus Chinensis*, Saponaria, &c. (from a reserved stock in nursery-beds for the purpose), over the surface of those beds where the bulbs are to remain several years together. Slightly turn the surface of the beds as soon as the flowering is over, and prick the annuals (in a thin crop) all over the said beds, without mutilating the leaf and flower stalk of the bulb crop, which cut clean down as soon as it dies off, and not before ; and meanwhile the crop of annuals is coming on. But I would add that it is not favourable to perfect bulb-growing to overcrop the beds; the ground requires rest as well as the bulbs. Beds of choice tulip, anemone, ranunculus, &c., should be turned up, and left till planting season comes again. The "Dutch garden" is an exceedingly interesting thing, causes very little trouble, and is also very profitable to professional men,

THE EVERLASTING FLOWER-GARDEN.

I HAVE given it this impossible name because this garden possesses a selection of perennial plants that are of indefinite duration. This is a garden that will accommodate itself to the majority of Flora's lovers, from the fact that it entails less yearly expense, and affords an equal diversity of beauty and richness of colour. A flower-garden of this kind is especially suited to people with small means, "villa gardens," and .those who have no plant-glass, &c. Upon the whole, this garden surpasses the Compound and American and Italian Gardens in many points, composed, as it is, of plants of protracted flowering qualification, viz., the herbaceous Phloxes, the Antirrhinum, Pansy, Œnothera, Veronica, Iberis, Pentstemon, Pinks, Carnations, Lilies, Wallflowers, Dyanthus, Hydrangea, Double White Rocket, *Lychnis fulgens*, and *Chalcedonia pleno*, several Potentillas, which are beautiful, blue and pink Hepaticas, Aquilegias, *Dielytra spectabilis*, Iris Flower-de-luce, Susiana, Pæonias, Anemone, Japonicas, *Campanula carpatica*, Cam, Coronaria, *Delphinium formosa*, *D. Hendersonii* and *Grandiflora*, *Lupinus polyphyllus*, an exceedingly beautiful thing ; Sweet-williams, various Dianthus, Sweet Alyssum, beautiful German Daisies, *Chelone barbata*, and Lily of the Valley.

Many others may be introduced here, such as roses, chrysanthemums, hollyhocks ; and flowering shrubs, such as *Berberis Darwinii* and *Japonica*, Daphnes, *Deutzia gracilis*, Kalmias, Azaleas, Rhododendrons, Genistas, Hibiscus, lovely shrubs ; *Ribes sanguinea, Pyrus Japonica*, Andromedas, Helianthemum, double yellow, white, and orange ; Veronicas, &c. In this list of flowering plants and shrubs will be found the foundation for a really good, permanent, and lovely perennial flower-garden, and these may be multiplied in variety to a considerable extent; of the Phloxes alone, for instance, a selection can be made consisting of variety enough to furnish an ordinary flower-garden, and yet not be wanting in contrast or perfection; thus, one might plant a whole bed of Beauty of Milkig, white; Countess of Holme, white, dark crimson centre; Rubra, Dianthiflora, and so on; so also by Antirrhinums, Pentstemons, Potentillas, Campanulas, and Delphiniums; and so also by the flowering shubs, all of which are beautiful in species and numerous in lovely varieties. Comparatively inexpensive, of little trouble, and long duration, a good, well-devised pleasure-garden, planted with a judicious selection of these species, would form a feature not frequently seen, and would not be without flowers from March to November. I particularly recommend this style of garden to all who want a good garden, of great beauty, without much expense after once planting it. I am well aware that beds and borders of mixtures of these are very beautiful; but I always recommend an entire bed of a sort as the most effective, and consequently the most desirable, both for economy of time and material; for generally where there are mixtures of species and varieties, they outgrow each other, impose upon each other in every way, and miserably detract from each other when in flower, besides causing constant vacancies, so that a compound bed or border of this sort may be said never to be perfect.

The beds for these plants should be dug deep and well manured, and if the land is naturally heavy and stiff, add some coarse sand, and peat, and leaf-mould to the beds where the Pinks, Carnations, Lilies, Hydrangea, Rocket, Lychnis, Anemone, Delphiniums, Dianthus, and Phloxes are to be; in fact, all flowers will do well in a soil of this sort. The shrubs named may be planted in beds of three or more ; but each sort must have the soil best suited to its nature ; thus, the Rhododendron, Azalea, Kalmia, Daphne, Deutzia, Andromeda, and Hibiscus, will require peat alone, or three-fourths ; and the other shrubs will do in good common garden soil and maiden loam. Some Standards of the Genista, Hibiscus, Pyrus Japonica, and Cotoneaster, and Roses of a pendulous habit, on seven or eight feet stems, add considerably to the beauty of such a garden, on a neat lawn.

Œnothera macrocarpa and *Taraxacifolia* are two dwarf plants, scarcely three inches high, of extraordinary beauty, with flowers of pure white, and clear, bright yellow, as large as a small saucer. Plant them six or eight inches apart in good soil. The *Lychnis fulgens* is a rare plant, the best of the whole, a dwarf plant, with very large scarlet flowers. Plant in peat loam and leaf-mould, six inches apart. *Chelone barbata* is a tall-growing plant of singular beauty, very uncommon. The Delphiniums surpass everything for richness and intensity of colour. There are no flowering plants that can excel a good full bed of *Delphinium formosum.* This may be raised from seed, and planted in peat and loam, or good common garden soil, of a light nature. If the soil is heavy add peat and leaf-mould. Plant six inches apart ; well drain the bed, so that the plants will pass through the winter safely. They are not tender, but super-saturation of the bed with water is very injurious to all plants in their dormant state. The campanulas are a lovely class of plants. The carpatica is a very low-growing variety, and free of flower. It is well adapted for small beds. Plant them in a well-drained bed of peat, loam, and dung. The hepaticas are a most desirable class of plants, especially the double blue. The single blue is a lovely thing for early small beds. Plant thickly, four or six inches apart, in good tender, sandy, garden soil. The

Gentian is another of these desirable, early, and rare old plants of great beauty. Nothing can excel the beauty of a few small beds of this lovely tribe. *Acaulis* is stemless, as the name indicates. It is a plant bearing a lovely blue trumpet flower of an immense size in proportion to the character of the plant as far as stature goes, and in consequence the flower becomes most conspicuous. In some localities this plant is said to be difficult to grow, and more difficult to induce to flower; but if it is planted somewhat in a shady aspect, in soil composed of good friable loam, a little peat, and some road sand, with a little old lime rubbish, sifted and well mixed with the rest, draining the bed, it will succeed well. The chief thing is not to disturb it often. Plant it well in the above compost, four or six inches apart, and let it remain for several years together.

The good old-fashioned Double White Rocket is a plant to be coveted by every lover of flowers. At the time of year that this flowers (May and June) there is no equal to a bed of this in full flower, for effect and fragrance. A singular peculiarity belonging to this good old flower is that it assumes additional power of reflection towards evening. If you go towards a bed of this plant in flower, between light and dark, that is, just after sunset, you will find it has some power which acts upon the sight, different from that of bright light, and it also assumes a greater degree of fragrance at that time. Plant them in good friable loam, with a little old dung added, and some sharp sand. Plant six or seven inches apart, during March, or early in the autumn, if the roots are strong; although it is best to make a new plantation every season from the old stools, after they have flowered. I wish the trade would revive this old favourite, and show what it is worth, by cultivating it high; I am sure it would be in great demand.

I need not say much of the Lily of the Valley; every one

knows very well what that is; but as there is some difficulty experienced in some instances in growing this little favourite well, I will just add that I cannot see why it should be more difficult to grow in one place than another, providing it has a shady border and good sandy loam, and a little leaf-mould to grow in, well planted, and seldom disturbed. It is one of those plants that do not strike root very quick after transplanting. Do not bury it above an inch, or one inch and a half below the surface. A good drainage must be secured, and the plants well bedded in firmly. Beds of polyanthus, double lilac, and crimson primroses are exceedingly rich in colour, and very effective. Plant them six inches apart in good ordinary ground. The Aquilegias are both curious and beautiful, embracing a variety of colour. There is something uncommon-looking about this flower; the beautiful character of its foliage, with its exquisite and peculiar flower, thrown up so completely above the foliage, and flowering so profusely as it does, certainly adapt the tribe to bed and border purposes, especially the Glandulosa (Grigor's). This is a beautiful dwarf-flowering variety, and highly recommended. A bed of this has a charming effect. It is perfectly hardy. Plant one foot apart, in any good common garden soil of a light nature. Propagation takes place by seed and offsets. (See " Plants by Seed.")

The Potentillas are rich in colour and diversity, and beautifully marked. These continue in flower a long time, and are perfectly hardy. The blue, white, and scarlet Pentstemons are really a most beautiful class of hardy plants, particularly adapted for bedding purposes. The varieties of blue are most lovely, and very uncommon. I cannot account for this, as they can all be raised in abundance from seed, and propagated by cuttings. *Speciosa purpurea atrocæruleum* are fine blue varieties, and the scarlet varieties are lovely plants for large beds. Plant in good loam and peat, one foot asunder, and cut back (as soon as the first principal crop of flowers are off) to keep the plants dwarf, or the cutting back may be left till March or April, which perhaps will be most advisable in late counties and cold soils.

Then there are the *Ranunculus uniflora*, the stocks and wallflowers. Of the stocks (which require sowing every season) choose the Intermediate and the purple Brompton. Sow these in June and July, and plant them out six inches apart into the bed they are to flower in as soon as large enough. Should the weather prove severe in the winter, protect them by covering the beds with furze, laid all over the bed carefully, and over this a Russian mat may be laid on severe nights. The stocks are not tender; but the sudden changes, and the influence of the sun upon any-thing frozen, causes death or some less important injury. (See " Effects of Frost, and how to Avoid it.") Let the soil be of a porous nature for these stocks, such as good common garden soil, into which introduce a good propor-tion of old lime rubbish, freestone, cinders, and broken brick, and some sand of a sharp nature. This applies to heavy soil or a cold subsoil in some of the midland and northern counties ; but in the southern and western counties the land is generally sufficiently porous enough. If these purple and scarlet stocks get through the winter they will form very desirable objects in the following early summer.

The *Helleborus niger* is a useful flower during the dull months of winter. This Christmas rose, as it is called, has a very singular palmated leaf, which is of a deep green, and large. The plant produces a white flower of a large size, and single. Any common soil of a sandy nature suits it. Its nature is very hardy and of long duration. The chrysanthemums are too well known to require com-ment ; but the pompone varieties make the most lovely beds, by constant stopping up till the end of July, and watering with liquid manure as soon as the flower-buds are half developed. The large-flowered varieties answer admirably for large beds, by pegging down, which commence as soon as the young stuff is long enough. Good friable loam, and sand of a sharp nature will grow them well.

The beds of this garden may be made very pretty indeed, by planting crocuses, snowdrops, winter aconite, and some of the variegated-leaved plants round them, which will have a very pretty effect on a well-kept lawn. A single plant or two here and there of the double blossom furze, and some beds of dwarf perpetual tea-scented roses, will add materially to the beauty of this garden. When once planted, very little expense attends it, beyond stopping, watering, tying up to sticks, and an annual trimming and dressing after the plants have done flowering. The name of " everlasting garden " has been given to this section because it contains a class of flowering plants hardy and of long duration, both as regards their flowering season and constitution.

THE GEOMETRICAL GARDEN

Is very well as a picture on paper, and easily constructed, but rather a difficult thing to manage if the idea is stringently carried out ; and even then it is too much like patchwork, and so adverse to nature, that I think it most pleasing by its absence. Mechanism in flower-gardening is even worse than no rule, for mechanism is too much wanting in natural effect. I have no objection to any pretty geometrical design for beds as a design, but to endeavour to carry it out is as much against nature's laws as it would be to endeavour to build a house without a plan. No doubt our predecessors worked hard to produce such a garden, and thought themselves rather clever in turning out such a pretty thing, which now-a-days is easy enough even for a carpenter to do ; yea, he is the proper person to produce such a design, while the naturalist, as a gardener, feels it difficult to bend his ideas to such whimsical shapes. But all this while, perhaps, some of my young readers are asking, " What is a geometrical garden ? " Why, a number of flower-beds arranged so as to match in twos, fours, sixes, or more, of precisely the same proportions, and are struck out by rule and compass. This garden must be on a large scale for convenience, therefore not at all suited to one pleasure-ground out of one thousand, but just the reverse.

THE ITALIAN GARDEN.

THERE are many imitations of this garden, but few worthy of the name. To form a good Italian garden takes some time and some material too ; for to have any effect worthy of a name, it must be on a good scale. It is not absolutely necessary to build a succession of terraces to make this garden beautiful, but quite the contrary (in my humble opinion). Choose a flat for effect ; enclose this with a neat hedge of Irish yew, common yew, privet, laurel, &c. ; lay it out into beds and walks, or beds on grass ; the outlines should be straight, with a five or six feet walk next the hedge ; which hedge must be kept trimmed, upright, and neat ; not clipped if of laurel, but cut in with the knife. The beds may lay in lines forming a succession of lozenges, angles, or squares, and a broad space between each of these lines of beds. These spaces are for promenades, and may be of gravel ; if so, all the beds must be edged with box, thrift, or some of the edging plants of the variegated class, &c. ; but they may be of grass, as I said before. These spaces should be broad walks, and should be wide enough to admit of a row of large pots, tubs, or vases in a straight line up the middle.

L

These vases, &c., contain straight-stemmed Portugal laurels, five or six feet in height, clear in the stem, with a head cut over into the shape of an open umbrella, of a very neat, symmetrical shape, with the knife.   They have much the appearance of fancy grown orange trees, and answer admirably for the purpose. A good deal of time and trouble attends the production of the trees; the stems must be attained by cutting off all the branches clean while coming on. This may be done while the plants are in the open ground, shifting them every two seasons till of the desired stature, then potted into pots, vases, or tubs, during the months of October and November. These must be well watered during summer, and one or two liberal waterings with liquid manure to preserve the deep green. Nip the points of the young wood out as it advances, to preserve symmetry of character. These may be planted out permanently if preferred, or two rows of Irish yews may be planted in perfectly straight lines (not too near each other), ten or twelve feet from row to row, and eight or ten feet from plant to plant. If this garden is on a good broad scale, several of the broad walks will be required. In one of these spaces (as I call them) may be the plants already named; in another a row of permanent pillar roses, trained very neatly to twelve or eighteen feet straight and stout larch pillars. These will form exceedingly fine and grand objects if managed well. Plant them with the Dundee Rambler, Rose Angle Blush, Queen of the Belgians, The Seven Sisters, Laura Davoust, and *Felicite perpetua* (these last two are most lovely and vigorous roses), Rampant, and Scandens, and *Sempervirens odorata.* (See " Roses.") These columns of roses will give contrast, beauty, fragrance, and charming effect to this garden, and will not be out of place if managed well; but as peculiar neatness is a characteristic of no ordinary appreciation in this garden, it must be especially maintained about these pillar roses. This is easily accomplished by due attention to training.

Large ornamental vases may be placed over the area, filled with plants of the season. So also the beds, according to fancy; but in this case, as in all others, there is nothing like whole beds of a colour. Blue, yellow, and white crocuses make a lovely display in the season. Annuals (in lieu of bedding plants) may be sown, selecting those of clear colours, dwarf habit, and free to flower. A list of what is really good, and a list of the "good-for-nothing" will be found in this work.

THE WILDERNESS AND HOW TO MAKE IT.

IF roses, climbing roses, and other plants were allowed to grow according to some people's theory, we should have plenty of wildernesses everywhere, and even where they would not be at all agreeable; however, this is not the way in which I should make a wilderness : there is as much trouble in forming a well-devised wilderness as a good pleasure-ground, and perhaps a little more. In the first place, choose the spot best suited; and this should be away from the dwelling-house, in some secluded locality, on low ground if possible, as the most appropriate for the plants that should grow here. These consist of climbing roses, clematis, honeysuckles, double flowering brambles, solanum, ivies, passifloras, periploca, ampelopsis, atregene; these are all climbers, and should occupy different positions; some climbing up stumps of old trees inserted in the ground for the purpose, and others rambling over heaps of old logs, stones, and earth. Then there are weeping willows and thorns, the laburnums, the *Leycesteria formosa, Pyrus Japonica,* and pyracantha. And the fir tribe, such as the hemlock spruce, *Pinus insignis, Taxodium sempervirens, Juniperus pendula,* and *J. sabina prostrata.* Then comes the dwarf species and varieties, such as Butcher's broom, cotoneaster, St. John's-wort, Berberis, wood-laurel, vaccinium, genistas, ferns, &c., &c. ; with the grasses, such as the pampas, and a variety of hardy herbaceous plants.

Now it would be as much out of good gardening policy to jumble these together in any confused and injudicious manner, notwithstanding it is for a wilderness, as it would be to plant them with a regard to nothing but compactness, and stringent mechanical order, although a due regard to order is as necessary here as in any other department of gardening. The scale of land for such a thing should be broad, as will be seen by any one acquainted with the classes of plants named ; broad walks and bold features are indispensable here. These are formed by clumping or grouping ; stems of old pollard trees set up on bold mounds of good earth, on which plant the climbing roses in separate groups, and the other climbers in groups, and some on single stumps of these old trees half lopped, and others trailing over heaps of earth, logs, and stones. The *Pinus insignis* must have a good broad, flat space to develop itself in ; the junipers a proportionate space in single plants, and the dwarf sorts planted in compound groups on heaps of stones, around the sides of which plant ferns and other plants. The walks should be moderately broad, and made to pass irregularly in and out among the groups, mounds, and single plants of a large character.

It is impossible to give a plan for such a thing, as the locality, situation, and the immediate circumstances must dictate in a great measure what is best ; form has but little to do with it, although a or oblong square would be most convenient. The exterior of this should be skirted with forest trees, such as Oak, Birch, Beech, Larch, and Spruce Fir, Lime, Evergreen Oak, Turkey Oak, Acacia, Laburnum, and thorns, keeping the most ornamental next the interior.

Good draining and double trenching will be necessary for the well-being of the plants, and good hearty soil too. Get a large quantity (in due proportion) of old logs (crowns of trees), &c., and place them in heaps where large clumps are desirable, and then cover these with several feet of good earth and dung, lime and stones, broken bricks or clinkers, all mixed together, forming the clump in the ordinary way ; the trunks of the old pollard trees being let into these clumps of earth against which plant the group of climbing roses, and so on as named before ; taking the precaution not to plant two opposite characters of plant on the same clump, nor at the same pillar; different coloured roses may be planted together, but of the same disposition ; that is, of the same growth. Just so in cases of the other climbers ; for instance, the Clematis and Honey suckle and *Passiflora Cerulea* may be grouped together, and the Cotoneaster, *Genista procumbens*, *G. Sagittalis*, and *tinctoria*, St. John's-wort, *Vaccinium*, and *Polygonum vacciniifolium*, may be planted on the sides of the clumps, and on heaps of stones and earth by themselves ; and various ferns should be planted in many places. Nothing suits the wilderness better than an abundance of ferns and grasses ; an ample supply of the splendid fern, *Osmunda regalis*, should be at hand. Abundance of this noble fern may be had for the trouble of getting, by obtaining leave of the owners of the estates on the borders of the river Dart, in Devonshire, where thousands grow in great luxuriance ; but it must be borne in mind that this fern must have a shady and damp spot to grow in, and a large proportion of river or pit sand mixed with the soil. Then there are the different hardy perennial plants, consisting of the Potentillas, Valerian, Aquilegias, Vincas, Lythrus, Œnotheras, Wallflowers, common White Lilies and coloured ones, Lily of the Valley, Iberis, Acorns, Aster, Anemones, &c., all of which are adapted and desirable for the wilderness. The surfaces on which the roses, ferns, and these perennial plants grow should be kept clean, otherwise it will be a " wilderness of confusion," and " without order" indeed. The walks should be broad, as I have observed before, and made of good gravel; the whole should be tidy, but not rigid. Very little pruning is required in this department, but training must be resorted to, or the roses and other climbers will not accomplish the object in view; but when they are once fairly established, and fairly cover the pillars and trunks, &c., no more training will be necessary, for, as I said before, if no trouble is taken to prevent it, these plants grow beyond what is desirable, even for a wilderness. In my opinion, as well as in that of better authorities, there are few things prettier, or more worthy of practice, than a wilderness of this sort, where the premises are large enough.

THE ROSARY; what it should be.

THERE are two kinds of these beautiful gardens, each formed with the same material; both are beautiful and interesting, but one is nothing more or less than a nursery where roses are propagated and grown for sale, and these rosaries are to be found all over the country, and some few persons have become notorious (almost proverbial) for this kind of thing; as Rivers, of Sawbridgeworth, Paul, of Cheshunt, and a few others; not that better roses are to be had here than elsewhere, for the trade generally get their stocks of these noted nurseries, so that the same sorts can be obtained almost everywhere. The kind of rosary I am about to recommend is a somewhat different thing from a nursery; it is what may be called the " flower," while the other is the " bud." The form of this garden is immaterial; the chief thing is suitable land. It is a fact within my own observation, that the same rose is not so perfect in some counties as in others ; and it is equally true that roses will wear out much sooner in one county than in another ; where the dog-rose is to be found in more abundance, there the cultivated rose will do best. But some will say, " Wear out ? I thought roses would last always !" Well, when I say wear out, I do not mean that the plant itself will wear out, but the flower degenerates more rapidly in warmer climates, than in colder ; at the same time it is a fact that the development is more rapid and greater in the flower of the same rose in the warmer than in the colder, and, as a matter of course, this is the chief cause of quicker degeneracy in roses on the dog-rose. I have seen good double roses degenerate into poor semi-double ones, in Devonshire, after standing a few years on the same spot ; this is partly owing to the soil, as well as the exhaustive nature of the climate ; which being salubrious, continues to excite, so that there is scarcely any definite resting season. Roses are best on their own roots in such climates and poor soils.

The dog-rose flourishes in cold clayey subsoils. This sub-soil is everything in rose-growing. The soil for a good rosary of a lasting nature should be good tender loam, and the subsoil of a cool nature, that is, free clay ; the ground for a good permanent rosary should be double-trenched, and well drained ; for although the dog-rose is fond of abun-dance of moisture, it is still impatient of stagnated water.

Roses planted in graduated beds, like the nurserymen grow them, are too formal for the well-devised pleasure-ground of the private mansion. Embankments of roses are very nice ideas, but generally the banks are too high and dry for the well-being of the roses in the long run ; a flat area, deep soil, well drained and well laid out, planted with a good selection of French, Provence, Moss, Bourbon, Perpetual, and Hybrid Perpetual and China roses, is certainly a most interesting thing.

So much has been said on this "Queen of Flowers," that I think it quite superfluous to add anything more; nevertheless, as I see still so little of the thing I mean, and scarcely ever have had the pleasure of late years of seeing a good collection of French roses, or a good rosary containing a well-assorted collection of perpetuals, I am thereby urge·1 to remark that I cannot tell how it is that our good gardens should be so wanting in these unique things as they are at present. I refer more especially to the "Gallicas," as they are called—that is, the French roses. It is true these are superseded by the Perpetuals (as they are called), simply because of the protracted duration of their flowering season, but there is little or no comparison in the quality of the flowers in these classes. The beautiful and rich "Gallica Roses" are among roses what the Camellia is among flowering shrubs, and the Ranunculus among flowering bulbs,—so symmetrical in form and rich in diversity of colour, that many of this class are justly designated "Ra-nunculiflora." I will not attempt to describe these splendid roses, and need not, for they have been described by many, and more particularly by that celebrated rose-grower, Rivers, of Sawbridgeworth, in his useful "Rose Amateur's Guide." However, I may just add that some of this class of roses are so much like a double ranunculus as to be mistaken for one; while others so nearly resemble a carnation as not to be distinguished from some of these flowers, so distinctly and exactly striped and flaked are they; while others are beautifully spotted and mottled. These are qualities that more particularly give the French roses the pre-eminence above all others.

Although a rosary, then, may or may not contain these to make it worthy of the name, yet I could not consider one complete without them. A rosary, then, should contain a due proportion of each class to arrive at perfection; for the most beautiful and perfect roses are among the Gallicas, Provences, Moss, Bourbon, Hybrid Provence, and Hybrid Chinas, and of this last, I may add, too much cannot be said by way of praise ; some of the largest, most noble, and perfect roses are to be found here. I cannot help feeling puzzled to conceive how it is that perpetuals should be allowed to supersede these grand, symmetrical, lovely, and constant summer roses. Where among all our new perpetual roses can we find one to compete with Cupe d'Hebe, Chenédoleé, Brennus, Lady Stuart, Great Western, &c., &c. ? Then there are the Unique Moss, and curious Provences, of which I must name the lovely "Crested" variety, so singularly beautified by the uncommon mossy calyx enveloping the beautiful bud, which always makes this rose a favourite.

The most pleasing and agreeable style of rosary is that of large and small beds of a circular form on a neatly kept lawn, allowing good room between the beds for perfect freedom to two or three of our modern ladies walking at leisure. These beds should (for perfect effect, as well as for the convenience of character) consist of classes of roses only ; for instance, let one entire bed (large or small) be filled with all Gallicas (French), because these grow similarly and flower at one time ; another bed of Provence and Moss ; another of the Hybrid China and Bourbon, Perpetual and Tea-scented Chinas, and so on. The beds should be at such a distance from each other as to admit, not only of walking with ease and freedom between them, but that each bed may be equally an object of attraction, and not dependent upon its neighbour for assistance, nor lending to it. I always find that every class of flower, whether in or out of pots, makes the greatest display and produces the best desired effect at a nice distance from the eye ; hence the importance of adjusting the scale of the clump of roses to the general scale of the garden.

I have said something about this "scaling" of beds under the head "The Flower Garden and its Defects;" thus, with the rosary, a disproportionate bed either has a heavy, or too poor and light an appearance, according to its disproportion. Large beds at a greater distance from each other are far better than small ones closer together, for these present a confused idea, and are disagreeable for walking amongst, besides a total loss of any good effect and of good flowers, on account of the limited space of the roots. Everything mechanical should be obviated as much as possible. Some good single standards, eight or nine feet high, on stiff, straight stems, should be planted here and there, in open and broad spaces; these may consist of the Hybrid Chinas and Noisettes, such as Brennus, Beauty of Billiard, Belle Parabere, and Fulgens; and of Noisettes, the following,—Aimée Vibert, La Biche, Luxembourg, Lamarque, and so on, which will form most lovely objects as pendulous standards, if carefully and well planted, fed, and judiciously pruned, merely thinning the branches out, and not cutting all the wood back, as in the case of general rose pruning.

Another unusual, grand, and lovely class of objects in the rosary are the noble pillar roses, fifteen or twenty feet high, trained to stout larch pillars, let into the ground (previously charring the end), sufficiently deep to keep them upright against a strong wind. These larch poles should be six or seven inches in diameter at the thick end, and may have the branches cut off six or nine inches from the stem, leaving snags; or may have some holes bored through them at right angles, and crossed at every fifteen or eighteen inches with oak pins, to form double pegs on the pole. These will greatly assist in holding the roses, as they are trained around the pillar between these pegs, over and under. These pillars should be planted in corners and entrances, with some of the fast growers, such as the

Ayrshire, Multiflora, Boursault, Hybrid Climbing, Hybrid China, and Noisettes; and in some warm and sheltered spots the Yellow Banksian. From the Ayrshire family, choose Dundee Rambler, Rose Angle Blush, Queen of the Belgians; and of Multiflora, choose Seven Sisters, Laura Davoust, and Fragrans ; of the Boursault, choose Amadis, Gracilis, and Elegans ; and from the Hybrid climbing varieties choose Well's White, Garland (Wood's), Queen of the Prairies, *Rosa craculatum ;* and of the Hybrid China, choose Brennus, Great Western, Blarii, Petit Pierre ; and of the Noisettes choose Ariel, Clarisse Harlowe, Jaune Duprez, a remarkably fine, rich, and fragrant rose, and Lamarque and Luxembourg.

All these pillar roses must be on their own roots, and planted in rich land. If it is not so, add good maiden loam and rotten dung, and water them once or twice during the season with some liquid manure; guano is as good as anything,—two or three ounces to the gallon of water; given the first time as soon as the flower-buds are fairly formed, and again a month or six weeks after they have shed the first crop of flowers. This applies to those sorts that give a second batch, viz., the Noisettes, &c. Each application should be a thorough soaking, and should not be too late in the season. The chief thing is to encourage as much long-rod growth of the season as possible, at the same time training these long flexible shoots round the pillar as they advance. It is easier, quicker, and safer to follow this timely training, than to let them grow on till they become confused. If a suffi-cient supply of new rods can be insured, say three, from the bottom to the top of the pillar during the season, the old ones may be cut out clean down to the ground in the autumn or spring, as these long rods of a single season's growth will give more flower than the old ones cut back to spurs, which must be the case if sufficient new growth cannot be secured to cover the pillar from bottom to top. If a sort of less vigorous growth than usual be planted against an extra high pillar, one that cannot ordinarily make wood from bottom to top in one season, as may be the case with some of the Hybrid Chinas and Noisettes, a rod or rods must be permanently laid in, and made to reach the top of the pillar by degrees, and judicious spurring in resorted to year after year. The pruning must be carefully done, being ruled by the disposition of the subject, otherwise all the flowers, or a great proportion of them, will be lost. Short-spurring will be necessary in some, and long-spurring in others. This is the secret of flowering roses. Some roses will never give a flower if pruned too severely. Two or three eyes, or buds, are enough at each spur on some of the Noisettes and Chinas, while some of the rapid climbers, as well as some of the Hybrid Chinas, Banksia, &c., must not be cut to within five or six buds or more.

It will be observed that the roses that give very long and flexible shoots, naturally must not be cut in so close as those that give wood less rampant. Nevertheless, it is necessary to cut some spurs in pretty close, to provide for flowering wood for the ensuing season, or you may find a difficulty in keeping home, or being obliged to cut away the flowers, or, at least, the wood that bears them. But the first plan here given will be found to answer best for flowering pillar roses, viz., the long-rod system.

Few things can compare with these grand objects of nature on fifteen or twenty feet pillars, forming column roses, which eclipse everything else in the way of roses. A plot of ground entirely devoted to these, and single large standards, as described, would be no mean thing. In planting beds of roses, plant moderately thick, according to the character. The Gallicas may be planted thicker than the Hybrid Chinas and Noisettes. A little judgment, and the knowledge of their natures, is alone necessary to prevent overcrowding or deficiency. The pruning of some roses requires caution, as I have already observed, more particularly with the Hybrid Chinas, whose shoots must be merely half cut back, and some of the shoots thinned out to provide stock-wood for flowering the ensuing season. Just so with the Briars; but the French, Chinas, and the Perpetuals, and Moss, may be cut in to within two, three, or four buds, according to the strength of the wood, pruning so as to keep an open head.

It is of very little use to be constantly cutting the suckers off at the surface of the ground, as they appear frequently from worked roses on the dog-rose. They may be pulled up sometimes, as a means of getting rid of them. If this does not succeed, take the plant completely up, cut the suckers clean out at the base, and plant it again. But the chief reason for suckers arising is a want of depth of good soil; they will not trouble you much if the subsoil is good. The time of planting depends pretty much upon the sort and the locality. In all cases it is best to defer this business till the month of April for tender roses on their own roots, and February or March for tender roses on the dog-rose; but the Hybrid China, Gallica, Provence, Moss, Hybrid Perpetuals,—in fact, all but the tender Tea Chinas may be planted in the months of November and December. In choosing roses, select those standards that have straight, clean, and stout stems, such as will not require a stake to support them, especially for the full standard. Do not apply dung immediately on the root of the dog-rose; but lay it (viz., good rotten dung) on the surface of the bed during December and January, after the bed has been forked over for the season. The pruning of all roses is best deferred till February or March.

The protection of the beds of tea-scented China rose is simple : get some furze and lay over the' bed, covering the heads moderately thick. If they are on half-standards (about 2½ feet high), and this is full high enough for this class, the furze must be tied to the stem below the head, then slightly tie the furze above; thus the head will be enveloped and secured from the frost, and free circulation to the dry air be still admitted. It is not so much the cold itself that destroys them as it is the retention of water which presents a destructive medium through the action of the frost distending the tissue, and causing death as soon as the sun's rays reach it. All the tender teas on their own roots must have a well-drained bed. Put abundance of old lime rubbish, broken bricks, old mortar, &c., at the bottom of the bed first, then fill the bed up above the level six or eight inches with loam, turf and all, with one-third leaf-mould well mixed.

The budding and grafting of roses is very simple indeed; of course it requires the knowledge of the character of the sort and its adaptation ; this gained (which is simpler still), the next thing is to observe the condition of both stock and bud, and one rule serves for both, viz., the maturity of the bud and the freedom with which the bark leaves the stock, which is easily proved by merely sticking the thumb-nail into the young wood five or six inches from the upright stem. If the bark leaves the wood freely it is in the proper condition for budding and grafting. The bud is in the proper condition for budding when it is " well up," as gardeners call it, that is, when it is perfectly full-sized, and the bark of the wood will leave the young wood on which the buds are. These are the certain rules, a deviation from which involves uncertainty in the results. The bud must be cut off an inch long with a fine-edged knife, preserving the bud about the middle, having the one or two branches nearest the top of the stock prepared by rubbing the leaves and prickles off, and the bark slit for an inch and a half from the stock upwards, and a cross-cut made in the bark at right angles at the top of the long cut; lift the bark (I used to do it with my thumb-nails), then cut off the bud; pull out the thin piece of wood inside the bud, and slip the bud into the stock quickly, pressing it gently toward the stem, and tie it with best matting or cotton or thick worsted; tie moderately tight, winding it round above and below the bud, and giving a single tie underneath, just to prevent it undoing for a month, when the bandages may be taken off, and if the bud has done well it will be safe by that time.   Do not shorten the young wood of the stock at the time, as this induces the bud to push at once, forming a shoot even before the bud has properly united itself to the stock.

The stock must be kept clear of all young stuff other than that budded; the budded stuff must be cut back within two inches of the bud during the following winter before March, and the dead part of the stock above the buds cut out.

Grafting is seldom resorted to with roses out of doors, but it is exceedingly useful in the propagation of choice and rare sorts indoors, using nice little stocks in small pots three to five inches in diameter.   The Dog-rose may be used of a dwarf size, small and sound, but stocks of the quick-growing Boursault are the best.   The stocks should be potted early from cuttings made in the last spring.   Grafts of any desirable variety may be worked on them, merely subjecting the stocks to a slight heat, or a close pit or frame without heat.   Cut the stock partly down, and cut the graft with a single bud, which insert in the stock close to the pot; slip the bud off similarly to one for budding, but with the wood attached to it; cut a similar bit of the stock, and match the bud and stock; tie it in, and use grafting-wax made of 1 lb. of Burgundy pitch, ¼ lb. common pitch, 2 oz. beeswax, and ½ oz. mutton fat, melted. (*Rivers.*) This grafting-wax must be put on with a small brush while warm, not hot, or clay may be used. This is a very rapid way of producing pot-roses, and also very interesting.

The propagation of roses by cuttings is simply selecting the ripened wood of the last growth, and dividing the bottom of the cutting at right angles with a sharp knife just below a bud, preserving one, two, or three above, according to the strength of the wood, and inserting this cutting in a pot of leaf-mould, dung, and loam, half filling the pot with crocks first for a perfect drainage, inserting the cuttings round the pot, pressing the soil firmly to the cutting, watering, and plunging the pots in sand, sawdust, or cinder ash. A very little heat indeed will serve to strike cuttings of roses, and none at all is required for many, but merely selecting cuttings of the summer's growth with two to five or six buds; trim off the leaves from the lower half, leaving the top ones, and insert them in similar soil to that described for pots, on a south border. Plant them one and a half or two inches asunder under a hand-light in September and October. Give some air as soon as they commence growing; take them up, and pot them or plant them out during April.

The raising of new varieties from seed is a good speculation often, and simple. Save the hips in the autumn and preserve in sand. During January and February break these hips and sow the seed in pans or wide-mouthed pots, in good soil, covering the seed with half an inch of earth, and set the pots, &c., in a frame with a slight heat, or in a shady house at work, keep the surface moist, and the seed will soon vegetate; the seed will grow without heat, but slower of course. The second year they may be planted out into fine beds of earth to flower.

ROCKERIES, and how to Make them.

THESE ornaments of the garden are not absolutely necessary things; nevertheless, they are objects of import-ance in a good-finished pleasure-ground, and indispensable to those gardens where a class of plants can only be at home upon them. It is not necessary to form one of granite from Devonshire, nor from Derby; neither is it necessary to build one as large as the Rock of Gibraltar, nor to provide water at the foot of the rock. If we are to be ruled by nature, we may or may ·not imitate a rock in the water. A rockery, then, can be out of place nowhere, still there are conditions in which a rockery certainly dis-plays itself to better advantage, and that is when it is backed by evergreen trees and shrubs, and overhung with laburnum or willow; these not only afford an agreeable accessory to a good piece of rockery, but a most desirable shade for the plants that furnish the rockery. A bit of rockwork may be made to imitate a large stone rising out of a pool, but unless it is of a different class from one of the inland kind, and furnished accordingly, it is out of place· If rock-constructors would gain a knowledge of natural rockeries, they would find it not so difficult to accomplish their object; this is easily done now-a-days. Photography is a boon in this respect; fac-similes of anything can now be had for a trifle, which if properly defined will illustrate what I mean, as well as be a good guide.

The difficulty of constructing a good rockery in some parts of the country is much greater than in others, for want of stone; but I think I can suggest a plan (not new, I believe) that will answer equally well when no stone can be found suitable.

There are two ways of doing this : one is by building with hard, coarse brick with cement, and facing it over with

M

cement after ; the other is by collecting first a lot of coarse
sand and stones, providing a stout box of any desirable size,
of a square form (say fifteen inches square, cubic, which is
quite large enough for handling), provide a clean-planed
board larger than the outside of the box (this is what may
be called a large mould like a brickmaker's, except that
theirs is oblong),—several of these bottom boards will be
required ; place the mould on one of these ; now having
some Roman cement, water, stools ready, and two men and
a boy at hand close to the mould, put out a quantity of
cement on a large smooth board, add water, and work it
into a thin mortar quickly, take it up and in with it into the
bottom of the mould ; enough to form a layer five or six
inches thick, in with some five or six inches of the coarse
sand and small stones well mixed, when the man at the
mould, having a moderate sized rammer in hand, must
proceed to drive the sand and stones into the cement till it
is well combined, and so proceed with layer after layer till
the mould is full ; let it stand for a few minutes, and then
by means of handles on the box (mould) lift it off, and let
the concrete stone remain till dry. If any difficulty is
experienced in getting the mould off, it may be made with
four hinges and hooks, by which it may be opened and
taken off; thus a sufficient quantity of stone can be made
to form a good-sized durable rockery at a little cost.

These concrete stones with the coarse sand and small
pebbles, &c., in them exactly imitate some of the coast
rocks, and are equally durable, and thus a good bold-
featured bit of rockwork can be built easily with cement, fit
for any place and to answer any purpose. No rockery
can be built well worthy of the name without cement, but
with this any class of rockery may be made. Any shade of
colour may be added to it by merely adding soot for
darker and chalk for lighter. Recesses and ledges must

be formed for the different plants ; the most effective style of rock is that of perpendicular, and finishing in heavy heads above.

The furnishing of the rockery is another thing, still it requires either the builder to be acquainted with plants, or that the building is under the immediate superintendence of one who knows what rock plants are. The planting of these is best done with cow-dung and loam made into a thick mortar, bedding some sorts (those suited for exposed ledges) in it ; of course the interior of the rockery is filled up with good earth, and some plants planted in the fissures and openings left for the purpose. The list subjoined will be found to contain a suitable and good variety.

1.—Genista procumbens.
2.— „ tinctoria flore-pleno.
3.— „ triquetra.
4.—Cistus calycinus.
5.— „ nigrescens.
6.— „ purpureus.
7.— „ flore-pleno.
8.—Berberis repens.
9.—Erica cinerea alba.
10.— „ atropurpurea.
11.— „ coccinea.
12.— „ tetralix.
13.— „ „ alba.
14.—Hypericum calycinum.
15.— „ uralum.
16,—Cineraria maritima.
17.—Antirrhinum, various.
18.—Pentstemon, various.
19.—Iberis Tenoreana.
20.—Wallflower, various.

21.—Veronica, various.

22.—Alyssum saxatile.

23.—Saxifraga umbrosa.

24.—   „   moss-like.

25.—Polygonum vaccinifolium.

26.—Soldanella Alpina.

27.—Erinus   „

28.—Arabis   „

29.—Sedums, various.

30.—Dianthus, various Alpina.

31.—Crucinella stylosa.

32.—Statice, various.

33.—Asplenium adiantum nigrum.

34.—   „   capillus Veneris.

35.—   „   various.

36.—Linum Alpinum, white and blue.

37.—Linaria vulgaris.

38.—Myosotis Alpina.

Also some summer plants, such as Lobelia gracilis, verbenas, and fuchsias. No. 16 is a free-growing hardy plant with ample white foliage, remarkably suited for bold features, and will grow large. Nos. 1 to 22 are all of a somewhat shrubby and half-shrubby nature, varying from six inches to one foot in height. Nos. 1, 2, and 3, are very hardy and beautiful yellow-flowering, trailing shrubs, and will form a fine feature on the rock, two or three feet from the ground. Nos. 23, 24, and 29, are fit for bare points that project. No. 25 is one of the most lovely rock plants that can be had, as hardy as a holly, and a free grower; it should be planted in a prominent place, in a good crevice of peat and loam, three feet from the ground level, where it will make a lovely display with its pink flowers. Nos. 33—35 are ferns, of which No. 34 is the handsome little plant found in such great abundance in Devonshire, on the old walls, &c.; it prefers shade, therefore plant in small crevices.

The rockery should be built during the summer, and planted in the month of March or April following. In planting shrubs, &c., that are to be set on exposed parts of the rockery, jutting points, &c., and small crevices, puddle the roots of the plants (unless they are in small pots) in a thin mortar of cow-dung and clayey loam, and bed the plants for the bare stone in a thick mortar of the same, using small stones outside to prevent the earth being washed off, and some moss outside to ward off the influence of the sun, and to prevent the earth from drying till the plants get established.

FOUNTAINS, AND HOW TO MAKE THEM.

AMONG garden ornaments there are none of greater use than fountains. There always seems a peculiar agreeableness about these accessories of ornamental water; and certainly they are of the utmost use; not only as appropriate objects, but as serviceable ones also, for flowering plants and water are first cousins in one sense, and water is the life of the former in another sense, although this is not the case under all circumstances; for if water of an uncongenial nature is given to the plant, instead of facilitating its development it will deter it; for instance, draw some water out of a well of " hard water " (as it is appropriately termed) and immediately water the plants with it, and you will observe the plants to either stand still or lose one part while they slowly make another; water is rendered fertile by exposure to the air and sun, hence the second important use of fountains; then there is a third important use they have in a flower-garden, viz., the saving of time, by the water being brought to the very spot without labour; this is an item of no small moment in most places, as one man will

do as much watering in the same time as two, and perhaps
three, if the water has to be fetched far to the spot where
wanted. Here there are three reasons why fountains should
be constructed in every flower-garden, yet many look at
them as impossibilities, and others as too expensive for
them. I am not going to divulge anything uncommon or
new, but I would just reply that a fountain is neither an
expensive nor an impossible thing anywhere where there is
a house, or any point of ten, twelve, or fifteen feet elevation
above the level of the flower-garden. They may be had
already made of iron and stone, and they may be made on
the spot of brick and cement, or they may be made of
galvanized iron and let into the ground; neither of these
methods is expensive, but the last named is the easiest,
cheapest, and most durable. A very good one with an
animated figure with the jet may be built for the sum of
£20 or less, and the supply may be had from a water-tank
fixed up so as to catch the rain-water from the house,
conducted to the fountain by a small pipe of lead or gutta-
percha; a large barrel holding a hogshead or more is as
good as anything, fixed up on four stout oak posts, with a
waste-pipe and a stopcock to the fountain, so that the
water can be turned on or off at leisure; the basin should
be eight or nine inches above the surface of the lawn (pre-
suming the fountain to be on the grass). Nice little fountains may be bought for from £5 to £10.

AVENUES, AND HOW TO MAKE THEM.

THERE is but one way of forming these, although of
different materials. One of the largest and most complete
extent is at Torquay, in Devonshire, on the Cary Estate.
This is of considerable length, and is formed of lime trees
almost completely. I should scarcely have thought that
the lime tree would have attained to such a magnitude in

this country, had I not witnessed it in this case. The girth of these limes, the age and health is surprising, feathered (as we call it) completely down, and forming a complete arcade and conical outside. The lime, then, is particularly adapted to avenue-making where a shady arcade is desirable. Another kind may be formed of deodars. These will form one of the most lovely avenues for a broad carriage drive with an open top ; there is no plan better suited to the formation of an evergreen avenue than this.

The next class of avenue is one formed of cedar of Lebanon ; for an evergreen class this forms a most durable and noble avenue, differing from either of the others in colour and appearance as well as character. As such an avenue advances to maturity it will be necessary to shorten some of the lower branches on the inside ; that is, next the drive. If obscurity is desirable, constantly nip the points of these lower branches out while the plants are comparatively young ; if it is desirable to get a view from the interior, cut the lower branches off close to the trunk when they intrude upon the drive, leaving all untouched at a convenient height to admit of vehicles passing ; thus a grand evergreen avenue, with a most lovely arcade for a summer promenade will be secured, excelling every other kind of summer walk. Nothing equals the richness of the green of this tree.

Beech forms a beautiful avenue with its lovely light green foliage, but it is very wintry-looking when the leaf is off. The horse-chestnut forms a rapid noble avenue, but carrying so much leaf, and being of a brittle nature, the large limbs are apt to get blown off during heavy gales, which frequently causes a gap in the line never more to be filled up. The deciduous cypress also makes a lovely avenue, with a striking light green leaf. This plant is of a very agreeable character ; the leaf is beautiful and graceful. The tree has the general appearance of the fir tribe in habit. But for richness and grandeur there is nothing to equal the noble cedar of Lebanon. Next to this is the beautiful *Pinus insignis*, and then comes the lime tree. These last two will quickly form a grand feature if the ground be deep in staple soil and of a sandy nature.

Avenues may be planted in double rows, triangular; but the single row is best. The distance from the road to the plant, and from plant to plant, depends upon the nature of the plant and the object in view. The road for a private drive should be not less than twelve feet wide; the plants may be planted six feet from the sides, nearer if it is desired to form an arcade quickly. For this purpose the lime, the *Pinus insignis*, and the elm should be used, and the lower branches stopped as described when they intrude upon the drive.

SPECULATIVE GARDENING.

This includes the very interesting art of raising seedlings, which is not only interesting, but attended with profit. At present this kind of gardening chiefly belongs to the nurseryman, simply because he has the greatest facility for doing it, and he throws his energies into the business of raising new varieties, knowing the chances of certainty better, perhaps, than those who merely grow plants for pleasure alone; yet the amateur has the same advantages as the man who grows for sale, and he has more quiet leisure time, and no fear of his plants being sold before he has obtained his object, nor of his process being interrupted. I do not know anything in gardening more interesting or more profitable than the following up of this branch, especially among florists' flowers. Many a little fortune has been made in it, and even great ones are possible. Certain conditions are requisite for success. Hybridization is the instrument, and perseverance the guarantee. First of all there must be some ground to work upon, that is, two plants (at the least) of the same genus, species, or order; for instance, there must be two or more roses, geraniums, fuchsias, calceolarias, primulas, &c., &c.; or there must be two plants having an affinity for each other, as in the case of the turnip and cabbage, and cherry laurel, pear and thorn, kidney bean and common bean, pansy and violet, lily and tulip, gesneria and achimenes, carnation and dianthus, &c.; and any of the same species may be crossed of course with certainty, that is, any of the different sorts of roses of an opposite character and colour, and of the geranium, fuchsia, and calceolaria families, &c., to accomplish any desirable object in view. Where there is no affinity existing between the classes, there can be no chance of crossing the two; for instance, you cannot cross the carnation and the geranium, the fuchsia and gesneria, the rose and the thorn, and so on. But geraniums of all classes may be crossed, all the classes of dianthus, of primula, and so on.

This is the drift of producing new sorts possessing different qualities and characters. Thus, if you wish to produce a new calceolaria possessing the beauty of the greenhouse varieties, with the hardiness of the shrubby sorts, cut the anthers out of the latter, and dust the stigma of the flower with the pollen of the former. So with everything else, whatever difference is desired from that existing in either of the two must be obtained by this process, and even to a far greater extent in this way. Let the anthers of the polyanthus and auricula be cut out (before they burst), and the pollen of the *Primula Sinensis* be put into the stigma of the two former, and some pretty varieties will be obtained, possessing the beauty of the *Primula Sinensis*, with the hardiness of the two former. This is the principle, of which there are many details to work out, according to the object in view, and only one rule by which to work, viz., the most fit condition to operate upon the flower.

There is a nice time for this, which, if missed, it will avail nothing to operate at any other time. The proper time may be ascertained by a lens, by means of which you can observe whether the stigma of the flower is expanded, and whether the pollen on the anthers is ready. This is known by the anther presenting a powdery appearance, and advantage of this should be taken immediately after the anther has burst. Clip them out with a fine pointed pair of scissors, and dust the stigma well with it, placing a small bit of coarse gauze over the flower, to prevent mischief being done by insects for a day or two. If it is desirable that the seedlings should partake of both parents, let the stamens remain in the plant that is to bear the seed. If all the rest of the flowers, besides those operated upon, are cut off, it will be so much the better, as the seeds will possess additional strength, and probably additional quality. Now this is the whole art of producing new plants. It is old, and well known, but little practised to the length it might be ; for any one can practise it who possesses two plants of one class, a purple stock and a white or scarlet one ; a white and red rose ; a white and a crimson carnation ; a white and a red fuchsia, &c. No one is bound to these colours, but the more opposite the colours are, the better the chance of some pretty varieties.

THE BEST PLANTS FOR WINDOWS.

WHEN I say " window plants " 'I do not mean plants that must be first raised and grown till they are in flower in heat, and in a greenhouse, and then brought into the sitting-room, but plants that may be propagated, grown, and flowered in the window of any cottage or sitting-room by any one following the instructions given under their respective heads further on, and in some previous articles in this work, except in the case of the *Achimenes;* this must be started first in a moderate heat, and then potted into six-inch pots, and then it will answer admirably for any window. (See the article on the same.)

DIVISION I.
PLANTS FOR SHADY WINDOWS.
(*The months denote the time of flowering.*)

Mimulus, various, and Musk (June to September).
Begonia semperflorens, and various (May to August).
Daphne mezereum, cneorum, and odora (April to July).
Primula Sinensis (December to May).
Auricula alpina, &c. (May to July).
Myosotis palustris (forget-me-not), (June to August).
  ,, azorica (June to August).
Pansies, various (April to August).
Arum, various (June to August).
Snowdrops, double and single (February to April).
Ferns of all sorts.
Lycopodiums (mosses).
Sollya heterophylla, a very pretty half-climber of an evergreen character, and blue flowers (June to September).

DIVISION II.
PLANTS THAT WILL NOT DO WITHOUT THE FULL SUN.

Mesembryanthemum speciosa (May to October). This is a fine half shrubby variety.
Oxalis florabunda (May to September).
Violet, Tree, Double Russian (April to June).

Mignonette, common (March to September).

*Tropæolum Jarrattii (June to September).

*   „   General Havelock (May to October).

*   „   Lili Schmidt   „   „

     „   Elegans, dwarf (June to September).

Mimosa armata (Soldier's Bush), a very pretty half-hardy shrub (May to July).

Acacia lophantha, a lovely, tall-growing shrub.

Anagallis, Eugene and Napoleon (June to September).

DIVISION III.

PLANTS THAT WILL DO IN A WINDOW WITH A SHARE OF SUN DURING THE DAY.

Geranium, fancy varieties (June and July).

     „   Scarlet, many varieties (June to September.)

Fuchsias, many varieties (June to August).

     „   fulgens minor, a lovely plant when small for the window (July to August).

Fuchsia fulgens major, a tall-growing, lovely sort, if the leader is trained up to five or six feet high and then stopped; when a head will be formed that will have a charming effect when in bloom (July and August).

Aloysia citriodora (lemon-plant).

Verbena, many varieties (July to September).

Achimenes longiflora (July to September).

Petunias, various double (July to September).

Antirrhinums, various (July and August).

Chrysanthemum, large-flowered (September to November).

     „   Pompone.

Carnations, various; clove, &c. (July and August).

Pinks, various (July and August).

Campanula pyramidalis, a most grand and lovely object (August to October).

Campanula pulcherrima (July and August).

Campanula Garganica (June to September). This is a free-flowering trailer; a lovely thing for pots for the window (June to September).

Dielytra spectabilis, a flesh-rooted perennial plant, ot great beauty in early summer (June to August).

Delphinium formosa, one of the loveliest coloured plants in existence; grow it in a six or eight inch pot, and feed well (July to September).

Delphinium grandiflora, ditto.

Lobelia cardinalis fulgens, a lovely, scarlet-flowered, tall-growing variety (June to August).

Lobelia gracilis, a lovely, blue-flowered trailer, forming a lovely object (June to September). This is a beautiful object in the window outside during the summer months; feed it once a week with manure water.

Cyclamen Persicum. This is a beautiful early flowering bulb of a half-hardy nature, especiallv adapted for the window (flowering from March to April).

Cyclamen Coum. This is a very pretty red-flowering variety, and hardy and early (February and March).

Calceolaria aurea florabunda. This is a very dwarf and amazing free flowerer (July to September).

Calceolaria Prince of Orange. Another of the same class as the one above, but of a darker colour; a fine sort for window work.

Calceolaria St. Alban's. Similar habit as the two former ones, but of a crimson colour.

Calceolaria Gem, a fine dark variety. The above four are dwarf, shrubby varieties, especially adapted for the window, and propagated by cuttings. Then there are the herbaceous varieties that are raised from seed generally, which require a little heat and some especial care before they can be ventured in the window.

Senecio (Double Groundsel), purple and crimson. This

makes a very fine plant for the window with little care
(June to September).

Cactus in variety (see Sorts and Culture).

Rosa Lawrenceana, Pallida, and Nigra, and Caprice des
Dames are the smallest tribe of roses, particularly adapted
for the window (see Rose Culture).

Rosa Chinensis, Tea-scented China, a most delicious and
lovely object for the sitting-room window (flowering from
June to September).

*Maurandia Barclayana, a very pretty flowering half-hardy
climber; fit for the broad trellis in the window (flowering
from July to October).

*Sollya heterophylla. This is a lovely, blue-flowered,
half-creeping evergreen shrub, well adapted for the window
(July to September).

*Passiflora cerulea, one of the loveliest fast creeping
plants extant; train round the window near the glass, inside
or out.

*Lonicera coccinea (trumpet honeysuckle), lovely
moderate climber (in pot) for window.

Lilium lancifolium album, punctatum, rubrum, and
many others (see Culture). These are all fine subjects for
the window (July to September).

Coronilla Glauca, an old window plant well known; will
grow anywhere (July to October).

Hydrangea hortensis, a well-known plant; well adapted
for the window. See Culture, and how to produce the blue
(August to October).

Oleander. This is an old favourite, although it seldom
flowers with cottagers, although it may be made to do so.
See the Culture (August and September).

Neirembergia gracilis, a very pretty free-flowering dwarf
plant; will do well in the window in a six-inch pot, and
loam and peat (July to September).

Violet, double Russian, and Tree (see the Treatment).

Pentstemon gentianoides coccinea, atrocæruleum, purpurea magnificum, delicatum, and many splendid sorts, all lovely objects in six or eight inch pots in the window ; good loam and peat, and feed them once a week with manure-water during blooming season (July to September).

Hepatica, single blue, double blue, and double peach, and white, all very hardy and very beautiful for the window anywhere ; feed them during early spring before they flower (March and April).

Wallflower, blood-red and golden yellow, fine for pots ; feed them well just before they flower.

Stocks, purple and scarlet Brompton, and ten-week, and intermediate ; excellent things for the window in pots and boxes (see " Culture ") flower from May to September.

Aster, Bouquet de Flore, Chrysanthemum flowered, and Truffauts Peony flowered. These are three exceedingly fine sorts, will do well in 6-inch pots if fed once a week, commencing a little before they flower (see " Culture "), August and September.

Viscaria, a beautiful annual for the window ; sow in the pot (July and August).

Fenzlia, a beautiful half-hardy annual for the window (July and August).

Schizanthus retusus, venustus, &c., very pretty annuals, particularly " retusus ; " sow the seed in pots in the autumn or very early in spring.

Nemophila insignis, this is a most lovely free-flowering plant ; sow the seed in six or eight inch pots in September, this will flower early in spring ; sow again in February or March to flower in June and July.

Nemophila maculata, most beautifully spotted.

Discoidalis, singularly bordered.

Dianthus Chinensis, Heddewigii, extraordinary large and

beautiful, fine for pot-culture and the window (July to October).

Clarksia pulcherrima, a most lovely object for the window when sown and grown in eight-inch pots. Sow the seed in March, and thin the plants to two or three, or even one if you can make sure ; soil, loam and leaf-mould, and some pulverized dung. Feed with manure, water once a week, commencing just before it flowers (July and August).

DIVISION IV.

BULBS FOR THE WINDOW.

Crocus, a variety ; plant six or seven in a six-inch pot of sandy loam in November (February and March).

Hyacinths, various, one in a pot (January and February).

Iris susiana, a grand old flower, plant one in a six-inch pot (May and June).

Dens canis, dog's-tooth violet, various ; this is not a violet at all, but more like a reflected lily ; a lovely and interesting little plant, beautifully spotted in the leaf, which is similar to the dwarf tulip leaf. The flowers which are thrown up above the leaf are either purple, rose, or white. Plant these bulbs in the autumn in a five-inch pot.

Scilla præcox, this is an early and beautiful light blue dwarf plant; put one in a six-inch pot in the autumn, and feed it with manure water just as the spike of flower shows (February and March).

Ranunculus, anemone, and narcissus are all suited well for the window (May and June).

DIVISION V.

FLOWERING SHRUBS, &c., FOR THE WINDOW.

Myrtle, narrow and broad leaved ; nip the points of the

young wood out to induce compact plants and lovely evergreens.

Mimosa armata, a beautiful half-hardy evergreen dwarf
shrub, with yellow, woolly, ball-like flowers ; plant in pots
of peat (May to June).

Mimosa lophantha, a lovely tall-growing mimosa, very
different from the last in the appearance of the leaf, which
is as handsome as a tree-fern—by seed sown in spring on
heat, same soil as the other (May to June).

Kalmia, pink and red ; this plant is the most lovely and
unique extant, when in flower there is nothing that possesses
such a degree of exquisiteness in the individual flower as
this plant possesses. Get nice dwarf bushy plants and place
them in good-sized pots with pure peat, it is quite hardy ;
feed with manure water.

Azalea pontica, yellow ; grandiflora, white ; atro-rubens,
red ; crocea, orange ; and many others, are all most splendid
in early spring and summer ; get small plants in nine or
ten inch pots, using peat, and feed with manure water.
(May to June).

Daphne mezereum, a well-known shrub of great beauty
and fragrance in early spring.

Dentzia gracilis and scabra, two exquisite white-flowering
dwarf shrubs ; pot in loam and peat, and feed with manure
water (May to June).

Genista tinctoria flore pleno (double-flowering) ; this is a
remarkably pretty dwarf free-flowering plant, very hardy,
and fit for . the outside of exposed windows ; feed with
manure water.

Hibiscus, double blue carnation, striped ; lilac striped,
pink striped, purple, red, and white, and a variety beside.
These lovely and superb plants may be called trees of
carnations, for although the leaf of the plant is very
unlike, yet as respects the open flower they very much

N

resemble carnations, and are a most beautiful class of plants. Pot in sandy peat and loam, supply the plants well with water during the growing season, and feed with manure water (July to August).

Jasminum humilis (dwarf jasmine).

* Westeria sinensis; this is certainly the most lovely climbing plant of a hardy nature; grow it in a nine or eleven inch pot of loam and peat, and train to long rods, corkscrew fashion, round three stout and straight sticks four or five feet high, stuck at a triangle in the pot close to the sides, thus forming a moderate column. Spur in these principals as the laterals appear, like as a grape-vine is pruned; this will form a lovely object when in flower ; feed well during the growing season (May to June).

* Hoya carnosa (honey-plant). Although this is a hot-house plant it can be grown in the window of the sitting-room, and I have grown and flowered it exceedingly well in an ordinary greenhouse ; give it a good share of sun and manure water, and it will flower nicely ; it is a lovely flower of the most unique class and of long duration, and it is remarkable that this plant bears flowers several successive years on the same foot-stalk, which should not be cut off when it has done bearing; grow in peat (August to September).

Camellia in varieties (see " Culture ").

Plumbago capensis. This is a lovely blue-flowered half-hardy low shrub ; will do well in the sunny window, grow in peat, stop it constantly to make bushy plants, and feed it once a week with manure water during the growing season (August to September).

Orange. The orange plant may be grown with ease in any window (see " Culture "). May to July.

Kalosanthes miniata. This is a most lovely, rich, and sweet-flowering, thick-leaved, and free-growing plant ; and if grown in heat and watered with manure water once a week, it will do well in a sunny window.

Polygala dalmaisona, a very pretty shrub indeed, of a half-hardy character, light foliage with pretty rosy-purple flowers, and easy of culture ; put into a six-inch pot, peat soil, and frequently stop the young shoots to induce dwarf, bushy plants (June to August).

Corrœa longiflora, a pretty half-hardy shrub ; stop the shoots frequently to induce dwarf plants (May to June).

Rhododendron, in variety ; get small plants of any of the sorts, and put them into nine-inch pots, grow them on every season, so as to obtain an inch or two of new wood, or no flowers can be had; feed and water the plants freely immediately after the flowering is over, but do not feed them after they have once started the new growth ; use clean water freely, plunging the pot, and set them in the full sun.

All those marked with an asterisk (*) are climbers, and there are no plants mentioned here that may not be grown and flowered in the window of the cottage and sitting-room of the villa by a little care and trouble.   I have grown most of these plants with less than the ordinary means, therefore I can recommend them for the window.

HOW TO AVOID USING LARGE POTS.

I GREW some camellias once in the same pots for seven years, and the pots only thirteen inches diameter; this was small compared to the size of the plants, for some of them were fully six feet high, and full of leaf down to the pot ; of a robust deep green, and in the season abundant flower. And I never saw such healthy plants in pots of so large a stature ; this was the result of feeding, as I call it, with half an ounce of guano to one gallon of water, once a week. Many other things I have grown in pots of a comparatively small size, and still have had equal success in flowering the respective plants. I mention this as proved by my own experience, that it answers equally well, if not better, to use small pots for plants to flower in, and at the same time admits of the convenience of housing a greater number. And this is particularly convenient for window-plants, and everywhere. An Azalea, Rhododendron, Kalmia, *Mimosa armata*, Daphne, Genista, Kalosanthus, *Plumbago Chinensis*, Epacris—in fact, anything, may be grown to fine large specimens in comparatively small pots, by adopting the feeding system. None need shift the plants nor fear any unfavourable results, and it is particularly convenient for exhibitors of plants, especially to those who have to carry them far to the show. Any amount of size can be realized by feeding the plants ; for instance, an Azalea can be grown three feet in diameter and proportionately high, a Rhododendron, Plumbago, Kalosanthus, Genista, Epacris, Mimosa, the same, and the Westeria ; and such climbers will cover an extra large pillar or trellis by feeding ; and form extraordinarily fine specimens, if only grown in eleven or thirteen inch pots, and no shifting will be required for ten or twelve years.

THE CULTIVATION OF MIGNONETTE.

THERE are two distinct seasons for sowing this favourite. For Mignonette to be strong and in flower during the winter, sow some seed in five or six-inch pots, well drained, filled with maiden loam, leaf-mould, and a little sand. Do not sift the soil for the pots too fine ; press it moderately tight into the pots ; water the pots of soil previously to sowing ; let the pots drain for an hour so, then sow the seed thinly over the surface ; and use enough fine soil to cover the seed fairly, and no more. Let this be done in the middle, or so, of August ; set the pots in an open sunny spot, lay a thin covering of moss over the pot till the seed is up, as that

prevents the surface drying.   Remove the moss as soon as
the plants are fairly up, and thin the plants out in an angle
to three in a pot, and as far asunder as possible ; encourage
the plants as much as possihle, and nip the points of the
leaders out as they get an inch or so long; stick some neat
sticks a foot long close to the main stem of each plant ; tie
the middle leaders to these neatly ; nip all the flower off as
it appears.   As soon as cold nights and cold autumn rains
come on, remove the pots into the cold frame, conservatory,
or into the sunny window.   This will be about October.
Commence in November a weekly watering with half an
ounce of guano to one gallon of tepid water—the " horticultural manure " will do, but great care must be taken not
to use any of these manures too strong.   Give water enough
to keep the Mignonette growing, but do not let the pots
stand in pans; let there be free drainage secured to the
pots, previously to sowing the seed, by putting a handful of
broken crocks in the bottom of the pot.   By attention to
these things good Mignonette may be secured throughout
the winter.   Sow again in February for summer Mignonette
for the window and the conservatory.   These sowings may
be in boxes as well as pots ; sow again in March and April
in the open ground ; the February sowing is intended as an
auxiliary to the August sowing, in case it may not hold out ;
but if due attention is given to feeding and watering, these
plants will continue to give flowers till Mignonette can be
had naturally ; but take care to nip all seed pods off, as the
seed will prevent the plants flowering.

THE TREE VIOLET.—How to Get it.

THE tree violet is obtained by training a Double Russian
Violet to what is wanted.   First select some good, healthy,
long runners in the month of May ; cut them off the old
stool, and as long as is necessary, trim and plant them in

good soil, on a south side, and give them a good soaking with water. Plant the whole length of the cutting within an inch and a half into the earth; let the soil be fine and deep, and plant six inches asunder. Keep the young plants clear of runners, and encourage the leaders as much as possible; set, if you have one, a handlight over them, they will strike without, but slower. The young plants may remain till September; then take them up and pot them into six-inch pots, using good maiden loam and leaf-mould, or old pulverized stable dung,—such as old cucumber-bed, &c. Previously to potting, trim everything clean off the stem to the root; reserve the leader till it has attained the desired height, which should not exceed fifteen or eighteen inches; then nip the point of the leader out, the tree will then be formed, and should be tied up to a straight stick. It will take, at the least, two years to obtain a good flowering plant; it will then be a plant that, with care, will last for years; but, to maintain vigour, feeding must be resorted to.

THE NEAPOLITAN VIOLET. —Cultivation.

It is propagated in the same way, and at the same time, as the Tree Violet, except that the cuttings of the Neapolitan are taken off the old stools as short as possible to insure success in striking them. Let the soil for striking the cuttings in be good and light, with sand in it; they may both be struck, first under a handlight and then planted out six or seven inches asunder. Keep these clear of all runners—nipping them out as soon as they appear, and let the young plants be kept moist during the summer; and by the autumn they will have become good, stocky, entire plants, fit for either potwork or bedding into a frame. I prefer potting them in September into six-inch pots; taking them up with a nice compact ball of earth. The ground must, if at all dry, be thoroughly soaked previously to taking up the plants; using the same kind of soil in potting them. Give them a good watering, and set the pots in the full sun for a month or six weeks; then remove them to the cold frame, greenhouse, or window; give manure water once a week. Keep all runners down, and abundance of good Violets will be produced on these lovely Neapolitan pot plants during the whole winter.

Cottagers, and those who grow them for sale, can obtain abundance of both Neapolitan and Double and Single Russian Violets by first planting out the half-rooted runners as here directed, and planting them out on a full south border under a wall, hedge, or the house; and then building a turf wall a foot high in front, and giving the border on which the Violets are planted a sharp incline to the sun; using a good proportion of leaf-mould in the border; plant them six inches asunder; a small border will at this rate take a great number of plants, and this distance apart is full enough. Plant them into this quarter in September; keep all runners clean off, and provide some straw mats to lay over them on temporary rafters (broomsticks will do) laid across the border, resting on the front wall. These mats will shoot the water, and form a good protection; but they must be removed daily in mild weather. As glass is now so exceedingly cheap, there are few indeed who cannot provide enough of this useful article to grow sufficient Violets to pay for it the first season. One hundred square feet, in squares seven inches by five and more, can be had in boxes cut to the size, for about twelve shillings; and any man can make the woodwork and do the glazing himself. One hundred square feet—that is, eleven square yards, will be no small surface of glass, and at such a small cost, for violet-growing. Six hundred strong plants can be bedded into this glass-covered space. The Violets will in due time make room for growing cucumbers and late melons. Thus a little glass can be made most profitable. The artisan, cottager, and small villa resident can, if desired, have violets for pleasure and profit too.

THE CULTIVATION OF THE STOCK.

THERE are too many varieties of these things. Among the biennial kinds there are none better than the purple and scarlet Brompton. For those that prefer the purple, few things can compare to a thickly planted bed of the lovely and fragrant purple Brompton, when it consists, as it should do if judiciously managed, of double flowers. The scarlet Brompton and Queen stocks and the Intermediate are good stocks, the latter partaking of the nature of both the ten-week and Brompton ; it is more dwarf than the former, but this depends upon the strength of the land. There are also the English and German ten-week ; the latter nearly all come double, and produce many shades of colour. The climate and culture are the cause, doubtless, of the German varieties coming three-fourths double ; and those who grow them for the sale of the seed, which is in great demand, on account of the lovely varieties and the quality it produces, find it worth while to take extra pains to produce seed that can be warranted ; and this can be done in England, although the climate has a great deal to do with it. No seed can be had from double flowers ; but if the stock can be cultivated sufficiently high to produce flowers with five or six petals, such will produce three-fourths double flowers for the next growth ; as the high state of the temperature with the care bestowed will produce the desired effect. The additional heat appears to affect the colour ; for good in some, and for worse in others ; hence some are muddy-coloured, as they are called ; that is, a combination of scarlet and white, of purple and white, and so on ; or it may be the effect of hybridization ;

if so, it does not prove in many cases much good taste in the operator, but a mere wish to produce a something new ; but be that as it may, the German ten-week stock is a beautiful thing for beds and pots during summer. English gardeners should cultivate reliable double-stock seed, as there is nothing to prevent it in this country more than in Germany, except the climate. This in the colder counties may be an obstacle ; but may be overcome by care and a little more trouble than it probably costs our friends over the water. If any seed can be produced that will bring double flowers, it is probable that, if more pains are taken, it will produce more double flowers.

To be sure of seed that will produce double flowers in the next growth, sow the ten-week English stocks in March in pans or pots ; and when large enough to handle, plant them out into beds consisting of good sandy loam and some lime rubbish, or rather sifted old lime. I noticed many years since the marked effect of this on some scarlet ten-week stocks. When the stocks flower, if they are all single never mind ; look for what five or six petalled flowers you can find, and cut all the four-petalled flowers off with a pair of scissors ; and as soon as the seed-pods appear, feed the stocks with some guano and water, one ounce to one gallon. Give this twice during the seeding, once as soon as the petals fall, and once again when the pods are half grown ; and you may depend upon a generation of double stocks next season : this is applicable to all stocks. The biennial kinds must be sown in the April previously to the year they flower ; that is, they should be sown one year and flower the next ; and then they generally die. The Inter-mediate may be sown in the months of July and August for early flowering in pots ; and some may be sown in June, for good stocky plants to flower in pots during the winter in the greenhouse ; and some ten-week may be sown in June to flower either in pots or boxes for the window in the autumn.

In sowing stock seed use loam and leaf-mould, sifted through a quarter-inch mesh sieve : sow it on the ground in the spring, and transplant the young stocks out into their quarters as soon as possessed with six or eight leaves, and into six-inch pots, putting three into a pot. This applies to the Brompton, Emperor's, and Queen's.

There are two distinct seasons for sowing the ten-week and Intermediate ; viz., February and March, and July and August. Those of the first sowings flower during the summer and autumn, and those of the latter flower during the winter and early spring, and must be potted for that purpose. The former sowings must be made in pans or pots, and either set in the window under a hand-light or in a cold frame. The Brompton, Emperor, and Queen stocks must be sown but once, and that must be during the months of March and April, to flower the following spring and summer, as I have already noticed.

Stocks delight in good maiden loam, a little sandy ; feed them with half an ounce of guano to one gallon of water as soon as the flower-buds appear ; and fine flowers of the double will be the effect. Stocks of the double may be perpetuated by cuttings when you can get them, which frequently offer themselves after they have flowered. Select the young stuff with some ripened wood at the base, and insert them in pots ; which set in a slight bottom heat, and keep close. Plunge the pots in a tan-bed ; sometimes they will strike root without bottom heat ; but, as the cuttings cannot be often had till towards the autumn from outdoor stocks, there is not time for the cuttings to strike before the season declines too far into cold, lifeless autumn or winter. Nothing will repay those who grow them better for pot-work and market purposes.

There is still another safe way of filling pots with double stocks. Plant the seedlings out at six inches asunder on good maiden loam of a fine texture, in a sunny, open spot; let them remain till the flower-buds can only be just observed; then go over them, and pick out a single bud with a pointed pair of scissors; put the bud between your front teeth, and gently press your teeth into the bud cross-ways. Listen to the sound; and if there is a slight grating, the bud is of a single plant; if no noise is heard whilst the tooth is pressing the bud, it is from a double flower. Give the ground a thorough soaking with water, and next morning take a garden trowel and drive down, first on one side pretty closely to the plant, and then drive it down on the opposite side of the plant; carefully lift it with the ball of earth entire, and, having some five-inch pots at hand, place each plant in them, having some fine sifted loam to fill up all the spaces in the pot with a small stick. Water the pots well, and set them in the shade for a week if necessary, and then bring them forward.

THE CAMPANULA PYRAMIDALIS.—PROPAGATION, AND HOW TO GROW IT.

THIS is a plant of a thousand, alike suited to the cottage window and the conservatory of the mansion, and a fit occupant of both; one that will bear hardships and the indulgence of a greenhouse; and is certainly the most noble member of the whole family, and equally good in its fair white and deep blue, which are of longer duration than most of the rest of its tribe. These extraordinary good qualities in a single plant, together with the ease with which it is propagated and grown, excites in one no ordinary degree of amazement that so little of it is anywhere seen, either among gardeners or amateurs. Those are to be pitied who leave this good old-fashioned perennial for some new thing, that must sink into complete insignificance, and are mere weeds in comparison. The Chimney Campanula, as it used to be called by my old gardeneress,—and a very appropriate name it is indeed for it,—is indicative of its character. There is no excuse for any one not possessing a good Chimney Campanula, the stature of a man every season. It may be raised from seed, by cuttings of the fleshy root and by offsets—that is, shoots, or young stuff produced at the base of the flower-spike. These are taken off after it has done flowering with a sharp knife with some of the old stool attached ; trim these, and insert them, one in a small, 60-sized pot of good peat, and a little silver sand ; press the soil close to the base of the cutting; water and set them on a slight bottom heat, or under a bell-glass, hand, or striking light, in a shady side. These, with the plants propagated from the cuttings of the pieces of the thick root, may be kept in the small pots till spring ; then shift them into six-inch pots, using loam and dung, or good peat and loam, and a moderate drainage.

Get a shilling paper of seed in March or April, and sow it on the surface of some two or three wide-mouthed pots, or nine-inch pans filled with fine sandy peat and a little leaf-mould, sifted fine ; water the surface of the seed-pans, so as to soak the soil through previously to sowing the seed ; let the water thoroughly drain out for an hour, then make the surface even by pressing it gently with some flat surface, sow the seed thinly and evenly over the surface, and as the seed is very fine, be careful not to bury it too deep ; have a little very fine sand and leaf-mould, and slightly sift through a gauze sieve a bare covering over the seed. Set the pans or pots in a slight heat, if not lay a square of glass on each pot or pan and set them in the full sun, shading them by a slight covering of moss from the influence of the sun. This is an excellent plan of raising seeds that require some heat when there is none at hand. The flat square of glass should completely cover the pot or pan; this prevents evaporation of the moisture exactly suited to the rapid germination of the seed. As soon as the seed is up shift the flat piece of glass a trifle on one side, or lift it up by placing a small stone, or wedge of wood, under it; this will admit a due proportion of air, and prevent the seedlings damping off; but continue the shade of moss for a while till the seedlings get strength, then remove it and shift the seed-pots to a shady spot for a week or two, after which they may be brought forward again and kept moist, taking the precaution not to super-saturate the soil.

Small square boxes, nine inches high at the back and four and a half in front, twenty inches wide, and twenty-four long, glazed with four squares of glass, are excellent things for placing seed-pans under, and for propagating numbers of plants; they are easily made, and cost but a trifle. I used to make my own, and found them more than equal to the ordinary handlight, the cost not exceeding one-fourth the price of the ordinary handlight. The seedlings must be pricked out as soon as they can be handled, and finally potted into five or six inch pots, where they may remain till the spring following. Then shift them into nine-inch pots and push them on by liberal waterings with manure water, half an ounce guano to one gallon of water, given once a week. Those that will flower will soon show it, and those that will not will not be prominent in the heart of the plant; discontinue watering these with manure water, let them stand over till next season, when they will make finer specimens still by shifting them into pots one size larger. Set the flowering plants in the full sun and free from every obstruction to the spike of the flower attaining symmetry of character, sheltering it from dangerous winds. As the old flowers die off clip them out with a pair of scissors to give room for the development of fresh ones; and to give a neat and clean appearance to the plant in flower; besides, the flowering season continues longer by daily looking over the spike of the flower and clipping all fading flowers off. Continue the weekly waterings of guano water. The plant will commence flowering the end of July or so, and continue in bloom till October. The flowering season will be prolonged by setting the plant in a shady part of the house, the window of the sitting-room, or in the light entrance hall of the mansion. There are two distinct varieties of this, viz., white and blue.

THE HUMEA ELEGANS.

IF the word "graceful" is an appropriate word for a plant at all, it certainly may be used to describe this lovely plant, although it is seldom indeed that we see a specimen of one of these plants worthy of such an appellation. The little success that is met with in the attempted cultivation of this plant, and the consequent failing beauty of one that has no rival, I suppose is the chief reason why we can never, or seldom, find a plant of this deserving the name graceful. I would add this to elegant as appropriate terms, for it is both elegant and graceful. A half-grown plant of this is very unattractive, but one grown out, as gardeners call it, is no mean thing, and is certainly worthy of a place in the conservatory, hall window, or entrance of the house, however honourable and graced by grandeur and titles. Get a shilling packet of seed by post, or otherwise, in the month of March or April, and sow it carefully in a shallow seed-pan or wide pot; put a handful of broken pot shreds in the bottom, also a thin layer of coarser soil such as will not pass through the sieve ; then fill the pot or pan up to the rim with fine sifted maiden loam and leaf-mould, two parts of the latter to one of the former, and some silver sand well incorporated; knock the pot on the table or potting-bench, to settle the soil moderately firm in the pot, make the surface level, and water the soil with a fine rose water-pot, gently, and to soak the soil through let it stand for an hour, then sow the seed evenly over the surface of the pot; take a gauze sieve with a handful or two of the fine light sandy soil, and sift enough to barely cover the seed, then set the pot in a frame at work, and shade the pot or pan with some moss. The seed will soon vegetate, after which remove some of the moss, and in a day or two remove it all, but protect the seedlings from the sun's rays by shading the lights. As soon as the seedlings are strong enough to handle, prick them out five or six into a five-inch pot, and return them to a frame to establish them, and then harden off and remove the pots to a cold frame. When the seed-lings have attained two or three inches of growth, pot them off singly into five-inch pots, using soil rather stronger, say two-thirds loam and one-third rotten dung, old hotbed stuff; next shift them into nine-inch pots, set them in the full sun, and far enough asunder to admit of the influence of both air and light to surround each plant; give liberal waterings and manure water once a week; by the month of October the plants will have attained from two to three feet of growth, and should present a fine robust appearance, with foliage down to the pot; discontinue the weekly watering with guano and water for a time, and remove the plants to some cold frame, pit, or greenhouse. Do not expect things as a matter of course, but do by these as you would by a choice collection of geraniums, give them light, air, and water in due proportion with other good plants. No more shelter is necessary than will secure them from frost through the winter. As the spring advances, about March, shift them once more into eleven-inch pots, and resume the liberal waterings with a half-ounce of guano to one gallon of water once a week till in flower; set them out as soon as all fear of frost is gone, and fine six or seven feet specimens of a fine colour will be the result, and they will prove splendid ornaments for the conservatory, and for low vases in various outdoor places through the summer, waving and reflecting various shades of colour at every breeze of wind.

THE ACHIMENES.—Its Uses.

THERE are many beautiful varieties of this, but none better suited for the purposes I am about to name than the grand and lovely old longiflora (a large and prolific blue-flowered variety) and longiflora alba; each of these is exceedingly fine, but especially the blue, being more robust than the white, and comparatively hardy. These flowers are generally of the hothouse class, but I for years have grown them in a cold greenhouse and in a common house window in splendid perfection. My plan of management was, in the month of March to get some nine-inch seed pans, two inches deep, and fill them with pure leaf-mould and silver sand, and sift the leaf mould through a quarter-inch mesh sieve, and then mix it well with the sand. A hole should be knocked with the hammer through the bottom of the pans for drainage, lay one crock over this, and cover the whole bottom of the pan with some of the siftings, not too coarse, then fill up within a half-inch to the rim of the pan with the fine soil, press it moderately firm into the pans, make it even, and set the little bulbs on the surface, gently pressing them into the soil one inch or one and a half asunder, then cover them over half an inch with the same soil. Then set the pans in a frame at work where they will soon begin to shoot, and show themselves above ground. If the soil is not too dry when the bulbs are inserted in the pans, no water will be required till they are an inch above the soil. The soil must not be too wet nor too dry, but of a nice medium moisture. Shade the pans when above the soil by coverings of moss from the influence of the sun; when water is required give it liberally with tepid water, and admit air as the plant advances, as is done with cucumbers and other things; as probably they may be in the same frame, where they do well.

Harden off during May by shifting the pans to a cooler place, and by the end of the month they may be potted off, placing three in a five-inch pot, six in an eight-inch pot, and so on, where they will flower well and make fine objects for the sitting-room window and conservatory. There is still another use to which these plants may be applied, viz., that of bedding in baskets. The baskets may be of wire, which can be obtained of those who manufacture them, and of ironmongers in general, and also of most seedsmen and nurserymen, and they are cheap and very ornamental; the baskets may also be made with willow and the wild rose; first forming a hoop, say twelve or fifteen inches diameter, then crossing some more in a half-circle to form the basket; tie or nail them to the hoop which forms the rim of the basket, the hoop forming the ring must be stout, to hold the nails, and to hold a stout wire handle by which to suspend the basket. These baskets can be made during wet weather, when no outdoor work can be done.

Those who prefer the lighter and more elegant forms made by the professed manufacturer should send to them for illustrated catalogues from which to choose. Having the basket suspended at a convenient height in the tool-house, and the soil and some moderately fine moss at hand, commence filling the basket by laying a good bedding of nice close green moss, then some plants, preserving as much of the soil about the root of the young plants as possible, breaking them out carefully; tuck the tops of the plants just through the wires, a layer of plants, some moss, and earth, bedding the plants carefully; and when it is completed it will, being all green, present a very natural appearance. Water it well with a fine rose water-pot soaking the entire ball, let it drain for an hour and remove the basket by suspension wires to the roof of the conservatory, where the plants will grow and flower for a long time, forming the most lovely objects imaginable. Water must be given to the baskets frequently, and once a week give them some guano water described before ; this will assist both the plants in the baskets and in the pots. As soon as the achimenes ceases to flower discontinue the watering, let the flowers die off gradually, remove the plants a fortnight after flowering to some sunny place in a dry pit, or frame, &c., let them remain till November, or to the end of October, then remove them, after cutting off the dead tops, to a dry part of the greenhouse, where they may be turned on their sides and packed close for the winter ; this is the safest way of keeping them till wanted again, and a marvellous crop of young bulbs of a large size will be the result. The achimenes delights in partial shade in the growing season, and in moss to grow in, and looks well any way, is not expensive to obtain in the first instance, and is easily multiplied, and is fit for whole stands in the greenhouse, pots for the window, on a trellis or hanging down, and for baskets as described.

THE TROPÆOLUM JARRATTII.

THERE are many varieties of tropæolum, but considering its adaptation and general beauty, none to be compared to the achimenes, which continues with an abundance of bloom and is peculiarly suitable for pot-culture, both for a good window and for the conservatory, and is well adapted for a show plant. All the tropæolums, even the common nasturtiums, are lovely things, but this one is especially charm-

ing. Get a bulb of this of any of the bulb-sellers in January
or February, and a six-inch pot filled within an inch and a
half of the rim with maiden loam, leaf-mould, and peat, in
equal parts, first putting a handful of pot-shreds in the
bottom of the pot; let the soil be moderately fine, such as
will pass through a half-inch mesh sieve, place the bulb on
this in the middle of the pot, with the crown uppermost;
press it into the soil in the pot, and cover up to the top of
the pot, then place the pot into a warm frame, pit, or house
at work. Those who have not this convenience should get
a neighbour to set the pot in his frame for a week or fortnight, as probably might be done for little or nothing. Just
to start the bulb harden off a little, then bring it into the
window or conservatory, and place some kind of a trellis to
it,—a flat or a salver-shaped one is, I think, the best, but that
is a matter of taste: it will, if a good strong bulb, cover a
trellis two feet high, and as wide; water may be given it
pretty freely as it advances, and some guano water as soon
as it has half covered the trellis; due attention to training is
necessary, for it will, when growing vigorously, quickly get en-
tangled so as to be past art, when the leaders merely want
guiding in the direction required, so as to fill the trellis; by
attention to these particulars one of the finest specimens of
tropæolum will be formed.

As soon as the flowering is over, and the plant begins to
assume a yellow appearance, discontinue the watering, and
let the plant die off maturely; then take the bulb out of the
pot and keep it in perfectly dry silver sand in a pot or box,
and in a cool room.

There are only two ways by which this plant can be
propagated, viz., by seed, which it gives very sparingly, and
by young bulbs, which are created by layering the vines;
that is, by laying some or all the vines of the plant down on
a bed of leaf-mould and sandy peat, and covering the joints

with some of the same soil, which must be kept slightly moist, the light of the frame kept moderately close, and the plant slightly shaded during the mid-day sun.

A little bottom heat will facilitate the formation of young bulbs. The whole of the vines must not be entirely but only here and there covered with soil. These soon form flowering plants, but those from seed will not flower for three or four years.

THE ORANGE TREE FOR EVERY ONE.

I MUST notice the orange plant not for the sake of the fruit, but for the blossom ; and I particularly recommend it to all classes for its delicate nature, white colour, strong fragrance, and blooming at a time when flowers are most in request—viz., winter. There are numbers doubtless would fancy an orange tree, but do not indulge the idea from the impression that a great difficulty has to be grappled with ; but for their encouragement I would remark that I have grown the orange plant in a house with the camellia, where it has borne a number of good-sized fruit. The orange plant will not bear frost, but it will live and continue in good health in forty degrees of heat, or even less, which is a lower temperature than that of an ordinary dwelling-house, so that the orange plant may be grown with ease in any window or conservatory. The plants may be obtained for a trifle in six-inch pots, where they may for convenience remain, and they will, by feeding them with guano water once a week (half an ounce to one gallon of water) grow in nine-inch pots and do well for many years. To keep these pretty dwarf plants within the limits of a window, or any prescribed space desirable, nip the points of the leaders out ; this will keep them dwarf. As soon as the month of June comes set them out of doors in the full sun, water and feed them well all the summer, and take them in again about the end of September or the beginning of October. The plants may be raised from seed and then grafted as soon as the stock gets as large as a goosequill. The grafting is performed by the usual whip grafting, using grafting-wax prescribed for grafting roses, which should be done in the spring, and the pots placed if possible in a little heat, or in a close, cold frame. I cannot understand why our growers of plants for sale do not grow numbers of these most desirable plants in six-inch pots for market as well as the French, who find a ready sale for these pretty little miniature orange trees, with some two or three good-sized fruit upon them. The fruit is not of much value, but the novelty and the fragrance of both fruit and flowers make them desirable and very tempting.

Sow some orange pips filled within an inch of the top in a pot in February and March, with maiden loam, pulverized dung, and peat, made moderately fine, put a handful of crocks in the bottom, fill the pot, knock the pot on the bench to settle the soil in the pot, sow the pips, and cover three quarters or an inch with fine earth, and set the pot in a frame at work ; they will come up without heat if set in the sun, but not so quickly. When the seedlings get large enough, pot them off into three-inch and afterwards into five or six-inch pots, then graft them, choosing some clean young stuff that has ripened and become firm. The orange is subject to the scale. (See remedy under the head, " The Gardener's Enemies, and how to Destroy them.")

THE CAMELLIA EASY TO GROW.

THE camellia has been and still is looked upon as a difficult thing, and almost an impossibility for most to grow I cannot understand this, except from the rarity and the goodness of the plant, but there are numbers of plants more

difficult to grow and considerably less worthy. The commonness of a plant makes it appear easy to cultivate ; take
for instance the fuchsia or geranium, these are common
everywhere, but upon the whole are considerably more
difficult to grow well than the camellia. The camellia will
stand several degrees of frost, but the others will bear none
without suffering ; either of the former two attains to perfection much quicker than the camellia, which is the cause
of its being brought before the public more frequently, but
the camellia outlives both these with one-third the trouble ;
in fact, there is no comparison between them, and little
existing between the character and quality of them. The
camellia is amongst greenhouse plants what the rose is
amongst hardy flowering shrubs. " The Queen " is preeminently so, with its deep green and rich foliage, always
the same, and its grand and exquisite flowers of nearly
every tint of colour, from deep and rich crimson to the
fairest white, and some possessing the most exquisite markings of a superb carnation.

The camellia is one of the easiest things possible to
grow ; and there is only one critical time in the cultivation
of this lovely plant, and that not half so difficult as that of
producing a cucumber in March. The difficulty of stimulating the camellia to produce new growth after blooming
for the purpose of insuring a crop of flowers for the ensuing
season has been made greater by some writers than is
necessary. In my own experience there is no question
about as to either the time or how it should be done, for I
never failed. After camellias have done flowering, induce
them to produce some new growth by shutting them up
close in the greenhouse, pit, or frame till the new growth
has started ; then admit air, and frequently syringe the
plants overhead. After the new growth has formed the
terminal bud, which will be about the end of May or the

beginning of June, turn the plants out and set them behind
a south wall ; that is, under a north wall for the four summer
months, and give them liquid manure once a week ; and
then in this situation they will do exceedingly well, and be
of a fine healthy green, and full of bloom-buds by the month
of October ; when they may be removed to the house, pit,
or frame, where they will flower in due time. Continue the
weekly waterings with half an ounce of guano to one gallon
of water. Those who follow these instructions will, no
doubt, have abundant occasion to thin the flower-buds.
A little heat may be applied to the house ; but I have found
very little necessary ; and, indeed, none at all to produce
new growth after the flowering was over. The propagation
of camellias is simple too ; stocks may be raised from seed
obtained from single ones, and from cuttings ; I prefer
raising stocks from cuttings of the single and semi-double.
Take off these cuttings as soon as the wood is ripened,
which is known by the hardness and by the terminal bud
being formed. Cut it off with a sharp knife at the base ;
that is, immediately below the new growth, preserving a
little bit of the old wood ; cut the base of the cutting clean
through at right angles close at the base of the new growth.
Trim the leaves off, leaving one or two at the top part of
the cutting ; then, having some five or six-inch pots filled
with good clean peat sifted fine, and of a sandy quality,
place a few pieces of pot-shred in the bottom of the pot, and
a handful of siftings ; then fill up to the top of the pot with
the fine peat, make it firm, and insert the cuttings five or
six in a pot ; nine if a six-inch pot. Let the cuttings into
the pot half their length with a planting-stick ; close the
earth firmly to the base of the cutting ; then thoroughly soak
them with water by watering with a fine rose water-pot ; let
them drain for an hour, and plunge the pots up to their rim
in sawdust, tan, or sand on a slight bottom heat and set a

hand-light, bell-glass, or striking-light over them, and keep close for a time till signs of growth appear; then give a little air, and pot off singly into three or four-inch pots, using peat and a little maiden loam during the following autumn; that is, twelve months from the season they are struck; and many of these may be grafted. The whole will be ready the September following; that is, within two years. The grafting is performed by splicing the graft on the stock by the whip-grafting method, still retaining the whole of the top of the stock, which is cut down to the graft after it has fairly united with the stock. The young ripened wood is selected for the purpose. The stocks should, when done, be in a growing state, and kept close after for a few weeks in a cold frame. Bind the grafts firmly, and use the grafting-wax mentioned for roses.

THE HYDRANGEA, AND HOW TO PRODUCE THE BLUE.

THERE is a particular sympathy among all lovers of flowers for blue. I suppose this happens in consequence of all flowers, whether species or genera, running principally upon every colour and shade but blue; but in the case of the hydrangea there is good cause for the want of blue, as there are no true blue species or varieties. Especially in some localities a blue hydrangea is a difficult thing to obtain; and when it can be got it is considered a thing out of the common way; and, of course, the grower has good credit attached to his genius. I do not know if I am philosopher enough to show cause why this colour is con-stantly produced in some localities and not in others. I know of a locality where lovely blue hydrangeas are natu-rally produced; that locality possesses a large amount of iron, tin, and mundic in the soil; and although peat, it will not grow heaths at all. This occurs in consequence of the soil becoming surcharged with acids, by the combined minerals lying in such soils to the detriment of some plants, while this very element conduces principally to the production of the blue in the hydrangea; simply by the plant, no doubt, having an affinity for this acid, which is conducted over the whole plant, and held in suspension by entering into the component parts of the plant, and being acted upon by the influence of the atmosphere (the blue rays of light or the element producing blues), the thing is produced—which, however, is not permanent; and this accounts for the blue going back to white and pink when the principal constituents fail. This is my view of the thing. (See " Why Plants are Green,"&c.) This blue may be produced anywhere by first growing the hydrangea in peat, then supplying it with the necessary element; and this can be produced artificially by keeping tin and iron ore in the water with which the plants are watered, and probably by strongly impregnating the water with carbonate of iron and iron filings; but I advise those who wish to grow this for blue flowers to get some of the peat described, so famous for producing it, from Dartmoor, where it constantly flowers blue.

To grow the hydrangea well in pots, take in July and August some cuttings of the young wood off three or four inches long, and strike them in five-inch pots, using peat. Set them on heat if you can; if not, cover them with a hand-light, and keep them close and well watered; but the heat will cause them to strike much faster, which is a thing of some importance; for these cuttings must be grown mode-rately fast, and care taken to maintain a healthy degree of circulation of the juices (sap) through the winter, main-taining the leader in good condition. Let them remain in these pots all winter, and feed them once a week with half an ounce of guano to one gallon of water—iron-water. In the spring shift them, and watch the leading bud; see that this starts well; then you will be right for a fine specimen of a plant with one head of flowers, which by growing in a six or nine-inch pot will attain to an enormous size.

THE CARNATION, PICOTEE, AND PINK.

As a class there is scarcely anything amongst florist's flowers to compare to a collection of these favourites. A collection of lovely Roses possesses beauty, form, and fragrance, but such a prize is within the reach of only a few. But nearly every one having a square rod of ground, or even those who have none at all, may have a collection of these beautiful flowers, the Carnations, Picotees, and Pinks, for they can be grown equally as well in pots and boxes as in the open ground. I particularly recommend these for beauty, ease of culture, and convenience, as well as for duration. The Carnation and Picotee have the advantage over the Rose, as they suit the convenience of all, and any one can culti-vate them, and they are of longer duration than, and not inferior to Roses. I do not wish to over-estimate the character of the carnation; but I do not understand why they are so exceedingly scarce, and how it is the trade do not endeavour to bring them forward. Why let this diver-sified class of easy-to-be-grown plants remain rare, and only a few growers, comparatively, possess them? For there is nothing will better repay the grower of them for sale, and the amateur grower of them for exhibition, by the grati-fication they afford, and facility for the introduction of new varieties. I will not describe their varieties, as descriptive catalogues of what are good and worth having may be had of growers on application. Turner, of Slough, and many other growers of them for sale, will, if required, forward their descriptive catalogues with prices for selection. The cultivation of the Carnation and Picotee is nearly the same as that of the Pink. There are those who will supply pipings of all by post. I would warn my readers, not against dishonesty on the part of the advertisers, but on the probable disappointment to be met with, both in sorts and success in striking them when they get them; but probably the greatest disappointment will be in the quality of the flower. I do not wish to infer that no good sorts of Carnations, Picotees, and Pinks, are to be obtained of the advertisers of them by pipings, but the best sorts are scarce, and their best growers never publish them this way. I would therefore recommend my readers to go to first-class growers of them, as they will be glad to supply their customers with good show sorts, at perhaps a less rate per dozen pairs than worse ones can be had elsewhere. Confidential growers will charge as much for pipings as they will for struck plants in pots. Those who wish to form a good collection of either would do well to order, say, one dozen pairs or more, as the case may be, at the price named. The prices run from £1 4s. to £1 10s. per dozen pairs, Carnations and Picotees, first-class sorts; and the Pinks, 9s. to 18s. per dozen pairs. To work on a scale of economy, it will be found that one dozen pairs of each contain a nice variety to begin with; these may be propagated quickly, and if multiplied by six, will probably give one hundred or one hundred and twenty plants by the autumn of the same year—one hundred and twenty plants per each dozen pair. It will thus be seen that a good collection, though small, may be increased to a sufficient quantity to fill a good bed or two. If purchased in the month of March, the plants will be in small pots; shift them at once into nine-inch pots, using good maiden loam, some good sharp sand, and old dung; that gathered from the road, and laid up for a twelvemonth, is excellent, if well mixed with the maiden loam, which should be moderately fine, but not sifted; put a good handful of broken pot-shreds into the bottom of the pot, and then some coarse turfy loam ; fill in enough of the fine compost, and set the pair of plants in the pot ; fill up, water, and set them in a cold frame, if you have one, or outdoors, on cinder ashes, in the full sun ; and when the plants commence starting for flower, commence a weekly watering with half an ounce, not more, of guano to one gallon of water.   In the month of July some pipings will probably be ready to take off.   Carefully cut these off with a sharp knife, and strip the leaves off from the two lower joints ; giving them a short jerk to prevent the leaf stripping the bark of the piping below.   Cut the piping at right angles immediately below the third joint from the top ; when suffi-cient are done to fill a five-inch pot, insert them ; or they may be struck singly in small sixties ; or in pairs, in large sixties ; in fine soil of the same description as that in which they grew, except a little more sandy and fine.   This soil must be sifted through a quarter-inch sieve, and having previously put a handful of small pot-shreds in the bottom of the pot, put a little of the siftings over the drainage ; then fill the pot completely up to the brim ; settle the soil in the pot by knocking the pot a few times on the bench, and pressing the fingers in the pot of earth.   Make the earth level, take a small waterpot, with a fine rose to it, water the pot or pots of fine sandy soil, so as to soak through the soil in each pot.   Let it stand for ten minutes or a quarter of an hour, then take the prepared pipings, and gently press them into the earth without making any hole with a stick, as they will go into the earth by a gentle pressure while the soil is wet.   Let them remain so for a few hours, then gently water them with a fine rose, to settle the soil about the cuttings ; and remove them to a frame where a little heat is on, and keep them close for a fortnight.   Or they may be set on a warm border, under a wall-house, &c., and covered with a close and airtight hand-light, bell-glass, &c.

and slightly shaded during the mid-day sun, but too much shading will prove injurious, care is required in this. All the hardier and common sorts will strike freely here, and may be struck in the open ground, or rather in the border without pots—preparing the soil as for the pots, and of the necessary depth — marking the space by the bell-glass, hand-light, or striking light, after the soil has been watered, and previously to the insertion of the pipings ; then press the pipings of Carnation, Picotee, and Pinks into the super· saturated soil in rows, two inches by one inch asunder; less will do for Pinks.

All the pipings are prepared the same, and may be struck as soon as they can be had, which is generally about July. After the pipings of Pinks are struck give air, harden off, and in the beginning of September plant them out into nursery beds, six inches by four inches apart, or they may be potted in pairs. The choice named sorts of Carnation and Picotee must be potted for the convenience of protection in cold frames during winter ; the common sorts will do very well in the open ground, in well-drained beds, with a good proportion of road sand in the soil. Raising new sorts is attended with more than ordinary speculation where the seed is saved from really good shown flowers, and a little pains are taken to cross them, the Selfs with the whites, and so on.

The seed should in the spring be sown in pans of moderately light soil, set on a little heat, and when large enough to handle, should be pricked out, either in pots, pans, or on beds of fine earth.

THE AURICULA.—Its Uses.

The Auricula I call the masterpiece of the Primula tribe. Considering its adaptation to every locality, its exquisite character as a flower, the lovely diversity of the family, and

the ease with which it can be grown, it is astonishing that
a collection of this unique class can scarcely be found in a
day's march, or even in a day's ride.   Here is a tribe of plants
suited to every locality ; whether in town or country, for
rich and poor alike.   It is also suited to grow in pots or in
boxes fitted for the window, up stairs or down ; and being
an Alpine plant, and therefore adapted for elevated localities
or mountainous districts, it seems to be at home everywhere.
There is also such a diversity of character in this flower, that
a selection from the different sections of the tribe forms one
of the most complete objects of interest possible.   There
are the Green-edged, the Grey-edged, the White-edged,
Selfs, and what are called Alpines.   The Selfs are a rich
class, and the others are superbly unique beyond description.   The Auricula is a florist's flower with more than the
ordinary amount of sporting capability, and capable of
improvement or changing.   The plants may be had of some
noted growers of them for sale, such as Turner, of Slough,
and many others, who advertise them in the magazines and
florists' journals.   The prices vary considerably, in proportion to the quality, from 7s. 6d. each to 2s. ; but the same
varieties may be had for about 30s. per dozen.   A couple
of dozen would form a fine foundation for any one to work
upon in raising new sorts from seed, and for a stock of
plants for propagation by offsets, which are taken off in the
autumn, when the stock plants are re-potted.   Some use one
soil, some another ; but I have found nothing better than
one part good maiden loam, and two parts old cowdung—
that has been laid up for two or three years, and that will
rub up to dust when put into a sieve, through which it
should pass (quarter of an inch mesh), adding a moderate
portion of sand, old road sand with the droppings with it,
that has been swept up for months and laid up in a heap,
will do for this purpose.   The Auriculas will thrive well in

this, and better than they will in a lighter soil. If there are no cold frames for them to pass the winter in, turn the pots on their sides against a wall, or building, where they will be free from drips of eaves. Let the plants be outward, lay several tiers of pots if you have them, and a wide board on the top. In severe wet and cold, a straw mat may be set before them, and pitched against the wall; when the plants are turned up, which should be about March, bring them to a south aspect; stir the surface of the soil with a small pointed stick, and turn off the loose earth; then having some of the same sort ready sifted and mixed proceed to fill up the pot nearly full with the earth, settling it well in by knocking the pot a few times on the bench or barrow, and give a moderate watering with a fine rose water-pot. When the plants show signs of flower, commence a weekly watering with liquid manure; this may consist of half an ounce of guano to one gallon of water, or one peck of sheep's dung half or quite dry; put it into a tub holding seven or eight gallons of water, fill it up and let it stand for twelve hours, then stir well, let it settle, and use the clear liquid every week till in flower; remove the plants to a shady window, or when in bloom let them have shade during sunny days; this will prolong the flowering season, as well as preserve the beauty of the flowers.

Raising seedlings is simple and easy; first put a handful of broken pot-shreds into the bottom of a five-inch pot or a seedpan for drainage, and then some siftings from the same soil used for sowing the seed; then fill the said pan or pot up with one part of old pulverized cowdung, one part leaf mould, and one part maiden loam, with a moderate portion of silver sand; let these be well blended together and sifted, or sifted first, fill the pot or pan pretty firmly by knocking the pot on the table and slightly pressing in the soil with the fingers. Make it quite even, and water the soil with a fine rose water-pot, so as to soak the soil through; let it drain for an hour, then sow the seed thinly over the surfaces, and sift through a coarse gauze sieve enough of the same soil to cover the seed as thick as a shilling; set the pot or pan in a cold frame, or cover the seed with a flat square of glass, and shade by covering it with moss. Very little watering, if any, will be required till the seed is up. By the time the seedlings have small leaves remove the pot or pan for an hour or two, only early in the morning, to a shady spot where but little sun strikes upon them. The seed should be sown during March, and pricked out as soon as the seedlings are large enough to handle, and treated as the sorts named. Packets of good seed may be had through the post of growers and of respectable seedsmen for 2s. 6d., and sometimes for 1s. each, but I beg to caution those who are desirous of obtaining really good sorts of seeds in this way against having recourse to cheapness; there may be more seed in a 1s. than in a 2s. 6d. packet, but quality is or should be the first consideration, and if 150 or 200 good fair sorts afford the probable chance of getting a dozen really good sorts averaging 10s. each, surely it is better to give 2s. 6d. than it would be to give 1s. and not get one worth 1s. I have had some really good ones even from the 1s. papers, but the 2s. 6d. papers are warranted from stage flowers, that is, the best named sorts; therefore some dependence may be placed on these.

THE PRIMULA SINENSIS.—Its Cultivation.

THIS is a general favourite on account of its beauty, ease with which it is grown, and the duration of the flowering season, for it may be said to possess the advantage in this particular over every existing plant. Although it cannot be said to be in perfection all the year round, it may be said to always in flower ; but taking the family together, and looking at the successive adaptation of the plant by mere propagation in different seasons, it is a plant that may be had in full bloom the whole season (*i. e.* a year).   This plant also possesses many good qualities not to be found in any other ; first, it is easy to grow, has a beautiful leaf, which is ample and symmetrical, and has numerous charming and really lovely varieties to boast of; nor is it particular as to the situation in which to flower, so long as it is secure from the influence of frost.   Apart from the raising of this plant from seed, it can be grown by any one.   Raising it from seed is still easy, providing the pot or seed-pan can be set in a frame where there is a gentle heat, and it is shaded from the sun till fairly up : and that is best done by covering the pot or pan with a thin covering of moss, which should be removed as soon as the seedlings are fairly up.   Obtain the seed from some such persons as the Messrs. Hayes, Edmonton ; Wild, of Ipswich ; Turner, of Slough ; or any seedsmen who procure their stocks of these men for sale. Packets may be had through the post for 1s. to 5s. each, according to the requirements of the purchaser ; but do not seek for cheap shops.   Get the seed in February or March, and sow it in wide seed pots, filled with one part maiden loam and two parts leaf-mould, adding as much silver sand as will render it porous ; take, say one quart loam, two quarts sifted leaf-mould, and one pint of sand.   Let the whole be well mixed ; first put a good handful of broken pot-shred in the bottom, and on this put a layer of moss or siftings of the leaf-mould ; then the fine soil, pressing it moderately into the pot.   Make it even on the surface with a flat tool (I used to have for this purpose a little piece of smooth, flat board with a handle in it) ; then gently water the pot or pan of soil with a fine rose water-pot, so as to soak the soil through.   Let it stand for an hour ; sow the seed thinly over the surface of soil in the pot, and cover it evenly with the same soil the thickness of a shilling, sifted through a coarse gauze sieve on the seed. Set the seed-pot or pan in a gentle heat—a cucumber or melon frame of sixty-five or seventy degrees, not more. As soon as the seedlings are up, remove the pot or pan containing them to a little lower temperature, and give abundance of air. Shade from the influence of the sun during mid-day, and be careful in giving too much water; for if this is over-done, probably many of the young seedlings will, as it is called, shank off. Set the pot or pan upon a couple of bricks or on some inverted pots, so as to bring the seedlings near to the glass; this will secure a free circulation of good air around them, and prevent damping off. Those who have forcing-houses can give the seed-pots the benefit of such advantages, as more safe for the seedlings. When the plants possess four or six leaves besides the seed-leaves, prick them off into five-inch pots well drained, putting about twelve in each pot. Water, and shade them for a day or two. As soon as they fill these pots, pot them off singly into three-inch pots, and when they have filled these, shift them into five or six-inch pots, putting a good handful of broken pots into the bottom of the pots, and a little coarse siftings of the leaf-mould on the top to prevent the drainage getting choked. The security of thorough drainage is the chief thing with this plant. Give the plants abun-dance of air, moderate watering, a weekly watering with half an ounce of guano to one gallon of water from the time the plants show flower. The double varieties and the very choice single sorts may be propagated by cuttings taken off after the flowering is principally over, and struck in a moderate heat. There is no necessity to raise this plant annually from seed when the old plants, as they often do, give offsets.

THE GERANIUM.—How to Produce Fine Specimens.

I THINK most persons will admit that six well-grown plants of anything is better than twelve inferior ones. Some pride themselves on the variety they possess, while they never see the beauty of them. It is quite possible to enhance the value of an old passed-off geranium, and make it even a restored favourite by bringing it out, as I call it; that is, by developing its beauty such as was not seen before.

A geranium possesses a charm in its name; but by a perfect development of its capabilities it becomes grand in the estimation of its admirers; and certainly a well-grown geranium, whether it be a fancy, scarlet, or any of the new coloured leaved varieties, deserves admiration. To obtain fine specimens of geranium, strike the cuttings early—not later than May or June. Select nice short-pointed stuff; insert these in three-inch pots singly, moderate drainage; and fill the pot up with two parts of good sweet peat, one part maiden loam, one part old leaf-mould, and a little silver sand well incorporated, and sifted through a half-inch mesh sieve. Press the soil moderately tight into the pot; then insert the cutting with a small planting-stick one-third of the whole length of the cutting, and close the earth firmly about the base of the cutting, having previously trimmed the cutting by taking off one or two leaves at the base. Cut the cutting at right angles, immediately below the third joint from the top (although the second joint will do if no more can be had). Let the cuttings lay after they are prepared for half an hour; then insert them and water well. A little silver sand may be laid over the top after the watering, to exclude air, although this is not absolutely necessary. Set the pots in a little heat, or cover them with a hand-light, a bell-glass, or a large tumbler. Geranium cuttings will strike without this; but the exclusion of the air promotes the striking, especially some sorts that are more reluctant than others. Five or six cuttings may be inserted round a five-inch pot, and cuttings may be struck in the open ground during summer. When the cuttings have made an inch of new growth, give air, and nip the leader out. Pot them off into five-inch pots as soon as they are well rooted, and keep a constant eye upon stopping as soon as they have made half an inch of growth above an eye, or a new bud and half an inch of wood above it. Pursue this course up to March or April, bearing in mind that the longer this is continued the later the flowering. Let the plants remain in the five or six-inch pots till February or March, then shift them into eight-inch pots, using soil composed of two parts maiden loam, one part leaf-mould, and one part rotten dung — such as an old melon or cucumber bed. The whole of this compost should be proportionately mixed and chopped up with the spade, but not sifted. Let this compound be neither over wet nor too dry, but such as will sift clean if necessary. As soon as the plants get established in these pots, commence a weekly watering with some liquid manure; such as half an ounce of guano to one gallon of water, or some of the popular artificial manures recommended; or take one peck of dry or half dry sheep's dung, and put it in a tub; on this put eight or ten gallons of soft water; let it stand for twenty-four hours or so, then stir it well with a stick; let it settle; then dip the clear liquor off, and use it as required. This last is exceedingly good for geraniums. As the plants advance tie them out by a wire the size of the wires of a coarse stone sieve having a few wire pegs, with an eyelet in them, through which to run the wire that is to go round the pot inside. Cut the wire long enough to meet round the pot inside, having three or four of these pegs five or six inches inches long, with the eyelet turned; run the wire through one, stick that into the pot close to the side, then thread another, and bring that one-third of the way round (supposing there are three), and drive that down, and so on till the circular wire is complete. Let this wire be nearly close to the surface of the soil; this wire will save the trouble and unsightly appearance of a number of sticks that are frequently seen in the pots of large specimens. The plant can be tied out to this wire, and brought down to the very rim of the pot; thus a symmetrical plant can be formed without a single stick; early tying out, and constant stopping, with good feeding with liquid manure, will rapidly form a fine specimen of a dwarf character, full of bloom. This treatment is equally applicable to all classes of the geranium. After the flowering season is over, cut them back to within an eye or two, shake the earth out of them, trim the roots, and re-pot them into six-inch pots for the winter, and treat as before. The raising of new sorts is attended with a good deal of interest, and often with a large amount of profit. Many have made little fortunes by raising new geraniums. I know one who has been remarkably successful in raising splendid varieties, some of which are decided improvements on the class. Fertilization of the stigma with the pollen from another flower of the quality in request, and cutting the anthers out of the parent flower, so that the seed partakes more of the quality of the one from which the pollen is taken; and another quality that is found in the parent plant is called hybridization, and is the means by which new and improved sorts are produced. (See "Hybridization.") The seed of geranium should be sown in pots of fine soil—two parts leaf-mould, one part maiden loam, and a little silver sand. Take, say two quarts sifted leaf-mould, one quart maiden loam, and half a pint of silver sand. Mix well secure good drainage; fill the pot within

half an inch with the fine soil.   Sow the seed thin ; cover it
the thickness of a penny piece, and set the pot in a little
heat, or cover it up with a bell-glass or a flat square.   If
the seed is sown in March, shade it with moss, and cover it
as directed.   Set it in the sun ; and, if kept moist, it will
vegetate without heat.   Pot the seedlings off as soon as
large enough, and treat them as original sorts ; but, as it is
desirable to see what these are as soon as possible, do not
stop them, but let them flower first, which will be in the
early spring, or even in the autumn if sown in February ;
and set in heat.   All the varieties of geraniums are well
suited for window work, although there are some more
robust than others ; these, therefore, should be chosen for
this particular purpose.   When the leaves of geraniums
become foul with dust or mildew, wash them with the
syringe, using clean water for mere dust, and sulphureous
water for the mildew.   This is made by putting a lump of
brimstone into a gallon or two of hot water—put, say half a
pound brimstone into an earthen pot, jar, or some such
thing ; pour on this five gallons of hot water ; let it stand
twenty-four hours : then use it on the geraniums infested
with mildew.   This brimstone will bear several repetitions
of hot water, or take some of the Gishurst compound, sold
in boxes, and use the quantity specified on the box for each
class of plant ; viz., the hardy, tender, and very tender-
leaved.   Let the liquor settle ; then draw off without disturbing the sediment, and use it for mildew wherever it
appears.   Do not water the geraniums overhead when in
flower.   If spot appear on the leaves, it is generally for
want of energy in the plant ; therefore give them more
nourishment and free drainage.   These attentions preserve
the plants in a vigorous state, and prevent the attacks of
mildew, a disease resulting from ill health.   (See Mildew.)

THE CACTUS.—Its Cultivation, and How to Make it Bloom.

THERE is but one class of plants besides the cactus that possesses anything like the curious forms and shapes of the the cactus, viz., the orchideæ ; even these possess plant-like appearances, while the cactus on the contrary, may be compared to the leaf or branches of a plant whose character is always the same, and others are unlike a plant altogether. Take for instance the melo-cactus and echino-cactus, whose appearance is that of a torpid substance under certain circumstances. Then there are the creeping and erect cereses, some of which appear gigantic and nude, and others of a grotesque form, some attaining to an astonishing altitude ; for instance, the hexagonus (six-angled) will grow twenty or thirty feet high, a most gigantic monstrosity with its white flowers which are not so large in comparison as some others which are of humbler growth. Then there are others which creep and trail, and so on ; upon the whole there is no class of plants so diversified, displayed in not only a peculiarly different form from all other classes, but in some instances in most singularly curious forms, both in the shape the plant assumes, and in the wonderful development of the flower. I refer to " senilis " covered with long white hair. Others are developed in the most gorgeous colours, while some present more humble and congenial forms, which seem to say, " we as a class can suit every taste."

In considering the true physical character of the cactus family, they are found to be plants without leaves, a reason why they remain unaffected by heat and drought. The respirating and inspirating functions of these are so small that they suffer nothing by the same amount of drought that will actually kill most other plants, even though they may be able to resist many degrees of frost. This being the case, every precaution should be taken to secure perfect drainage, and the food, as it may be called, secured for them in the most agreeable form, which would be in a liquid state. Some contrivance should be made to regulate the supply of nutriment necessary for the development of the parts of this plant, such as old mortar, charcoal, &c., as these would become a suitable medium through which the plant would draw the required quantity equal to its necessities. It is an error to give the cactus a large quantity of nutriment in the form of consolidation, that is, rotten dung, &c. The plant cannot consume it in time to prevent sourness, therefore the best practical form by which to supply these plants with this element is to give them half an ounce of guano to one gallon of water once a week, and seldom or ever to shift them, except to give them a little change. The plants should be placed in the most sunny part of the house ; by the treatment I have described I have flowered some that were never seen in the locality to flower before.

The cactus is a general favourite among cottagers and villa residents, although it seldom or ever flowers with them. I gave some instructions in the "Gardening for the Cottage," which I repeat here in substance. The cactus may either be kept in the pot through the winter, or taken out in November, the soil shaken out of the roots, and hung up by the heels in some room secure from frost till March or April; then take them down, re-pot them, using one part maiden loam and two parts sifted leaf-mould, and one part sharp sand, with some charcoal, old lime rubbish, or cracked bones in the soil. The loam should be chopped up turf and all, with the spade, but not sifted : give water, and bring them to a sunny window, or greenhouse, forcing-pit, &c., and give them liquid manure once a week as soon as they begin to swell, and as much sun as possible all through the summer. Retarding and exciting are the only means by which constantly to succeed with the cactus family. If they are kept in the pots through the winter give them no water from November till March or April ; never mind their shrivelling or looking a little brown, they will soon change colour in spring. The chief thing is to perfect the flower-buds during the summer ; let them rest in the winter, and give the plants power to develop in the spring. They may be raised by seeds in heat in spring, and by cuttings during the summer ; let the cuttings lay (after they are prepared) for a week, then insert them in pots of the same soil, or peat.

THE OLEANDER.—HOW TO FLOWER IT.

NUMBERS of amateurs possess this plant, and justly feel a pride in the possession of such a plant, both on account of the good-looking character of it, and the flower that comes now and then, as if by chance, on this old favourite ; and it certainly does possess a large amount of interest, owing to its perpetual evergreen, and the rough treatment it will bear, but it is doubly interesting when it can be induced to flower freely. It seldom fails to produce an abundant show of flowers, but rarely perfects a single one. In the ordinary way it shows the signs too late in the season to perfect the blossoms, as they drop off ; and the question is often asked by cottagers and amateurs,—"What does the too late show of blossoms indicate?" To this I reply that more stimulant is required early in the season. Those who have the means of heat should subject the oleander to sixty-five or seventy degrees, and give an abundance of water and liquid manure ; but those who have not such convenience must have recourse to the next best expedient, that is, to place the plant in a southern window. Set the pot in a saucer, such as are sold for the purpose, or a deep dish, and feed the plant with liquid manure once a week, consisting of one ounce guano to one gallon of tepid soft water. Never suffer the plant to stand in cold draughts, and advantage should be taken of hot sunny days, when the plant may be brought out and set in a sheltered spot, but it should be taken in before sunset ; by this means the oleander will flower anywhere. No omission must be allowed in the supply of water, and especially the manure-water. Cuttings of the oleander will strike freely in a bottle of tepid water, or in a pot of peat kept moist.

THE TUBEROSE.—ITS CULTIVATION.

WHY this is called a "rose" I cannot say, except that it possesses the fragrance of the genus rose, as in this respect it is nothing like a rose in character, but it is more like a diminutive lily. The fragrance of this plant is its recommendation, as one well-grown plant is sufficient to perfume a large room or conservatory. This plant is imported by most bulb-sellers annually from Holland, and bulbs may be had for fourpence, and good large double bulbs for sixpence each. The bulbs should be procured in January, and the skin carefully taken off at the base,—that is, where the roots are emitted,—for if the outside skin is not taken off here it happens sometimes that the skin prevents the bulb striking root ; the consequence is it does not thrive. Pot a bulb, only half buried, in a five-inch pot of peat, and give good bottom heat ; no water till the bulbs have fairly started ; then they may be removed to a cooler atmosphere, such as that of a warm greenhouse, pit, &c. ; then, after a week or two, to a cold frame. As soon as the pots are filled with roots, shift them into nine-inch pots, using pure peat. Some care is necessary in shifting them from one pot to another to prevent the ball of earth falling to pieces. When the plants begin to run for flower give them liquid manure once

a week,— half-ounce guano to one gallon water, when fine
specimens will be formed, whose delicate flowers and fragrance will amply repay the trouble.

THE CENERARIA.—HOW TO GROW IT.

No class of plants are more easy or more worthy of cultivation. Too much nursing of this class would be equally
as bad as not enough.   Keep the plants as cool as possible
without exposing them to frost.   In growing from seed, I
obtained for 2s. 6d. the best seed to be had ; and I would
again remark that if first class plants are required it is best
to send to those only who are noted for growing none but
good flowers. Sow the seed the middle of May or the
beginning of June, on one part loam and two parts leaf-
mould, with a good portion of silver sand. Sift the two former
through a quarter-inch mesh sieve when it is three parts
dry, then add the sand.   Select a spot in the garden having
a west aspect, where the midday sun has no influence ; take
the soil above to the spot,—say a half-bushel,—and put it
down ; set up some bricks on edge so as to admit of a
handlight standing inside ; then spread the soil, make it
level and even over the surface ; gently press the soil to
make it a little firm, and water the whole surface with a fine
rose water-pot, so as to soak the bed of soil through.   Let
it remain for half an hour, then sow the seed thinly and
evenly over the surface, first making a mark with the hand-
light ; sow the seed within this, barely covering to the thickness of a sixpence. Set the handlight on, shade from the
sun's full influence, and give air as soon as the seedlings
are up, and more air as they gain strength, keeping them
sprinkled every day with a dew-pot or very fine rose water-
pot. When the seedlings possess four or six leaves prick
them off into thumbs (two-and-a-half-inch pots), or two into
a small sixty, or three into a large sixty-size pot, using the

same compost, and set them in a shallow cold frame facing the north. Keep them close for a few days, then admit air, and frequently sprinkle them. As soon as the plants meet or cover the top of the pots, shift them into six-inch pots, using the soil a little stronger,—one half leaf-mould and decomposed dung,—old pulverized hot-bed manure and leaf-mould, and maiden-loam one half, with some sand. By this time the plants may be set out in the open air in the full sun on cinder ash, and let them remain here till in danger of frost by night. As soon as the leaves cover the top of the pot (they may be flowered in these pots) or shift them into nine-inch pots. When there is danger of frost, remove the plants to the house, or into a pit or cold frame. Frequently syringe the plants over head, almost daily, as neglect of this leads to black mildew and aphides ; and this syringing should be constantly kept up with clean water till the plants are in flower, and even then the foliage would require it, as well as a free circulation of pure air. If insects should multiply in spite of the above precautions, recourse must be had, when the leaves are perfectly dry, to fumigating with tobacco. The ceneraria may be propagated by off-sets,— that is, young stuff that is seen after flower at the surface of the pot, which should be taken off and treated as seedlings. Among pot plants there are none more desirable than the ceneraria for early spring display, and good-named sorts may be had of most florists for 9s. and 12s. per dozen. The best time to purchase is during the early autumn, while the plants are in small pots ; the plants should be shifted into six or nine-inch pots at once. The ceneraria is an exceedingly good plant for exhibition purposes, and might with care be grown in the window. As soon as flowers are seen water weekly with guano-water,—half-ounce to one gallon of water.

THE CALCEOLARIA.—Its Uses and Culture.

This genus is composed of two distinct classes, shrubby and herbaceous. The latter are the most superb, and only fit for pot-culture, the former are fit for both pot-work and the flower garden. The shrubby can be grown by any, the herbaceous only by those who possess something more than a window ; this principally applies to the raising of the herbaceous from seed, which may be raised with care out of heat, but requires some gentle moist heat to succeed well with it, after which it can be grown and flowered in a good window equally with the shrubby varieties. The shrubby calceolaria is an exceedingly useful class for all purposes, and there is nothing better repays the trouble of bringing them to perfection, capable as some of them are of attaining to good bold features. Those who are desirous of possessing dwarf plants of a robust character and free of flower, should select " aurea floribunda," orange-yellow; "Prince of Orange," orange-brown ; " Yellow Prince of Orange," bright yellow ; " St. Alban's Pet," bright brown crimson ; " Negro," a rich crimson flower; " King of Sardinia," rich crimson, and " Gem," and " Hebe." There are many more varieties equally desirable. Get a plant of each during February, and put them in pots a size larger than those in which they are bought, using maiden loam and sand with a little pulverized old manure. Set the plants in a slight heat if you wish to increase the stock, if not the plants should be shifted from the small pots to six-inch (thirty-twos) and set in the conservatory, cold frame, pit, or window. Nip only the points of every shoot, as this will induce compactness of growth and promote the formation of a handsome symmetrical plant. Continue to stop the shoots as they get two or three inches long up till May, and freely water the plants, giving them once a week weak liquid manure water

from May and throughout the summer ; this may consist of
barely a half-ounce of guano to one gallon of water, or some
of the liquid made by the sheep's dung mentioned for the
auricula.   As soon as insects make their appearance smoke
them with tobacco, or use some of the insecticides before
mentioned ; but the best thing for single plants is to en-
velope the head of the plant in a soft, fine thin calico apron
or something of the sort, large enough to fairly cover the
whole head down to the pot, first sticking three small sticks
in so as to prevent the covering resting upon the young
shoots or flowers ; or the plant may be laid on the side on
the floor or table, and then covered quite close, and if quite
dry tobacco smoke through a pipe or fumigating bellows
may be blown in till filled ; then let it remain for an hour,
lift it off, and syringe the foliage of the plant.   All the cal.
ceolaria family are much better kept in cold pits or frames
through the winter and as long as it is convenient, but when
in flower of course they should be brought to the conservatory or window, and set out of doors, and if no other glass
than a window can be had, they may continue there for the
winter. · Plunge the pots of the shrubby varieties into the
ground during the summer, but let the herbaceous remain
behind glass.   In sowing the seed fill a shallow seed-pan
with two parts leaf-mould and one part maiden loam, with a
handful or two of silver sand.   Sift the two former through
a ¼-inch mesh sieve, mix well, and fill the pan or pot.
Make moderately firm and even, then water the soil, let it
stand for half an hour, sow the seed, and cover it the thickness of writing-paper ; set the pan in a gentle heat or in a
forcing-house, pit, or frame, or in a close box, or under a
handlight, keep close, and shade the pan during the day,
and cover up with a thick mat during night an hour before
sunset ; by this means the choice herbaceous calceolaria
may be raised without heat.   Slightly shade the pan itself

with some clean moss, and carefully sprinkle it when dry with water, but the seed will probably be up before any water is required, if the watering of the soil in the seed-pan is attended to previous to sowing of the seed. Carefully shade the young seedlings, give air, and prick them out ten or twelve into a five-inch pot of fine earth as soon as they possess six or eight leaves; then pot them off singly into large sixties, about three and a half inches; let them remain in these all winter in a cold frame or pit, keeping the frost from them, and shift them into six-inch pots during February or March; feed them with the guano water as directed for the shrubby calceolaria.

THE MESEMBRYANTHEMUM.—Its Uses.

UNDER suitable circumstances, that is in the full influence of a bright sun, of all the plants in cultivation there are none that can compete with the mesembryanthemum as a class for display. The lovely little M—— Tricolor, considering the character of the plant, surpasses everything in its glorious display, but the one to which I shall confine my observa-tions is a procumbent, half-shrubby variety called "purpurea speciosa," or showy purple. This plant is peculiarly adapted for the production of fine specimens for the conservatory and sunny window; it is somewhat a woody plant, con-sequently it is comparatively hardy, although it will not bear any frost; it strikes freely from cuttings of the young wood in pure peat and sand, and is a wonderful plant for bedding, and nothing among bedding-plants can compare with it for display during hot sunny days. And as a pot-plant it surpasses everything where the sun can exert its full power upon it. This flower in a dry atmosphere has a remarkable characteristic :—the blossoms that are ready to expand do not become deteriorated by the continued closing of the once expanded flower, although a week or more may elapse before the sun may shine, whose influence alone causes the expansion; it will expand and remain closed for a considerable time without injury.

If the plant is in a five-inch pot in March shift it into an eight-inch pot, previously putting a layer of three inches with pot-shreds for drainage in the bottom of the pot, and on this some coarse siftings; then set the ball in the middle and fill in with pure peat of a sandy nature; water, and set it in the conservatory or window. Stop any points that are likely to cause the plant to grow out of proportion, and train it a little to form a symmetrical specimen; give moderate waterings and some liquid manure once a week, and a fine specimen will soon be formed. After the chief of the flowering is over, which will be quite the autumn, cut the plant over, a little back, and encourage it to grow a little; then be sparing with the water for the winter, just keeping it in a healthy state, and using it freely with a weekly watering of manure water in the spring and summer, half an ounce guano to one gallon water. In using this plant for bedding purposes, strike the cuttings early in the spring (April or May) and get the plants forward for good strong plants in five-inch pots during the following summer, and turning these out into the beds in the following June. Put out the plants so as nearly to touch, and at the time of bedding out let the soil be loam and sand, or stony peat with one third small pebbles, or rubble gravel put into the peat, and a raised bed with a good drainage, and the plant will, during the whole summer on sunny days, throw everything in the flower-garden into the shade. The splendid little Tricolor must be raised annually from seed and grown in pots of free peat, with a careful drainage and watering. The flower is indeed one of the most lovely annuals.

THE FUCHSIA.—How to Grow it.

THERE are several classes of the Fuchsia. The grand old *fulgens major*, and the *minor*, are two very different plants,—one attaining to the noble height of ten or twelve feet. The plan by which I have succeeded well with it has been to induce the young plant to make rapid growth from the cuttings, preserving the leader till it has attained, say, seven to eight feet, and then to stop it; it will then branch out, and form a head, with a clean stem; from these branches will issue corymbs of flower, suspended on long footstalks, which will have a very pretty effect. Feed the plant with manure water during the summer, and grow it in a thirteen-inch pot of good peat and loam; this is the *corymbiflora major*. Then there is the *fulgens minor*, a lovely dwarf, rather shy flowering species. The way to succeed with this plant is to strike cuttings of the young growth in the spring, as soon as two or three inches long; two buds are enough; cut smooth at right angles, just below the joint, cut one leaf, or set of leaves, off, and let the top ones remain; pot each cutting singly, in three-inch pots, in pure peat and maiden loam, two parts of the former to one of the latter, not too fine; if they can be set on heat so much the better. They will soon strike, and flower in the same pots, which is very convenient for the trade, who grow them for sale; but if fine specimens are desired, they must be shifted from these cutting pots to six-inch, and be grown on through the summer, when they will flower in the autumn. Avoid watering altogether from November to February, and set the pots in a cool part of the house. Turn the pots on their sides under the stage, in the tool-house or closet; probably by February the plants will show signs of life, and some flower-buds; then bring them forward, turn them out, and shake the earth out of the roots; trim them a little and repot them ; water and set them on heat, if you have it, for a week or two, or in the hothouse, in the conservatory, or in a window, where the plant will do well.   Give liquid manure once a week, from the time the plant has fairly broken and started for growth.   The popular varieties or *Coccinea minor* and *major* are very numerous, and constitute the subjects of great interest, containing, as they do, an extensive and an extremely pretty variety.   Cuttings of some of the free growers should be struck early in February, using an inch or two of the tops of the young stuff.   Having some pots of one part maiden loam, and two parts good peat, sifted moderately fine, first put a good handful of crocks in the bottom, on this a layer of siftings, then fill in the fine soil, using three-and-a-half-inch pots, or five-inch will do ; fill up to the top of the pot, and make it firm ; then insert three or four cuttings in a small pot, seven or nine in a five-inch pot.   Water, and plunge the pot in mild heat ; keep close, and they will soon strike ; which, when fairly rooted, pot off into small sixties, then into five-inch pots, and from these to eight-inch pots ; using two parts chopped maiden loam and one part peat, and keep the plants up in the pot ; that is, do not sink the ball deep, or cover the original ball deeper in earth.   Water freely, put a long straight stick to the stem, to which tie it neatly but not too tight, and encourage it on in the window, conservatory, or deep frame or pit.   Give liquid manure once a week, half an ounce of guano to one gallon of water as soon as it fairly shows flower ; thus a fine specimen may be formed the first season from three to five feet ; but if the stem is preserved till the following spring, the soil shaken out of the root, and repotted into a pot one size larger, a little water given to start it, and some liberal waterings with clean water when it has fairly broken shoot, with some manure water once a week, and the laterals cut back to an eye or two at the most, a still finer specimen will be obtained in a short space of time. Never cut the side branches back in the autumn, but let them remain uninjured till spring. Fuchsias may be preserved very well for the winter, and kept nearly dry in the pot, in any dry room, closet, stable, and shed, where frost cannot get at them. Cuttings may be struck all through the summer without heat. The varieties of Fuchsia are so numerous already, and still new ones constantly coming out, that it is needless to enumerate any; but for the sake of those who may be desirous to possess a good permanent sort for special puposes, I may just point to the good old sorts Souvenir de Chiswick—dark, and Venus de Medici—light; two free flowers, and good character, which are not difficult to grow.

THE PHLOX.—ITS ADAPTATION.

THERE are two classes of this, the annual and perennial; both are exceedingly fine plants for bedding. The annual species called Drummondii is most desirable for the flower-garden, where it will flower the whole summer in profusion, if first it is sown on gentle heat in March, pricked off into five-inch pots, putting five or six in a pot, and then turned out into the beds during the end of May and beginning of June. To succeed well with this plant let a good portion of sifted leaf-mould be put into the bed, with some coarse sand, and nip the points of the plants out to induce a branching growth. The perennial species are remarkable and superb things, both for pots and beds. Few things can compare with well-grown plants of Beauty of Milrig—pure white; Countess of Home—white, dark crimson eye; Van Houtii—a lovely and noble striped flower; Queen of Beauties—white, violet eye; *Rosa compacta*, and many more. These Phloxes are rather gross feeders, therefore put them in nine-inch pots, and feed them constantly,—once a week, with one ounce of guano to one gallon of water. The cuttings may be struck during the summer; select the young stuff, two or three inches long, of a short joint, and a little solid; trim and place them either in pots of sandy peat and loam, or under a handlight or striking-glass in the open ground. Prepare the soil for these cuttings by sifting it through a quarter-inch mesh sieve, and add a moderate proportion of silver sand; insert the cuttings one inch and a half asunder; water with a fine rose water-pot, and cover close after the cuttings are dried a little; shade them from the full influence of the sun, give air as soon as the cuttings show signs of having struck root, which is known by the growth they will make. As soon as they are fairly rooted, which will be in the course of three weeks or a month, lift them with a small fork or trowel, and either pot them off into three-inch pots or plant them out into nursery beds six inches asunder; here, as well as those in pots, they will grow and form good stout plants by the autumn, when they will die down; in the spring following shift the plants that are in pots into six-inch or nine-inch pots, using two parts maiden loam, and one part good peat, with some road sand, give water, and set them in an open space. The potting and shifting should be done as soon as the plants have grown two inches. Only two principals, or leading shoots, should be allowed to remain for flowering. Use liquid manure as recommended, as soon as the plants begin to branch; fine and handsome specimens will then be formed fit for exhibition, the window, and other purposes. The Phlox may be propagated in spring for all purposes, by offsets from the division of the root. The Phloxes are excellent for rockwork and edgings; especially the procumbent varieties, which include *repens verna* and *nivalis; verna* is a very early and pretty variety, and should be in every garden.

THE CULTIVATION OF THE PENTSTEMON.

THIS is one of the most useful and superb hardy plants we possess, both for bed, border and pot culture, flowers for vases, bouquets, &c. ; and this tribe includes some of the most lovely things to be found amongst hardy plants, and is equally fit for exhibition, the ordinary flower-garden, the window, and the conservatory. The Gentianoides are a beautiful class of shrubby plants, very hardy ; but the herbaceous class varieties are grand and superb, being characterized both by noble form and beautiful colour. The Campanulata, for instance, though scarce, is a splendid plant for pot culture, of a class marked with various shades of blue and white. Take, for example, the *Purpurea speciosa* and Atroceruleum as types of this magnificent class of the Pentstemon, and we shall have specimens capable of throwing numbers of the new things into the shade,—a tribe of hardy plants at once worthy of a space in our best gardens, windows, and conservatories. I was struck with the superiority and capability of this class on raising some of the lovely blue-flowered sort from seed, and flowering them in pots ; having thus a fine spike of flower, three or four feet in length, well filled up, which was not a common thing amongst Pentstemons. This, with the beauty of the species, enhanced the value of the class as proper plants for pot-work and for exhibition purposes ; it is strange, therefore, that this beautiful plant is seldom or never seen. A sixpenny or shilling paper of seed of the above, or Violacea, Victory, or Magnifica, all in shades of blue, may be procured by post from any seedsman. Sow in seedpans or wide pots in March, and set the seed on moderate heat. First put a good drainage, then some coarse siftings, and fill the pan or pot up with one part maiden loam, two parts leaf-mould, and one part silver sand ; take, say, half a peck of sifted maiden loam, one peck of leaf-mould, and one quart of silver sand, rather than equal part of this with the loam. Mix all well together and fill the pot; make it moderately firm and even ; water with a fine rose water-pot, soak the soil fairly, let it remain for half an hour and sow the seed ; cover it the thickness of a shilling, and set the pot in heat. Give air as soon as the seedlings are up, remove them to a cold frame as soon as they get a little strength, and prick them out when they can be handled, using soil a little stronger—two parts peat and one part leaf-mould. Continue them in a cold frame for two or three weeks, when they may be set outside ; pot them off as soon as large enough into three-inch pots, where they may remain during the winter ; shelter them from heavy rains, and shift them into six or eight inch pots during March, using one-half maiden loam, and one-half pure peat ; feed them with liquid manure as soon as fairly established in these last pots, and some fine specimens will repay the trouble. The Pentstemon may be propagated by cuttings and offsets.

THE BOUVARDIA : ITS BEAUTY AND USES.

FOR simplicity of character, chaste elegance, delicacy of tint, and adaptation for its purposes, there is nothing among flowers to equal the unique Bouvardias. There is nothing difficult in the cultivation of this plant for pot-work, at all times of the year, by retarding and forcing, and for small beds, and it may be propagated freely. And yet, with so many inducements to cultivate this lovely plant, it is seldom to be seen either in a small bed or a pot, although combining usefulness and delicacy of colour enough to induce every lover of flowers to grow it ; take, for instance, *Longiflora*, a chaste white, of unique habit, for pots in the window of the sitting-room and conservatory, and for bouquets for the winter, when so little can be had of these colourless flowers.

Then there is *Oriana*, a lovely scarlet, and Laura, a delicate pink; Rosalind, a splendid salmon; Hogarth, shaded salmon; and Flava, pale yellow; all alike worthy of a space in the conservatory, the greenhouse, the window, and the flower-garden. A stock of these superb things may be obtained from the growers at a cost of about a shilling each; and as they will be in a dormant state by September or October, that will be the best time to procure them. Buy them in pots, with good stocky crowns, let them remain in the pots quiet till February or March, unless flowers are wanted in the winter; then shift them into pots a size larger, subject them to a moderate heat in November, and as soon as the plant fairly starts into growth give water, if the plants are wanted for summer ornament—whether for pots or beds—put the pots in which they have grown the preceding summer into a moderate heat in February or March. When they have fairly started, give water; and when the stuff is an inch or an inch and a half in growth, take it off with a little bit of the old wood—a sort of heel; trim it a little, and place them in either three in a 3½-inch pot, or one in the middle of thumb 2-inch pot; using pure peat, two parts; leaf-mould, one part; and a good portion of silver sand; apply water and plunge, or set them on a mild heat. When they are well rooted in these cutting-pots, if for bedding, shift them into large sixties, and into 4-inch pots if for potwork, and finally into 6-inch pots, using the same soil and good drainage, and feed them with half an ounce of guano to one gallon of water, when some splendid specimens will be formed. The plants must be kept from frost throughout the winter, but may be preserved in a tool-house or ordinary room, or in a cold pit, but no water, or but little, must be given them during their inactive state.

THE IPOMOPSIS ELEGANS: How to Grow.

This is one of the most splendid half-hardy biennial plants grown, and the most rare, in consequence of the peculiar tendency of the plant to shank off, which happens at a time least expected, and just when the plant has arrived at the first stage of maturity, which is in the autumn, when a degree of rest is required. I have had fine plants of this up to the dull months of autumn, and thought nothing could prevent my having fine specimens in the following spring and summer, when all at once one drops after another, till I have had perhaps only one or two left, and have managed to flower but one. I think I have discovered that the principal cause of this mischief has been a want of energy in the root and a healthy and active circulation of the vitals through the whole plant. It cannot be through too much moisture, for neither wet nor dry will save it; but of the two, it seems to suffer more from drought. There is no doubt every plant of this can be saved during the dull months if an active circulation of healthy air above the chills of an autumn night, and a sufficient supply of nourishment adequate to the demand, can be given to the plant. There is no difficulty in raising or growing it through the summer; what is wanted is to substitute as nearly as possible this summer element; therefore bring the plants into the pit or to the greenhouse before the energies of the plant become less strong and active by the chills of autumn. To succeed well with this plant, sow the seed in April, on heat, in pots of leaf-mould and loam and a little sand; prick them off, putting three into a large sixty-sized pot; then pot them off singly into large sixties, using moderate drainage and soil not too fine, and some charcoal the size of mazagan beans in the soil for potting; and give a weekly watering with half an ounce of guano to one gallon of water through the whole growth of the plant from the time they are fairly established in these last pots, or in forty-eights, which would be perhaps better for them during the winter. Good drainage, open soil, even temperature, not too high, a constant supply of nutriment, for the plant to be kept in an active growing state, and to be moderately supplied with water, are the most likely means of securing any number of this plant for flowering.

ALOYSIA CITRIODORA (or Lemon-scented Plant) ;
How to Grow, its Uses, &c.

THIS favourite never fails to sustain the pre-eminence over all the fragrant plants. Poor plant ! I have often felt sorry for it when I have seen it stripped and cut to pieces by the fair sex for hand-bouquets. There is, however, no beauty to lose, so the gardener has not that to mourn over; neither is there anything worthy of imitation in the character of the plant. But the charming and agreeable fragrance of this plant seems too captivating to resist the temptation to slip a sprig off whenever an opportunity offers. This is among scented flowers what the Camellia is amongst flowering ones—the masterpiece, and it should be grown in large quantities by the market gardeners for London and all cities. A sprig of this plant, a flower of the Lily of the Valley, and one leaf-bud of a Tea-scented Rose, two or three Neapolitan Violets, a sprig of Mignonette, a flower of the Heliotrope, a winter or spring Carnation, and a bit of Daphne in flower would be no mean thing, and something that would find thousands of customers—for who would not have such a small bouquet in a glass or porcelain vase on a table in the sitting-room ? Grow the lemon-scented plant, then, in good quantities. It is easy to grow ; select some of the short-jointed young wood at any time it can be had —early in spring or summer is best ; let them be two or three inches long—two inches is enough,—cut these off in the wood a little solid, and trim them at the base with a sharp, fine-edged penknife just below a leaf; having, say, nine cuttings ready, fill a sixty-size pot with two parts peat and one part loam, sifted through a quarter-inch sieve, and a little silver sand added, first filling the pot one-third full with fine broken pot-shreds. Make the soil moderately firm, put the cuttings in with a small, nicely pointed stick half their length, so as to admit of a striking-glass or a tumbler being placed over them inside the rim of the pot. Having inserted the cuttings, water them with a fine rose water-pot, let them stand for half an hour to dry a little, then place the glass over them to exclude air; set the pot or pots on a gentle heat and shade, or in a window. They will strike anywhere during the summer, but a gentle heat will promote the striking. Take the glass off every morning, wipe glass dry, and put it on again. Give a little water when necessary, and these cuttings will soon strike, which will be known by the growth they make; then remove the striking-glass, let them be well watered, and as soon as they are fairly rooted pot them off into small sixties singly. Stop them to induce bushy plants; give them when in these pots a little liquid manure, and encourage them on, so as to form good stout little plants, with as much ripened wood as possible before winter. These plants will give a considerable proportion of stuff for bouquet work the following winter and early spring if put in a brisk heat, and fed once a week with a half-ounce of guano to one gallon of water; but they may be shifted into 48s in the spring. This plant grows freely outdoors in the south, and against a wall in a southern aspect in the northern counties, where it will pass through the winter by matting up during a sharp frost. Cuttings of half-ripened wood will strike in the open ground during summer, but they are often too late for some who have no heat at hand.

THIS plant is particularly adapted for all classes. There is no plant that will, both in beauty and earliness of flowering, repay the trouble of its cultivation better than this; and it is a plant that every one can grow with ease, although there are but two ways of possessing them with any certainty, viz., that of buying or raising them from seed, although they will occasionally give offsets, but this and that of raising them from seed is slow work; it is best, therefore, to purchase a bulb or two of the bulb-sellers who import them from Holland, in the autumn, and when once possessed they will last a lifetime, unless some accident befall them, for the Cyclamen will live to a most extraordinary age. Be careful not to injure the crown, for if this gets injured so as to prevent it shooting for one season, probably it never will emit another leaf, although it may live for a long time. Plants of Persicum, white; and Coum, red; may be had for 1s. each in the autumn, which is the proper time; then pot the plants, first putting a good drainage in the bottom of a five or six inch pot, according to the size of the bulb; then filling the pot up with two parts maiden loam, one part peat, and one part leaf-mould, with some sand; let the pot be filled with this soil within an inch, then set the bulb on the top, and gently press it down an inch or so; then fill up round the bulb to the top of the pot,—thus the bulb will be about half-way clear out of the soil,—this will be proper, as the Cyclamen dislikes being buried completely. They may be started in a slight heat or not, or set in the window; a little water given as the soil gets dry, and more liberally as signs of growth appear; and when coming into flower, give some liquid manure once a week, consisting of half

an ounce of guano to one gallon of water : as soon as signs
of rest appear, which will be some time after the flowering
is over, discontinue watering with liquid manure, and let
the plant retire to rest gradually for a month or two ; then
repot it, and start it again. These plants are pretty hardy,
but will not endure frost. In raising them sow the seed
in peat, and a little leaf-mould and sand in pots, in March,
or before. Cover the seed half an inch with fine earth,
and set the pot on a moderate heat, and keep it moist,
and shade by covering the pot's surface with moss. The
seedlings are slow of growth, and should be left in the
seed-pan or pot for two years before they are fit for potting,
then put them into small 60s, and treat them as other
bulbs. The trade should import them in large quantities
from Holland, where they may be had of such as Messrs.
Krelage, of 146, Kleine Houtweg, Haarlem, by the 100
and 1,000.

MYOSOTIS, the Cultivation of.

(*Forget-me-not.*)

THIS is a hardy plant, and in general favour, and may
be grown in the ground or in pots, where it has an exceedingly good effect. I recommend it as a very useful pot
plant for the shady window in town or country. The
variety *palustris* is about the best for pot work, and forms
in pots one of the very prettiest objects possible. It can
be raised from seed, or by division of the plant. Sow the
seed in spring in pots or seed-pans of fine loam and leaf-
mould, and cover it the thickness of a shilling. Set the
pot under a handlight in a cold frame, or lay over it a flat
square of glass, and shade it with moss. The soil in the
pot should be soaked previously to the sowing, as it promotes quick vegetation. Give air as soon as the seedlings

appear, and prick them off when large enough into other pots, and finally into single pots, 48s, placing one or two large crocks at bottom of the pot previously to potting them finally, and the following season some handsome plants of Forget-me-not will be seen full of flower.

THE PANSY.—Its Uses.

(Heart's-ease.)

No tribe of plants is so well calculated to suit all classes of Flora's lovers as the Heart's-ease ; not only on account of the unequalled diversity of character and colour, but from its adaptation to every locality, whether in town or country ; any one possessing a narrow border, or a corner of the premises where a border can be formed to hold a few or many plants of Pansy, it can be grown, and will form a very interesting object, and one of diversified beauty. This charming tribe possesses the interesting peculiarity of change in feature and in colour, a peculiarity which no other class of plants possesses in anything like the same degree. Varieties of form and of colour follow each other in rapid succession, and each generation of these flowers presents some fresh novelty. In dealing with the pansy, .he cultivator has a broad field for experiment open before him, and at the same time one that well repays the trouble and attention that may be given to it.

The scarlet pansy no doubt may be produced by a judicious combination of the colours, and by a series of patient experiments. I do not profess to prescribe for the production of the long-sought scarlet pansy ; but it is probable that if a clear white and the pollen of a good crimson can be put together some approach to the desired hue may be obtained : it is the presence of too much yellow that interferes with the development of the precious colour, and the

different shades of bronze are produced instead.   Let this
be as it may, the production of new and choice sorts is
within the reach of every one.   To effect this recourse must
be had to good stocks, either by purchasing plants from
noted growers, or by raising them from seed produced
from the best sorts, for which 2s. 6d. or 5s. must be given.
And here I would caution all who are desirous of raising
none but good or moderately good pansies, not to rely
upon the common seed-shops who advertise 6d. and 1s.
packets for sale, such packets are no good.   Good pansy-
seed, or rather seed from really good pansies, is not easy
to get, and cannot be had at all for less than 2s. 6d. and
5s. per paper; and even this is really more advantageous
than buying cheap seeds, for probably out of 100 or
150 plants there will be raised from such a paper of
seed fifty worth 2s. 6d. each; and I have seen one plant
worth a guinea raised from such seed.   On the other hand,
I have raised 300 or 400 plants from a 1s. paper, and
not one of them worth a penny.   If the seed is saved
from any but the best sorts, there is little chance of much
good.   Send to some noted grower of this plant in the
northern counties in February or March, and sow the
seed in seed-pans at once.   Let the soil be one part maiden
loam, two parts old dung pulverized to dust, and one part
leaf-mould, and some silver sand added.   Sift the three
former through a ¼-inch sieve; fill the seed-pan or pots
with this to within half an inch, when it should be made
moderately firm, then water with a fine rose water-pot; let
it remain for half an hour, then sow the seed thin, and cover
over about the thickness of a shilling.   Set the pots or pans
in a cold frame under a hand-light, or cover with a flat
square of glass and shade.   When they are up the plants
must have air, and when large enough prick them out on a
north, east, or west border of fine earth, any common

garden soil that is good will do, adding some maiden loam and road sweepings, sand, &c.   Prick them out six inches by four asunder, till they have proved themselves, which they will do by the autumn, when the best should be taken up and potted into four or six inch pots, to be placed in a cold frame, or some sheltered spot for the winter ; and some may be placed in the window, or in front of a common greenhouse.   The choice sorts must be propagated by cuttings taken off during the summer, selecting the side-shoots of young stuff with short joints and solid (the old hollow stuff is no good for striking) ; just trim the leaves off a bit, and then insert the cuttings two inches asunder on a north or east border of fine earth, of the same description as recommended for the seedlings ; or it may be nearly all maiden loam, they are very fond of this, and will strike freely in it.   When they are rooted take them up and pot them into large 60s ; these will be found useful for the window, and for turning out into beds and borders in the following spring ; or they may be grown in 48s, and flowered well by feeding with the sheep's dung water, as recommended for the auricula, always selecting a shady aspect for the flowering of the pansy.

THE CHRYSANTHEMUM FOR EVERY ONE.

THE cultivation of this tribe is very desirable, and it may be well described as every person's plant.   As a class, it is most accommodating, as a flower most beautiful, in culture easy, and in colour rich and diversified.   There are two classes of this grand flower, viz., the large-flowered and the pompone ; each of these is beautiful, but the last-named is the favourite ; it is less noble than the former, but surpasses it in point of symmetry, in compactness of growth, and beauty of flower.   It is well adapted for the flower-garden, the conservatory, and the cottage window.   To meet every

requirement recourse must be had to propagation by cuttings.   This is done in February or March, and sometimes
in May; this last-named period for taking cuttings will
answer for very dwarf plants, and they may be struck as late
as June and July for mere miniature pot plants: they are
very dwarf and very useful for decoration of the greenhouse
and the window.   The striking of chrysanthemum cuttings
is simple enough: in February and March, when the young
stuff is rising from the old stool, select those which are
healthy, sound, and short jointed; cut them two or two and
a half inches long, no more; trim them a bit at the base,
and insert them in large 60s; put four or five in a pot,
having the pot filled with two parts maiden loam, one part
leaf-mould, and one part silver or road sand of a sharp
nature.   Make the soil in the pot pretty firm; insert the
cuttings one-half their length in the soil; water, and set the
pots on a mild heat, or cover them with a hand-light or
striking-glass, and shade from the full influence of the sun,
by all means keeping them moist.   Or the cuttings may be
inserted in the open ground on a south side, and covered
with a hand-light, &c, kept moist, and shaded a little during
the mid-day sun.   These will soon strike, when air must be
admitted and the shading discontinued.   As soon as the
cuttings are well rooted take them up and pot them off into
large 60s, nip the points of all of them out, give liberal
waterings, and set them in a cold frame; or they may be
set out in an open part, but if you have a frame at liberty
give them a fortnight in it, and then set them out in a sunny
spot.   When they have filled these pots with root shift them
into 6-inch or even into 8-inch pots, using good maiden
loam two parts, peat one part, and sand one part.   Keep
them in a full sunny place; give liberal waterings every
day, manure water once a week, and continue to stop
every shoot as it possesses two buds; the stopping may be

followed up till the beginning, or even the middle, of August, and fine healthy, robust specimens will be the result, which will continue to decorate the greenhouse, the window, and the flower-garden all the autumn months.

The cuttings struck in May and June will require but little or no stopping; these will be very pretty dwarf plants for the window of the citizen, the mechanic, and the artisan, and for dwarf beds. Plants of the chrysanthemum may be had for 6s. to 12s. per dozen; get them early, and grow them as directed.

THE ASTER, as a Pot Plant.

THE ease with which it can be grown, the beauty of the flower, the season of its display, and its adaptation as a pot plant to ornament the window of the cottager, the sitting-room, or the conservatory, should at once demonstrate the value of the aster. It is nearly always assigned a place in the open ground, simply because it will grow there very well; but in many instances the disposition of the plant to hold on flower in protracted flowering is considerably lessened in consequence of the unfavourableness of the season; and this is felt more by the superior sorts than by the common varieties. But if asters are grown in pots the misfortune of losing half the flower is not only avoided, but the full beauty of the plant is secured by being placed behind glass.

If three plants are put into a 9-inch pot filled with two parts maiden loam and two parts old dung pulverized to dust, and a portion of road sand added, and moderate watering; kept in the open till they show flower, then fed once a week with liquid manure, consisting of that made with the sheep's dung recommended for the auricula, or of half an ounce of guano to one gallon of water, or of any of the artificial manures recommended for such things, there will be few blooms that will give more satisfaction ; nothing among annuals, or even among greenhouse plants, will better repay the little trouble bestowed on them. Select *Bouquet de Flore* and *Chrysanthe Flowered.* Sow the seed in pots or seed-pans, of one part maiden loam and one part leaf-mould, and a little sand ; sift the loam and leaf-mould through a half-inch mesh sieve, and cover the seed with mould to the thickness of a shilling ; set the pot or pan on a moderate heat, or cover it with a hand-light, or lay a square of glass flat on the top of the pot ; shade, and set it in a sunny aspect. This applies to the raising of the plants without heat, which can be done equally well, only a little slower. When the plants are large enough to handle well, prick them off into pots, putting three in a 3-inch pot ; from these they may be transferred to the large pots, or to the beds. The ground for asters for beds must be of a tender and good friable quality.

CHOICE ANNUALS FOR BEDS.

BARTONIA aurea, a pretty free-flowering yellow plant of a foot in height. Sow moderately thick where it is to bloom, and in an open spot. Brachycome ibidrifolia and alba, two exceeding good things for small beds, may be sown where they are to flower, on fine soil, one part leaf-mould and one part good earth. Make the bed light with the leaf-mould and some sand, pit or road sweepings ; sift the leaf-mould if coarse. Make the surface fine, and sow the seed, in separate colours, on the surface ; then sift some earth (mostly leaf-mould) through a very fine sieve, so as to cover the seed the thickness of a threepenny piece, and shade the bed by laying a thin calico sheet or a newspaper over it for a few days, to prevent the surface drying and heavy rains disturbing the germination of the seed ; remove the shades soon after the seed is up. Or they may be sown in seed-pans or under a hand-light and planted out. These two make a lovely dwarf bed, the one clear white, and the other clear blue, and remarkably free of flower.

Calychroa platyglossa, a very pretty, free-flowering yellow plant about a foot high, with a fimbriated margin of white. Sow moderately thick where it is to flower.

Clarkia integripetala, a beautiful thing; a dwarf, free-flowering plant with rose-coloured flowers, which are very conspicuous. Sow where it is to flower on good and moderately fine earth; cover the seed the thickness of a shilling.

Collinsea Bartsiæfolia and multicolor, two very pretty free-flowering dwarf annuals for small beds. Sow moderately thick on a fine surface of good common soil.

Convolvulus minor, a very beautiful thing for a good-sized bed. Sow on a medium surface thinly, and cover half an inch.

Dianthus Heddewigii, ſacinatus, and Chinensis. The two former are exceptions to the whole genus in the size of the flowers. Where the true sort can be had, and grown on good sandy loam and leaf-mould, there is nothing among Dianthus that can match the size of this particular flower. The Chinese varieties are very unique in their markings, and a bed of these sown moderately thick is very attractive.

Gilia nivalis and tricolor, two very pretty dwarf varieties, well worthy of a place in every garden of annuals. Sow where it is to flower on good fine earth of a light nature.

Gypsophila elegans and G. muralis, two very pretty hardy plants of a dwarfish nature, and free to flower. The first mentioned is white and purple; the last pink.

Fenzilea dianthiflora, a lovely thing for pots and small beds. Sow in pots of leaf-mould and loam, and set on heat. Prick them out and then pot off singly, or plant out into the small beds.

Inopsidium aucule, the smallest perfect plant known ; a curiosity.

Larkspur in variety.   There are no annuals more worthy a place in the flower-garden than these.   Sow where they' are to flower in good, light, sandy soil ; if the ground is heavy, add a good proportion of leaf-mould.   Make the bed fine, and sow the seed moderately thick on the surface ; then sift some fine earth over the whole, covering the seed to about the thickness of a halfpenny.   Give liquid manure just before they flower, and continue this once a week through the flowering season.

Linum grandiflorum rubrum.   This is the best and most beautiful linum of the whole ; dwarf, free to flower, and very showy, being a deep scarlet, or rather a crimson.   Sow in April where it is to flower.

Marigold, orange African, striped unique, and dwarf yellow or pigmy, all exceedingly beautiful for good-sized beds.   Sow in wide pans or pots in two parts leaf-mould and one part maiden loam, and a little sand.   Cover the seed the thickness of a penny piece, and set the pan or pot on a moderate heat.   Prick them out when large enough, and finally plant out four inches asunder for the " pigmy,' and six inches apart for the others.   Give weak liquid manure once a week from the time the flower-buds appear till the end of the flowering season.

Nemophila insignis, blue ; maculata, spotted on white ground, fine ; discoidalis, black, white border ; all pretty, hardy dwarf annuals of superior merit, but the blue is the best.   Sow moderately thick on good mellow soil ; let the surface of the bed be only moderately fine and half dry.   Sow the seed over it ; then chop the seed in with a short-toothed rake, or beat the surface of the bed with the back of the rake.   Thus the seed will be covered without further trouble or raking.   These answer admirably for pots and for boxes for the window. Sow in August for winter and early spring flower; in February and March for early summer; and in May and June for autumn flowering. Feed once a week with liquid manure from the time they are half grown till the flowering is half over, more particularly those in pots.

Rhodanthe Marglesii. This is one of the choicest of half-hardy annuals; and, although it may be grown in small beds of fine light earth, two parts leaf-mould, one part maiden loam sifted through a half-inch sieve, or the leaf-mould sifted and mixed with good garden soil, and some sharp sand added, it is better adapted for pots, where it is beautiful. The border must be elevated by adding the leaf-mould to render it dry. Sow the seed in seed-pans or wide pots filled with two parts leaf-mould and one part maiden loam, sifted through a ¼-inch mesh sieve, and some silver sand added to render it free, previously putting some small crocks in the bottom of the pots so as to secure thorough drainage; set the pots on a mild heat, and shade a little with moss to prevent the surface drying. As soon as this annual is through the earth, take off the shade, admit air, and give water carefully. Prick the plants off, three into a three-inch pot, and finally pot them off into three-inch pots singly; from these turn them out into the bed in June, or shift them into forty-eights for the conservatory and the window. Give weak liquid manure once a week, free drainage, and moderate waterings.

Portulacca splendens, alba striata, two splendid half-hardy annuals of an exceeding showy character in an open sunny spot. Sow the seed in March in seed-pans filled with two parts fine leaf-mould, one part good peat, and one part silver sand; that is, take, say two quarts fine sifted leaf-mould, one quart peat, and one quart sand, or a little less; put good drainage in the bottom, a little coarse siftings on it, and then the compound soil. Make it moderately firm and even, and sow the seed. Set it on a moderate heat, slightly shade it to prevent drying, and carefully sprinkle with water, should water be requisite before the seed is up. Prick them off into three-inch pots, three in a pot; water, and shade for a few days. After a week remove the pots into a cold frame. Keep the frame close for a few days till the plants are hardened off; then admit air. In the month of June turn them out, ball entire, into the bed, which should consist of good garden soil, with a good proportion of leaf-mould and pit-sand worked into it. Let the bed be raised above the level, to secure perfect drainage; plunge the ball of three plants in the bed six inches asunder, and give water. If it is desirable to save seed, pick the pods daily before they burst.

Schizanthus grandiflora, oculatus, and retusus. These are very pretty hardy annuals, or rather, half-hardy. Sow where they are to flower in April on good, rich, and light soil, or they may be sown in pots and planted out. The retusus is a fine plant for greenhouse decoration if sown in August or the beginning of September, potted into forty-eights, using two parts maiden loam and one part leaf-mould. Kept in a dry, cool pit or greenhouse through the winter, and shifted into eight-inch pots in February, and fed with liquid manure—half an ounce of guano to one gallon of water; few things can exceed the beauty of this plant thus grown.

Zinnia elegans. This consists of the most beautiful and superb flowers imaginable, combined with grandeur and richness scarcely to be found among all our annual flowers. To have the advantage of this, sow the seed in pots of two parts leaf-mould and one part maiden loam, and a little sand added. Sift the two former, fill the pot within half an inch, make it a little firm; sow the seed, and cover it the thickness of an old penny piece with fine light soil, and set the pot in moderate heat. Prick them off into three-inch pots, putting three plants in a pot, and return them to a mild heat. Water a little, and shade for a few days; shift the pots to a cold frame when they have established themselves in these pots, and put them out into the borders or beds as June approaches; plant six inches asunder. The zinnia may be pegged down, when they make handsome dwarf beds for many weeks. Some liquid manure may be given them a few times during their flowering season.

Aster, double-quilled German and double globe—fine varieties for sowing in the open ground. Sow the seed in April on beds of good fine soil, consisting of common garden mould; dig it moderately deep, introducing a good portion of old rotten dung, some leaf-mould, and a portion of road sand into the bed a month beforehand; let it lay rough, fork it over a few inches deep, and make the surface fine. Sow the seed moderately thick, and cover with light earth the thickness of a penny piece, by sifting it over the seed through a $\frac{1}{4}$-inch sieve; thin the plants out to four inches asunder, and a fine bed will repay the little trouble. A 6d. paper will sow a good-sized bed.

CHOICE SUN-FLOWERS FOR BEDS.

By this I mean flowers that open only in the sun,—that is, while the sun shines, and closes in the absence of its rays. It is a notable fact that those flowers that open and close under the influence of the sun—open when it shines and close when its rays are prevented from pouring upon them—are among the most striking and brilliant colours. Take for instance the—

Anagallis Indica, bright blue ; grandiflora, crimson. Sow the seed on fine peat mixed with leaf-mould and some sand in a small bed in an open spot. Make the surface fine, sow the seed, and cover to the thickness of a sixpenny piece ; or sow the seed in pots or pans. Prick them out when large enough into other pots, and plant out in May and June. Very dwarf.

Calandrinia grandiflora and speciosa ; the first is a half-hardy perennial, and speciosa a brilliant annual. Sow them on beds of sandy soil with some peat in it. Sow on a fine even surface, and cover slightly with fine light earth, two parts leaf-mould and one part peat. These are very dwarf, and a most showy purple.

Mesembryanthemum tricolor and various, all sun-flowers. This splendid little plant (which I have made mention of before) is perfectly unique in its lovely flower ; the whole plant is a jewel among flowers, and when carefully and well grown, blossoms very freely. Sow the seed in pots (well drained) of two parts leaf-mould and one part peat, sifted, and one part silver sand ; let the pot be filled one-third full with fine broken pot-shreds and a little coarser siftings on them, then fill up with fine soil. Sow the seed (which must be taken out of the pots) on the smooth surface, and cover to the thickness of a sixpence ; set the pots in some mild heat, and shade with moss. Give air as soon as they are up, and carefully water. Prick them off, putting three into a three-inch pot well drained ; water sparingly, and remove them to a colder frame as soon as the plants have established themselves in these pots ; and finally turn them out into the small bed, formed of two parts leaf-mould, one part peat, and one part coarse sand. Let the bed be raised considerably above the level, and some coarse siftings of leaf-mould, peat, and stones put under the bed, having only three inches of fine soil on the surface, and let this be of a porous and open nature. Turn them out of the pots (ball entire) in June, where the full benefit of the sun can be had. They answer admirably for growing in forty-eights as pot plants. Sow the seed in March or April annually.

Oxalis floribunda. Sow the seed in February or March, in pots of peat and leaf-mould as directed for the last-named plant, except that less drainage is required. Set on a mild heat, and then pot off into single pots, small sixties; from these turn the plants into the beds in May or June, place them six inches asunder, in beds of good earth, with some peat and leaf-mould in them. (This is the shamrock species.)

Portulacca splendens. See page 265.

Sphænogyne speciosa; a very showy yellow-flowered annual. Sow the seed in pots of fine leaf-mould and loam, in equal parts. Cover the seed as thick as an old penny-piece, and set the pot or pots on heat. Prick the plants off into forty-eights, putting three in a pot, and remove them to a cold frame. Turn them into the beds in May or June, place them pretty thick, feed a few times with liquid manure.

Linums, various.

Eschscholzia crocea, compacta, &c. These are two very showy perennials, with yellow flowers, only fit for large beds, broad borders, rockwork, &c.

NOTES ON SCENTED PLANTS.

HOW TO GROW THEM.

THERE are but few plants that are without scent, either agreeable or disagreeable, in the flower or the leaf. The plants of which I am about to speak are those whose fragrance is agreeable and also perceptible at some distance. These are comparatively few. Why there are so few, and how it is that they possess their peculiar properties, is a mystery, except it is solved in this way. As soon as the organs of the flower are fully developed, the presence of heat extracts the essential oil, which is given off as the result of the condition of the surrounding atmosphere; hence mignonette and violets give their fragrance out in proportion to the heat by which they are surrounded, and the latter cease to emit any fragrance at all if deprived of sun and heat for a lengthened period. Some have doubtless observed that in the evening of a hot summer's day there seems to be additional odour from the mignonette, stocks, wallflowers, &c.; this is in consequence of the additional essence evolved by heat subsequently becoming condensed by the cooler atmosphere. Of scented plants mignonette is one of the chief. (See " Culture.")

The violet is another of these odoriferous plants. (See " Culture.")

Stocks also belong to this class. (See " Culture.")

Wallflowers are another lovely and very fragrant class of plants. (See " Culture.")

Pinks and cloves are possessed of a peculiar aromatic fragrance which makes them favourites, especially the white and true old pinks and the true clove. (See " Culture.")

Roses, tea-scented China, especially the old sort called " fragrance," and many of those lovely tea China roses possess a deliciously sweet and aromatic odour. (See " Culture.")

Orange tree. The flowers of this possess a peculiar pungent aromatic odour, so powerful as to become actually disagreeable to some sensitively constituted persons. (See Culture.")

Tuberose, double and single, are very agreeable rose-scented bulbous plants with white lily-like flowers. (See " Culture.")

Geranium tuberosum ; a bulbous-rooted geranium, with peculiar dull-coloured flowers, but with a strong odour, grow them in six-inch pots of peat and loam, starting them in a moderate heat. When in flower bring into the conservatory or window.

Heliotrope,—Beauty of the Boudoir, Miss Nightingale and La Petite Negresse; well known for "cherry-pie" fragrance : these are the only plants that possess this peculiar smell, identical with the odour of cherry pie. The culture is easy. Strike the cuttings of the young stuff in pots filled with sandy peat and loam, or peat alone. Set the cuttings on heat ; as soon as struck pot off into three-inch pots ; then shift them (as soon as they have filled these with root) into forty-eights, or six-inch pots ; stop them frequently to induce bushy growth, and feed them once a week with liquid manure; or turn them out of the small pots into the beds in June, nine inches asunder ; either peg them down or let them grow at will. This plant forces well, and may be grown in the window also.

Daphne Indica, mezereum, and many others; all peculiarly odoriferous, more particularly the mezereon, whose fragrance is discoverable at an extraordinary distance during early spring. (See " Culture.")

Syringa emodi. This is a most fragrant and free-flowering variety, the odour of which somewhat resembles the orange. A hardy shrub.

Chimonanthus fragrans. This is a highly and remarkably fragrant species, the flowers of which are insignificant, and appear before the leaf in the early spring. A hardy shrub.

Jasmine ; in variety,—well known.

Honeysuckle ; in variety,—well known.

Hoya carnosa ; one of the most extraordinary climbing plants extant, which bears most sweet and lovely flowers. (See " Culture.")

Datura humilis, double yellow. This is very sweet, even to a fault in the judgment of some people. Sow the seed in pots, and set on heat. Grow in six or nine-inch pots, or turn into the ground, good rich soil.

Sultan, sweet ; a half-hardy annual, with a particular

sweet, honey-like fragrance.   Sow on heat, and plant out in June.

Erysimum Perowskianum.   This is a remarkably hardy annual, having a scent resembling that of the wallflower; it bears orange flowers.   Sow on good ground where it is to flower, or sow in six-inch pots to flower.   Give liquid manure.

Schizopetalum Walkerii ; a very curiously modelled white flower, and very sweet.   Sow on heat, and plant out in good ground.

Scabious elegans ; several rich-coloured flowers, possessed with a very extraordinary sweet fragrance.   Hardy perennials.   Sow in small bed, and plant out where they are to flower.

Alyssum, sweet ; a dwarf hardy annual, with very sweet white flowers.   Sow where it is to flower.

Ageratum odoratum ; a very pretty light blue and sweet-flowered annual.   Sow on heat, and plant out where they are to flower in May.

Musk moschatus ; well known ; may be raised from seed and from parts of the root.   Grow in beds or pots, using two parts maiden loam, one part leaf-mould, and a little sand.

Pea, sweet ; various ; well known.

Clematis flammula ; a fine, hardy, sweet-scented climber, admirably adapted for climbing over arbours and doorways, covering old fences, walls, and buildings.   Propagate by layering the last season's wood.

GOOD CLIMBING PLANTS.—Their Uses.

HARDY CLIMBERS.

AMPELOPIS hederacea. This is the well-known Virginian creeper, a plant of a hardy constitution, which changes the green colour of its leaf to a crimson in the autumn; very striking and peculiar. It will answer well for rapidly covering any unsightly wall or building in any situation either in town or country.

Aristolochia sipho; a most nobly foliaged hardy climber, with curious flowers; a fine plant for covering a wall where boldness of feature is required.

Atregene Austriaca, Alpina, Americana, and macropetala; pretty-leaved hardy climbers, with flowers similar to a single anemone, but of white or some shade of blue; fine for covering pillars, archways, doorways, &c.

Clematis. All of this tribe are useful hardy climbers, but campaniflora and Sieboldii are two very pretty varieties.

Jasmine, officinale, chrysanthemum, and revolutum; well-known hardy climbers.

Honeysuckle, flexuosa, grata, evergreen, and the semper-virens; beautiful scarlet flowers, but the first two are the best.

Passiflora cærulea; a most rapid hardy climber in a sheltered aspect; flowers handsome.

Solanum jasminifolium; a very pretty, hardy, blue-flowered climber for a wall.

Tecoma. This comprises the bignonias or trumpet-flowers, a most splendid class of hardy climbers, which, however, require a south wall, and a sandy dry soil. The flowers are either red, crimson, yellow, blue, or purple.

Westeria Chinensis. This is certainly the best hardy climber we possess. Nothing can exceed the beauty of a

full-blown westeria, with its lovely lilac racemes of flower.
This plant possesses peculiar flexibility, and as in the course
of a single summer it will form a great deal of wood, it is
particularly adapted for twining round the pillars of an
entrance-hall, training over a window, over an archway, or
in front of a summerhouse or a garden temple, &c.   Plant
in any good sandy soil.   Propagate by layers and cuttings
of the young ripened wood.

Ivies: canariensis, Irish, rægneriana, — a very large-
leaved variety,—foliis argenteis, and foliis aureis,—gold
and silver-marked in the leaf; very pretty ; small-leaved.

Double-flowered bramble ; very pretty, but rather coarse.

Banksian roses ; double yellow and double white ; two
beautiful climbing roses ; the white is a lovely violet-scented
variety.   Both want a south or south-west wall; for covering a wall few things are more pleasing than these lovely
roses.   Do not prune till all danger of frost is over, and then
prune carefully.   Lay in all the long flexible shoots of young
wood that you can, and thin the old out to make 'room
for the young ; on this depends the crop of flowers.   Propagate by cuttings of short ripened wood after the flowering
is over.

Calampelis scabra.   This a very pretty, free-flowering,
orange-coloured, bignonia-shaped, half-hardy climber, and
free of growth ; fit for a south entrance to an arbour, or to
the house, &c.   Propagate by seed sown in early spring,
and by layers.

Pyracantha ; a hardy plant that can scarcely be called a
climber, still it answers admirably for slowly covering a wall,
where it has a very neat appearance.   It lasts a long time,
and during the late autumn and winter months looks very
pretty, with its clusters of vermilion berries.   Propagate by
seed and by layers.

Pyrus Japonica.   This can scarcely be called a climber,

still it is one of the most beautiful hardy plants for covering low walls, fences, &c., with its very early scarlet-crimson flowers, which are given in great profusion before the leaf. Propagate by layers, and grafting on the quince or pear.

Cotoneaster microphylla ; another pretty hardy plant that answers well for covering low walls, fences, &c., where neatness is required ; presenting a very pretty evergreen object, with its rose-vermilion berries. Propagate by layering, cuttings, and by seed.

Magnolia grandiflora exoniensis. This is without doubt the most noble evergreen white-flowered plant extant for covering a south wall. The leaves are as large as one's hand, of great substance, and profuse. The flowers are frequently as large as a half-pint breakfast-cup, a delicate white, and of delicious fragrance. Propagate by cuttings in heat and by layers. Grow in pure peat.

HALF-HARDY CLIMBERS.

Cobœa scandens. This is one of the most rapid climbing plants extant, with large bell-shaped flowers, which are purple ; must be raised on heat in March, potted into three-inch pots, and planted out in May ; well adapted for covering a pillar, an arch, or trellis-work, on a south side, good soil.

Lophospermum scandens, several varieties. This is a very rapid, pretty, neat climber, with light or dark rose-coloured flowers ; sow the seed in March in heat, and plant out in May, or propagate by cuttings late in the autumn.

Maurandia Barclayana, a very pretty, light, half-hardy climber, with blue and white flowers, in shape resembling the foxglove. This pretty climber is fit for pots for the conservatory, and for planting outdoors to cover a small trellis where the space is limited, and neatness indispensable ; sow the seed in pots in March, or before, and set on a moderate heat, or propagate by cuttings; good light earth and some peat.

Thunbergia aurantiaca and alba; two very pretty climbers for pots, with orange-coloured and white flowers; nothing can be prettier than these if well grown. Sow the seed in March in pots of two parts leaf-mould, one part maiden loam, and one part sand; cover the seed the thickness of half an inch, and set the pot in a brisk heat. As soon as they can be handled pot off into small pots, then shift to six-inch pots, and harden off; bring them to the conservatory and greenhouse; feed them with liquid manure once a week; train them on trellises, and frequently syringe to keep down red spider.

Loasa aurantiaca. This is a very pretty and handsome half-hardy climber for pots, with flowers of a peculiar shape; sow the seed in March, cover slightly, and set on mild heat, then put off, and grow on as for Thunbergia; or this climber may be planted out, strained on a small trellis on a south wall.

Ipomea elegans. This includes some of the most lovely climbing pot plants extant, nothing among dwarf and medium climbers can exceed this tribe for diversity of colour and display of beauty; sow the seed in pots in March and April, and set on a moderate heat, pot, and grow in six-inch pots in the greenhouse. Some will require a warm house to do well; give liquid manure once a week, and train to a ~~moderate heat.~~ *Trellis.*

Clianthus puniceus. This is one of the most lovely and rich medium climbers for pots, and for the trellis and pillars of the warm greenhouse and conservatory. It bears crimson pea-shaped flowers. Sow the seed in pots of two parts leaf-mould, one part maiden loam or peat, and one part sand. Cover the seed half an inch, and set in a brisk heat, or propagate by cuttings, and grow in six or nine-inch pots of loam and peat ; sprinkle frequently to keep down red spider, and give liquid manure. The climber is fond of warmth.

Convolvulus major. This is a section of the Ipomea, but will grow well in our gardens in the open ground, while the Spomeas all require continuous warm to do well. There is nothing more suitable than ten-feet snaggy pillars, a small larch pole, or three small, clean, straight poles set in a triangle eight or nine inches asunder, for these to grow on here and there about the ground. Put in the poles and sow the seed in good rich earth at the base, covering the seed half an inch ; sow in April.

Tropæolum Lobbiana, crimson : Lillie Schmidt, scarlet. Triomphe de Grand scarlet, and Canariensis, pretty yellow, all beautiful things for pot in the window and greenhouse, and the last named is very pretty for trellises. Sow the seed in heat in April, and propagate by cuttings of the perennial species.

WALL-PLANTS, AND HOW TO PLANT THEM.

Most of these are included in plants for the " Rockery," but as the walls of the boundary, the house, &c., require especial plants, I think it worth while to enumerate a few for the convenience of those who have no rockwork, and still have walls that they would be glad to hide or ornament.

The tops of brick walls and also stone walls may be furnished with the single wallflower, choosing very small woody plants and planting them early in spring or autumn, and the valerian will do well on the top of coarse stone walls. The saxifrage, or golden moss, will likewise flourish on the top of walls, also sedums, Scutellaria Alpina, Erinus Alpina, Arabis Alpina, and Antirrhinums ; all these must be bedded in mortar made of maiden loam and cowdung, and some little excavations made in the wall over the joints.

This will give the plants an opportunity of rooting into the wall.

Perpendicular walls may be made ornamental, and to present a pleasing appearance, by inserting small plants of Asplenium trichomanes and A Ruta muraria (wall rue), two ferns remarkably well suited for insertion in shady walls ; the first is a lovely little plant found in abundance in Devonshire growing on old stone walls, on old buildings, and on banks where stone form a part of the fences, which is generally the case close to the public roads , and the other may be found growing out of solid stone and mortar walls. This pretty little fern can be collected in Devonshire in the autumn or early spring. Another way of obtaining the plants of the lovely Trichomanes and Adiantum nigrum is to collect the fronds in July and August, and carefully preserve them in paper bags to carry them to their destination, and let the seed be sown on some rough peat and loam in a shady corner where a degree of moisture exists, free from heavy drips of trees, on an elevated sandy soil ; dust the surface by knocking the fronds over it, then throwing them down and leave them, and let all remain undisturbed for three or four years ; or, the fronds may be shaken over pots or pans of rough peat, and set in a shady part of the greenhouse, hothouse, &c., where probably some plants will soon appear. When plants of ferns are collected, let them be as small as possible consistent with strength, and with a nice little ball or fibre. Chisel some little recesses in the wall at the joint of the brick, puddle the roots in thin mortar made with loam and cowdung ; put some stout mortar in each hole, bed the plants in them occasionally, and syringe lightly during the first summer.

UNDER-PLANTS FOR SHRUBBERIES.

ST. JOHN'S-WORT, calycinum ; a very hardy and pretty dwarf thick-growing evergreen plant, admirably adapted for planting under larger shrubs ; it makes a very pretty covering for the ground, and it is propagated by division of its roots.

Aucuba Japonica. This lovely spotted evergreen dwarf answers very well as an under-shrub; propagate by cuttings and by layers.

Daphne laureola (wood-laurel); a beautiful plant for shady places, likes sandy soil, and should not often be removed ; fragrant and evergreen.

Ruscus (butcher's-broom) racemosus. This is a well-known evergreen under-shrub for permanency, as it does not like to be often removed.

Vaccinium (whortleberry plant). This is a most useful plant for an under cover for plantations and for game, as well as for domestic purposes, the berries being good for pies, and very juicy; it is a pretty, neat, low shrub, requires a dry sandy soil, grows in abundance in Devonshire.

Vinca (periwinkle), major and minor. This is a fast-growing and pretty under-plant for dry ground.

Ivies, English and Irish plain-leaved ; the former has very small leaves. Then there are some wide variegated leaves, all which make pretty underground coverings.

Cotoneaster microphylla, a very neat and durable shrub in dry places for underwood ; propagate by cuttings and layers.

Ferns, Filix mas, Filix fœmina ; two splendid plants for growing as under-plants in sandy soil ; plant in November or February and not later than March, choosing small plants.

Tussilago (coltsfoot alba), and variegated, a capital plant for covering the ground under trees.

Lily of the valley, well known.

Primroses, well known.

Digitalis (foxglove) should not be too much shaded.

Ribbon-grass, very pretty, not to be under too much shade.

Arum, British, well known.

Acorus calamus, a pretty iris-flowered bulb, bearing pods of vermilion berries.

Iris, various, blue mostly.

Daffodil, double and single.

The number of plants that will do well under trees under all circumstances is very limited. It will be observed that few indeed, if any, will live long on the ground occupied with the fir tribe. This is in consequence of the peculiar resinous property of the tribe, which poisons the ground. Even grass perishes under the fir tribe; these are therefore the worst class of trees for planting under, and the next objectionable is ash when thick. But where the plantation consists of not overcrowded mixtures the generality of these plants will be found to answer, and these trees form the prettiest ordinary home shrubberies if backed with laurustine, common laurel, bay, acuba, &c., and the recesses filled with daffodils, acorus, iris, digitalis, ferns, St. John's-wort, &c., in front; the associations thus combined are also most consistent with nature.

PLANTING IN GENERAL.

ONE rule is practicable for all planting, but not, as inexperienced observers remark, "plant less deep or less shallow than originally," as the one is equally as bad as the other. To sink a plant much below the original landmark would be as detrimental as planting less deep. Let the ball or original landmark be two or three inches (not more, especially for fruit-trees) deeper than the plant was originally, and never under any circumstances tread the soil in tight round a newly planted shrub or tree. When a fruit-tree is planted, trim off all lacerated and broken roots ; cut them back to a sound part ; put some good earth in the middle of the hole (which should be considerably larger than is wanted), so as to form a hillock ; make it moderately firm with the spade ; set the plant on it ; spread the fibrous roots out over this hillock ; they will tend downward as a matter of course over the sides of the hill ; then let an assistant throw some fine soil on to the root ; covering the whole five or six inches in depth. Now take hold of the plant with both hands, striding over the hole, gently lift, and shake the plant, this will admit of the fine soil sifting into the roots, and if the plant is large take a clean, stout stick, with a rounded point, and work some fine soil under the plant, and among the roots, then fill in a little more, and set the heel on in three or four different places nine or ten inches from the stem, merely to fix the plant ; fill up with the remainder of the soil, and let it remain to settle down by degrees ; do not tread the surface of the ground after, let it remain open to admit of sun, air, and water passing down freely for at the least a month or six weeks. If the planting is done late in spring, after five or six inches of fine earth has been put upon the roots, take a four or five gallon pot of water, without the rose, and pour over the roots, holding the pot up so as to give force to the water, this will wash the soil among the roots ; give in this way two or three pots of water, let it remain for ten minutes, then fill up to the top and let it settle. I have transplanted trees of a large size this way very late, without the least disadvantage. On the other hand, plants frequently die off, or make but poor progress, even though they are planted in the best season, when they are trampled in and the soil thus hardened,—and this is not to be wondered at, as the fibre is then excluded from the vital element " oxygen," which if prevented entering the soil the death of the plant must be the result, in consequence of the lifeless state of the aqueous matter, water, and watery matter, that subscribe chiefly to the formation of vegetable life. The surface of the earth being trodden down it is thus rendered non-conductive, and is impervious to both the fertilizing rains and the influence of the sun, the absence of which is detrimental to all vegetable life, but especially so to a newly planted tree. The fibre divested of its functionary organs (spongioles) requires additional assistance to stimulate it to reorganize itself speedily, or all must suffer ; this is best effected by allowing the surface of the soil to be left rough and open to the free reception of heat. All planting is doubtless best done at the nick of time, which is when new organs are about to be formed ; this is at the fall of the leaf in some, and when nature seems to retire to rest in others ; and it is disadvantageous for the formation of new feeders for the roots if after these special times.

Planting plants without roots, such as rose stocks and cuttings, requires different treatment ; these must have the earth made firm about the lower part of the plant or cutting, simply because the air that promotes activity and growth in due proportion to the necessity of the subject of rooted plants destroys or hinders the formation of the base of the root, viz., the "callus," which first forms on the base, and from which proceeds the root. If once the air exerts its full influence upon this, the cutting, or fibreless plant generally perishes, so tender and sensitive is this part of the plant. The chief cause of newly planted trees dying is being "badly planted."

USE OF SAND IN THE SOIL FOR CUTTINGS.

SAND is, or should be, entirely composed of stone ; this being the case, there can be no appreciable amount of nutriment in it ; still some cuttings will not strike root without it, because sand is a conductor of heat and of moisture, or regulates both by preventing too much of the latter settling about the tender callus, and by the free admission of due heat, and allowing a superfluous charge of both to pass off,—retaining a nice proportion ; but soft-wooded plants will strike root without sand, because these possess inherent juices of their own sufficient to sustain them during the time of suspension, that is, while they have no root; besides acting as a non-conductor of the external air proves highly beneficial in striking all hard-wooded cuttings, while using it for the same purpose in striking soft-wooded plants would prove fatal, because their inherent nature is different from that succulent nature which possesses a much larger proportion of sustaining and self-supporting power than hard-wooded cuttings.   Let a cutting of, say a heath, epacris, leucopogon, azalea, myrtle, &c., get once thoroughly dry, and nothing will revive it, or induce it to strike root ; but a cutting of a geranium, fuchsia, begonia, mesembryanthemum, or any soft-wooded plant will, under the same circumstances, quickly recover itself, and from the same condition, except it be one of entire destitution of all vitality.   Sand is useful for rendering soil friable (tender) and more easy to penetrate.   There is no virtue in sand further than in a mechanical sense ; it is a regulator of moisture, renders the soil easily penetrable by the tender fibre, and being of a fine texture, acts as a non-conductor of the external air, almost essential in propagation,—whether hard or soft-wooded sorts.   Hard-wooded cuttings, such as ericas, cannot be grown without sand ; this is owing to the nice regulation of moisture by the sand, which is almost essential to the existence of this tribe.   Hard-wooded cuttings should have a thin layer of fine, pure silver-sand over the top of the pot, say ¼-inch thick or so.   This should be laid evenly on the surface of the soil.   After the cuttings are inserted, and have been watered, let the water drain out for half an hour, then put on the sand evenly, as this will suck up the superfluous moisture, prevent damping off, and the external air penetrating the soil ; but this is not neces_ sary, indeed, it would prove fatal to many soft-wooded cuttings.

THE DIFFERENCE BETWEEN PEAT AND BOG EARTH.

THERE is so much difference between peat and bog earth that the one cannot be substituted for the other.   There is also a good deal of difference in the quality of peat. Thus the peats of Dartmoor are impure, and abound with minerals—mundic, tin, copper, &c. ; so that delicate Ericas, and many particular plants, refuse to flourish in it, while the same class of plants will luxuriate in the peats of Wimbledon Common, Epping Forest—near Highbeach, Wanstead Heath, and Bagshot, and some others.   But of all the peats I ever had anything to do with, that of Epping Forest, near the " Royal Oak," is the best ; this peat is positively highly nutritious ; it will grow cucumbers exceedingly well.   Good peat is something more than so much decayed vegetable matter.   It does not consist of decomposed and half-decomposed layer after layer of vegetable matter ; but it is an original compound earth, of fine pure sand and nutritious loam, salica, lime, &c.   Good peat is soft, and will, if it is half or three-fourths dry, slightly adhere together when taken up in the hand and pressed; it possesses a kindly power of self-adherence, inferior peat is harsh, and disposed to separate under the same circumstances; and the sand of inferior peat is coarse and impure.

Pure peat is found on a sandy gravel for the subsoil, and where the Common Brake grows, — *Pteris aquilina*, the Common Fern, luxuriates generally, and on dry and somewhat elevated localities, but never in low and swampy places, nor super-saturated localities. Many mistake this altogether, and go to swamps and low grounds for their peat because it is black and rich-looking. The colour of peat is no criterion for the quality. Bog earth is not the peat for any except those who grow aquatics, orchids, and ferns,—such as Thelypteris (Lady fern), which would do very well in it,—some sub-aquatics and so on. But, upon the whole, there are few plants indeed that will grow in this kind of peat, as some call it, and none but plants of a similar nature to those I have named will do well in bog earth.

Bog earth is naturally destitute of sand, and if added artificially it cannot introduce purity, except by a lengthened exposure to the sun's influence; and even then it is wanting the properties of good natural peat.

Peat is quite a different thing from bog earth,—the peat of some theorists, who recommend this peat for Rhododendrons, &c.; but neither Rhododendrons nor any other American plants will do well in this kind of peat, if peat it may be called, for mud is a more appropriate term, being a soil that is soured beyond remedy, and fit only for a small number of plants that thrive in it. There is no such thing as making peat good, it must be originally good, or it will be deficient of the necessary quality found in pure peat. Through ignorance of what really good peat is, some recommend what is positively injurious to American and other plants requiring pure peat. To grow Heaths, Rhododendrons, Azaleas, Camellias, &c., well, no reasonable expense should be spared to obtain a load or two of good peat, which, since the introduction of railways, is not now so difficult to obtain. A few sacks of pure peat, sifted through a coarse sieve, would go a long way towards growing heaths, &c., in pots.

CHARCOAL.—Its Uses.

CHARCOAL is very valuable for cleansing purposes; it possesses, like some things infinitely less durable, the power of affecting the unfixed and fixed vapours of the atmosphere, absorbing impurities and imparting a healthy tone. A piece of charcoal, thrown into a boiler containing a piece of slightly decomposed fish or flesh, will have the effect of restoring it to purity; and if some lumps of charcoal are put into a cucumber-frame, or a house, a portion of oxygen will be absorbed by it; and as charcoal is pure carbon, it forms the elementary compound carbonic acid gas, which, being absorbed and digested by the leaves of the plants, becomes a nutritious element, and contributes materially to the increase of the vegetable fabric. As plants give off oxygen again in a pure state, plants and animal life too under the influence of charcoal are naturally more healthy where plants and charcoal abound. Carbon has more influence over oxygen, which more rapidly carbonates in proportion to the quantity of charcoal present, so that confined plants are more benefited than those in the open air. The chemical influence of charcoal is very beneficial over water; its use, therefore, for the soil in which plants grow is of great advantage. In proof of this we have only to visit a spot where earth has been burnt in a field, or some old pits where charcoal has been made, say, fifty years ago; and it will be observed that the herbage and various plants growing there are of a more robust character and better

colour than they are on the land immediately adjoining, which
has not been affected by the charcoal: on an examination
of the charcoal buried there, it will be found that the fibres
have penetrated through the pores, and have wrapped
themselves round the outsides of the charcoal; which is
accounted for by the charcoal carbonating the oxygen and
hydrogen held by it, and thus creating suitable food for
plants, as it contains the most desirable element for the
nutriment of plants.   Charcoal, more than any other substance used for the purpose, also answers for drainage, and
is a congenial means of supplying suitable food,—holding,
as it does, sufficient moisture to sustain the plant longer
than that of anything else.   Ordinary crock-drainage is
good as drainage, but it has no food element in it.   A pot-
plant, in a pot containing small pieces of charcoal for
drainage, would live longer without a fresh supply of water
than in one with broken pot, brick, &c.; which is owing to the
charcoal containing in a liquid state food for the plants, and
it is besides the best possible form of preparation for plants
so situated.   Charcoal, then, in fact, is the happy medium
by which plants are most likely to be benefited, chemically
as well as mechanically.

WHAT MILDEW IS.—Its Effects and Cure.

If all Fungi are of the same nature as mildew, and mildew
is a Fungus, there is still an unsolved mystery connected
with this tribe of plants—if plants they are, viz., their
endurance and generation.   If mildew of any sort and
every sort is the production from seed, where is the root that
produced the seed, since no such thing has appeared in the
locality or on the vines for twenty, or fifty years perhaps?
and where did the seed spring from that produced the
mildew on your clean washed and boiled linen, and the
new sheets?   If mildew is perpetuated and propagated by

seed, how is it that it can be created anywhere and everywhere, and that it will pass through heat enough to dissolve
the woody fibre of vegetation unhurt and unimpaired,
although the tenderest and finest of all seeds.   If mildew is
produced from seed, how extraordinary its power of endurance, vitality, locality, and germination !   If the mushroom,
for instance, possesses seed, and is propagated by that seed,
why does not that seed become more widely diffused? and
why is it, year by year, to be found only in a few isolated
spots—in a field or common? and how can the seed
possibly retain vitality enough to grow after having first
passed through the stomach of a horse, and through fermentation sufficient to scald?   I think it is pretty evident that
if some Fungi are produced by seed, mildew is not.   Then
what is it? and how produced? are questions to be solved
by a different theory from that of propagation by seed.
Mildew is, I think, a disease generated by an impure air,
and some other unknown cause.

    With all our vigilance we cannot always avert mildew,
which is doubtless a disease, from the fact that it always
appears on the parts of a plant already wanting health;
peas and cucumbers, for instance, are first attacked on the
parts becoming inactive; it then proceeds towards the
more healthy parts, choking the organs of respiration,—the
destruction of the plant speedily following its inability to
throw off the surplus acid and watery humours, poisoning
also the surrounding atmosphere in which the plant exists;
thus the vine, peas, cucumber, and other vegetable produce,—hence the necessity of plants having a healthy growing atmosphere.   I once had the care of a greenhouse that
would scarcely grow anything free of mildew, and being
rather an unfavourable aspect it was considered a failure.
I thought otherwise, and commenced the daily application
of pure water with the hand-syringe.   This proved a com-

plete cure, and very soon there was as good a collection of healthy plants in this house as could be seen anywhere. A slow fire should be always kept in a house troubled with mildew, and the syringe used once daily, but the effects of syringing should be removed by drying off the plants quickly, and air admitted whenever at all practicable.

Cold and damp are prolific elements of mildew; pure water and a rapid circulation of the surrounding air are sure preventives, and a certain remedy when infected. When syringing cannot be practised, water impregnated with the fumes of stone brimstone will be found a preventive;—pour ten gallons of boiling water on three or four pounds of stone brimstone, and let it stand for twenty-four hours, then syringe the plants with the clear liquor; pour more hot water on the brimstone, then syringe again : this may be repeated three or four times with the same brimstone. Flour of sulphur may be sprinkled over two or three deep pans containing a pound of quicklime, and set in the house. An ounce, or even half an ounce, is enough for constant daily use. This will give off mild fumes, and in small quantities will be effective, and far better than applying large doses, which often prove destructive to fine and delicate-leaved plants.

THE EFFECTS OF FROST.—How to Recover from.

FROST, as is well known, will penetrate the vitals of every living thing till it perishes. This is not done all at once, but by degrees ; first, it attacks the object in spots—small points like needles : these stop circulation, the juices become coagulated, till by continued action of cold the thickened juices swell, and cause a rupture of the tissues,—rending them asunder. Then when the rays of the sun come to bear upon these parts death ensues, from the fact that these juices solidified, suddenly dissolve and cause a vacuity : the lacerated fibre is then exposed to the influence of a second attack of frost, which quickly destroys the plant by drying up the remaining vitals.   In the case of continued cold, frosty and cutting winds, the life of the plant is dried up by the action of such winds, carrying away all the juices and supplying none, acting precisely in the same way as continued drought upon the leaves and branches.   During continued frost large trees and stones will also burst asunder, in consequence, in the trees, of the dilated condition of the juices, but where there are no juices the frost has no effect ; hence we see the necessity of preventing such circumstances as will place plants likely to be affected by frost in a position for the effectual preservation of the juices.   Plants situated in low grounds, near the sea-shore, and those kept in a stimulated condition during frost or through the winter, are likely to be injured sooner, and with less frost, than those on high grounds and in a drier atmosphere.   The influence of the sun's rays striking the parts of a frozen plant causes the destruction of the plant, or a portion of it, as the same kind of plant placed in a position to avoid the influence of the sun's rays during frost will recover, whilst those plants affected by the sun will perish.   Brocoli would be saved from destruction by frost if carefully covered with Russian mats before the sun fell upon them ; or if some furze or spruce fir branches were put so as to shield them from the sun during frost.   Geraniums and other tender plants are easily recovered from the effects of frost, by shielding them from the influence of the sun, sprinkling them over with cold water, and placing them in a slightly elevated temperature, partially excluding light for a day ; they will then have so far recovered from the frost as to bear on the succeeding day ordinary usage.

ECONOMICAL GLASS FOR EVERY ONE.

THE window, both of the cottage and sitting-room, is adapted for the cultivation of many plants, but in a great number of instances it is difficult or quite impossible to raise many of our most beautiful plants from cuttings or seeds. It is not expected that all will become proficient gardeners, but I do think it possible that all having a sitting-room window may be fully able to raise all the plants required for every window possessed and for small gardens, by simply constructing useful glass frames, which should consist of small hand-lights and a second inner window. The hand-lights are simple enough, and can be made by any one. Take a nine-inch board of deal three quarters of an inch thick, and the length required for such a frame as represented in the margin : two feet by one foot six inches, and nine inches high at back, and five inches in front ; or use a board eleven inches wide, and 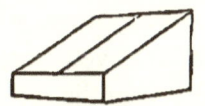 have the back eight inches high, and the front three inches, with one bar in the middle rebated to hold the glass ; or instead of rebating for the glass, nail on a narrow slip as well as on the sides. Thus a most useful light for raising seedlings, for striking cuttings, and growing cucumbers on the ridge may be made for about 1s. 6d. Another useful and almost indispensable kind of glass is that of sliding sashes, of a neat light cantling inside the window ; this forms one of the most useful plant cases possible, and behind which the most delicate exotic ferns, as well as others that will not flourish when exposed to the dust of a living room, may be grown ; and these light sashes may be in pairs to fold hinged on the fillets of the walls, and so turning back as required. There should be a glass

top as a cover, which may be hinged on to the middle half
of the window; and this, if hung so as to admit of the top
dropping down, will be convenient by raising the lower sash for
the admission of air into the room ; and this portable case
will also exclude dust, and prevent a too rapid evaporation
of the moisture, and will be equal to the interior of an
ordinary greenhouse for plant-growing in a small way.

HOW TO MAKE THE MOST OF HEAT.

WHETHER it is for a frame-pit or a house there is one
rule for economizing artificial heat.   The application of
heat is frequently of little use, and sometimes even injurious, for instead of answering the object in view, it
partially frustrates it, and engenders disease.   What is the
cause of mildew, and the host of insect pests ?   I reply,
fluctuating temperatures,—the high temperatures by day
and chills by night.

All plants, whether tender or hardy, will flourish best
in an even temperature.   Something approaching that of
the months of June and July; and this may be largely
accomplished by management.   Such low forcing-houses,
pits, and frames will be of more real benefit by careful
attention to covering up in due time than by keeping
up a strong fire heat; and closing and covering the glass
should be done an hour before the sun withdraws its influence.   This will be the most economical, as less firing and
labour will be required, and cucumbers, melons, or anything
else will luxuriate far better than by any other treatment,
and escape the evils arising from the neglect of these
particulars.   Melons and pine-apples, I feel assured, can be
grown successfully with comparatively little or no other
advantages.   Pines might want some slight heat during the

two or three dull months in midwinter, and melons can by this means be grown and ripened well. Covering up about three inches with dry hay, then with single or double mats, according to the season; and pinning the mats down back and front one hour or hour and a half before sunset is the secret of good success in framing, &c. The application of tepid water to the plants in all cases of forcing, whether of a high or low class temperature, also is most essential; and applying the water in the early part of the day. The temperature of the water should be about the same as the interior of the frame, house, or pit; or the plant will receive a check, and the atmosphere a chill, the fruitful source of disease and pests. Ventilation is another important necessity in plant-growing. Air from the exterior should be admitted into the house under the pipes, tank, or flues if possible, and the superabundant heat allowed to escape at the most elevated point; cold draughts will thus be avoided, fresh air admitted, and the impure air discharged, which, being supplied by the fresh and pure, will keep up the most desirable element for the prevention of disease of every kind. Plants in an impure air are like persons living in contaminated rooms, whose atmosphere engenders fevers and inflammations for the want of personal cleanliness. A pure atmosphere should, therefore, be maintained amongst plants, and the best means should be practised adapted to the nature of the plants; and such, as the results of the experience of many years, I have attempted to give in the foregoing remarks.

THE CAUSE AND EFFECTS OF PLANTS BEING GREEN.

THIS colour is produced by the foliage absorbing proportions of the three primary colours—red, blue, and yellow. The different proportions of these colours produce various shades of green, as seen in a variety of plants; and such as have variegated foliage are either diseased or have changed their functionary organs, and thus assume what belongs to the flower. By the application of art plants may, therefore, be made to assume strong tints of the flower of the identical plant. Green is the most agreeable colour that the eye can look upon without injury. The brighter the light, the deeper the green: a wise provision for man by our great and beneficent Creator, for which we cannot be too grateful.

LIST OF PLANTS SUITED FOR AMATEUR EXHIBITION.

Abbreviations :—g. h., greenhouse ; w, window ; g, ground.

Cineraria.   See Cultivation (g. h. and w.).
Calceolaria.   See Cultivation (g. h. and w.).
Achimenes.   See Cultivation (g. h. and w.).
Tropæolum Jarrattii.   See Cultivation (g. h. and w.).
Geranium, fancy and scarlet in variety.   See Cultivation.
Fuchsia in variety, both (g. h. and w.).
Mesembryanthemum speciosa purpurea (g. h. and w.). See Culture.
Leschenaultzia formosa (g. h.), a really lovely dwarf, freeflowering, scarlet-flowered plant, capable of a handsome growth, and moderate size in an eight-inch pot of good sandy, well-drained peat.   Moderate greenhouse in winter,

and shade in summer ; will strike freely by cuttings, peat, and even bell-glass.

Epacris in variety, very like heaths, but more hardy than many Ericas, and not so difficult to grow (g. h.) ; grow in peat. Stop the shoots frequently to form bushy plants ; keep moderately moist, and feed them once a week with weak liquid manure, and specimens of a large size will soon be formed.

Azalea Indica alba. This is a fine free-flowering and a good-growing variety. Grow in peat, eleven-inch pot, and frequently stop the points of the young shoots. Feed weekly with one ounce guano to one gallon of water, and a fine specimen will very shortly be formed (g. h.). Propagate by cuttings and layers.

Chorozema in variety. This is one of the most lovely genera we possess for exhibition purposes ; fine and hand-some plants of it may be speedily grown in an eleven-inch pot of one-half fibrous pure peat, one-third fibrous loam, and one-fourth sand, and with charcoal interspersed through the whole. Should have good free drainage (g. h.) ; propa-gation-seeds sown in March on heat, and cuttings of half-ripened wood during early summer in fine pure peat and sand under a striking-glass. Stop frequently to form hand-some plants.

Pimelea spectabilis. This plant, when well grown, is one of the most unique things possible to have in a greenhouse, but care must be taken to stop the shoots of the young wood while the plant is young to keep it dwarf. Grow it in pure peat and good drainage.

Plumbago chinensis (g. h. and w.). See Culture.

Kolasanthes miniata (g. h. and w.), a lovely thing, and a plant capable of attaining a large size. Stop frequently, grow in peat and loam, feed once a week with one ounce of guano to one gallon of water from March till after the flowering ; then cut back within two or three buds or joints of the old wood, and water sparingly throughout the winter.

Polygala Dalmaisiana. This plant will attain to a very large size ; it is a free-grower and perpetual flowerer ; has ample foliage, is of a pretty character, with pretty pea-shaped purple flowers. Grow in peat. See Culture.

Erythrina crista-galli. One of the richest and grandest half-hardy, crimson-flowered plants we possess, grow in an eleven-inch pot of peat and loam. Feed it once a week from the time it begins to make new wood till after the flowering season, with one ounce of guano to one gallon of water.

Fabiana imbricata, a lovely, free-flowering plant, and tolerably hardy. Propagate by seeds and cuttings ; use sandy peat under a bell-glass (g. h. and w.).

Pultenæa stricta, a very pretty yellow-flowered evergreen shrub from New Holland. Grow in equal parts peat and loam, using good drainage.

Genista Canariensis, a most lovely, yellow-flowered, and profuse-blooming half-hardy shrub, capable of becoming a handsome and large plant by growing it in an eleven-inch pot of good sandy loam, stopping frequently and feeding weekly with half an ounce of guano to one gallon of water (g. h. and w.).

Lisianthus Russelliana and nigrescens. The last of these is nearly black-flowered, of thin foliage, and with free-flowering character ; which is presented in a very pretty style—similar to that of the fuchsia. The seed should be sown in the beginning of March on the surface of pots filled with one-half maiden loam, one-fourth peat, and one-fourth leaf-mould and some silver sand. Make the compost fine, fill the pot up first, using good drainage, and put a layer of moss over to prevent the soil running among the crocks. Water the soil with a fine rose water-pot ; let it stand for half an hour. Sow the fine seed over the surface; cover very slightly; set in a brisk heat, and cover with a flat square of glass, to prevent the earth drying. As soon as they are large enough, pot off singly into small sixties. Keep them in a moist heat, and give liberal waterings; the next season they will be fine specimens if kept in a good warm greenhouse throughout the winter, in good lively heat during the spring, and if grown in an eleven-inch pot and fed well (g. h.).

Bouvardia longiflora, white, Hogarth's and Laura, salmon and pink (g. h. and w.). See Culture.

Siphocampylus lantanifolius, coccineus, two very fine varieties of a lovely genus, free to grow and flower in nine-inch pots of loam and peat; noble plants for pots (g. h.).

Senecio (double groundsel), purple and crimson. This is particularly suited for cottage cultivation and for exhibition; as it is capable of growing to a good medium size, is of easy cultivation, and a free flowerer; may be raised from seed and propagated by cuttings. Grow in loam and leaf-mould; stop and train early to any desirable shape (g. h. and w.).

Petunia, double varieties, General Havelock, crimson; Dr. Lindley, crimson; Antigone, white; and many others, double and single. This is a fine class of plant for decorative and exhibition purposes; a class at once easy to grow, free to flower, and capable of growth to any desirable size. Propagate by cuttings on a gentle heat during spring, or under a bell-glass in the summer. Grow it in six or nine-inch pots of maiden loam two parts, pulverized dung one part, leaf-mould and sand, one part; stop the young shoots frequently to induce dwarf and well-filled handsome plants: train neatly. Give a weekly watering with weak liquid manure, $\frac{1}{4}$ ounce of guano to one gallon of water, and not more than $\frac{1}{2}$ ounce to the gallon (g. h. and w.).

Begonia Rexii, a fine-foliaged plant. B. fuchsiodes, an

exquisite crimson-flowered species. This last requires a warm greenhouse in the winter, to be grown in peat and leaf-mould, well-drained, and but little water through the winter, and to be fed with half an ounce of guano to one gallon of water once a week through the summer (g. h. and w.).

Bignonia radicans and picta. This last is very pretty and beautiful, with its lilac striped flowers. If grown in pots, they must be eleven or thirteen-inch. A good cylindrical trellis, four or five feet high, should be provided, and the plant may be trained to wind round this. The first-mentioned is hardy.

Verbenas are exceedingly good things for exhibition purposes. Choose free flowering sorts. Grow them in six-inch pots; stop them frequently; feed with liquid manure. Keep down the insects. Train to a trellis adequate to the object in view, and grow freely (g. h. and w.).

There are a number of other things capable and equally worthy of growing for special purposes, most of which have been treated upon in the preceding pages, under the heads heads " Plants for the Window," " Plants for the Flower-Garden," " Annuals for Garden," &c.

In growing flowers for cut blooms for show purposes, or for fine specimens, such as Hollyhocks, Chrysanthemums, Campanulas, Dahlias, Perennial Phloxes, Antirrhinums, Delphiniums, Roses, Pentstemons, Lilies, Wallflowers, Stocks, &c. (nearly all of which have been treated of), it is requisite to give the plants additional room and good soil to grow in. They should be fed once a week with from one ounce to two ounces of guano to one gallon of water; commencing with this liquid water manure as soon as the flower-buds appear; thin out the stems and flowers if size of flower is the object desired. Some plants will take two or three years to form good specimens, while others will only take two or three months to do so. Roses, Azaleas, Rhododendrons, Heaths, Epacris, Chorozemas, Leschenaultzia, &c., will require from two to five years to form good bold specimens; while fast-growing things, as Fuchsias, Geraniums, Balsams, Tropæolums, Dahlias, Chrysanthemums, Petunias, &c., will form fine specimens, and produce flowers for exhibition purposes within twelve months,—in fact, in varying periods from two or three months to twelve. A great deal depends upon the manner of growing them; the rules laid down here will be about as quick a way as possible of producing the result. By growing these flowers in suitable soil, giving attention to watering, stopping free growing by the necessary heat required by some, cleanliness, stimulating in due time by the liquid manure prescribed for each kind, and by training, &c., fine specimens may be obtained in a much less time than by indifference.

CALENDAR OF WEEKLY OPERATIONS FOR THE YEAR.

JANUARY.

THE FLOWER GARDEN.—1, 2, and 3. During these three weeks continue to make whatever alterations and improvements are necessary,—such as laying lawns, making new gravel walks, digging vacant ground, making new beds and borders; every week sweep and roll the lawn and the gravel walks, after heavy rains. Dig flower-beds and borders deep, and leave the ground rough to pulverize; manure the beds and borders, as required, with rotten dung, maiden loam, peat, or leaf-mould, according to the nature of the land. Plant Roses, and prune them, if of the hardy kinds, and climbing sorts. Prune deciduous shrubs. Plant deciduous shrubs and common Laurel, and plant Box edging, if the weather be open. Land-drain the lawn if needful, and dress it with good old dung and fine sand, if mossy. 3. Sow some hardy annuals, to flower early in warm and sheltered spots.

The Frames.—Every attention must be paid to these humble structures at this time of the year. Where plants are kept for bedding purposes, admit air on all occasions of mild weather; give water sparingly, and dry the plants off as quickly as practicable, by admitting all the air possible, and carefully cover the frames up during cold nights. 3 and 4. Put in some cuttings of Calceolarias, Fuchsias, Geraniums, Neirembergias, Heliotrope, and any plants that are much in demand; and sow a little Balsam, Coxcomb Globe amaranth, on heat; and some Ten-week Stocks and Nemophila in cold frames in pans, for early flowering, and to succeed the autumn sowing for pots.

The Greenhouse.—The Cinerarias must have every attention,—by frequent syringing, occasional fumigating, and water and air. The Pelargoniums are very quiet; stop them as they advance, water sparingly, smoke them frequently, and admit air freely. Give the Camellias, Epacrises, Mignonette, and Primulas, liquid manure, and keep the air of the house healthy by keeping the fires on; close early, and guard against severe frost.

The Forcing-house or Pit.—This includes either of those structures where a higher degree of heat is kept up for bringing into flower, or to use the plants and fruits most wished for. Grapes, Cucumbers, Pine-apples, Melons, Rhubarb, Roses, Azaleas, Geraniums, Rhododendrons, Genistas, Pimelias, Narcissus, Stocks, &c., all of which may be easily forced, and brought early into flower and perfection by introducing them into these structures during this month ; but it should be borne in mind that all the flowering plants must be established at the least one season previous to their being brought into these departments; and many will force year after year if not driven too sharp, by too high a heat. A gentle rise of the temperature is necessary till it reaches 70° or 75°, falling at night to 60°. Avoid giving much water at first, and then always use tepid, and frequently syringe such as are coming into leaf with tepid water, and let it be pure. Do this in the morning; admit air by opening the house a little at top, and with the fire kept up the damp will soon be driven off. Keep some sulphur in very small quantities laid on some lime in the house or pit; the fumes will thus almost insensibly arise and circulate over the house, and prevent the progress of insect pest, and do no harm to the plants; this is far safer and better than to leave the pests alone till they form an overwhelming army, and then administer a remedy in large doses. Keep some good lumps of camphor in bags hung on the walls of the forcing-house. Give liquid manure as the plants advance. Propagate Roses, Daphnes, and Orange-plants by grafting, by seed, and by cuttings; and propagate whatever is most in request early.

THE KITCHEN-GARDEN.—During the whole month watch every opportunity for wheeling dung on during the frost; trench and rough dig all the vacant ground, fork over the ground between the rows of gooseberries, raspberries, and fruit-trees; plant and prune apples, pears, plums, and vines. Prune and train peaches, nectarines, and apricots; sow a few early beans and peas, plant some early frame and ash-leaved potatoes, and sow some of Wood's early frame radish upon them. Take up rhubarb and seakale for forcing; and cover them; sow mustard and cress once a week on heat.

FEBRUARY.

THE FLOWER-GARDEN.—The continuation of last month's work must be proceeded with in this department, and whatever alterations and planting is necessary in the way of free-growing shrubs, roses, &c., must be proceeded with as rapidly as possible. 3, 4, plant ranunculus, hyacinths, tulips, narcissus, anemone, lilies, &c., fork up beds of these that have been planted two or three months since. Sow a few hardy annuals and transplant hardy perennials.

The Frames. Plants in frames must be carefully looked after, by giving air freely and water cautiously. Remove all decayed leaves from the auriculas, pansies, calceolarias, picotees, &c., &c., and as regards bedding plants, the observations for last month are good here. "Frames," it will be observed, may and do consist of two classes, viz., "cold" and "warm." Thus when I remark upon the propagation of anything half-hardy under this head, I mean "warm frames," and when I mention auriculas and pansies, &c., &c., I mean "cold frames."

The Greenhouse.—The cinerarias must be well looked after now, and kept clean. The primulas will be in full flower now, and must have a weekly application of liquid manure. Some of the geraniums may be shifted and stopped for the last time if medium flowering is the object. Keep this house as cool as is safe for the well-being of the inmates ; give all the air possible and room for the plants, so that air and light can come at them.

The Forcing-house.—The last month's remarks are applicable here, except that some of the plants in flower must be hardened off by first removing them to the coldest part of the house and set on the floor for twenty-four hours, and then removing to the warmest part of the greenhouse or conservatory ; and the propagation of bedding and other plants gone into with more energy. A brisk energetic heat must be kept up in the cucumber and grape houses.

THE KITCHEN-GARDEN.—Last month's observations must be finished out as speedily as possible as regards dunging and digging, planting and pruning. Sow beans, peas, radish, carrot, and lettuce on a warm border; celery, brocoli, Brussels sprouts, and cabbage, the celery and brocoli in pans on heat. 3 and 4, transplant some beans and peas to a warm border, and sow some parsley; cover and uncover daily the early sown radish, using some old hay, oat straw, or ferns. The radishes in frames will require liberal waterings, and all the air possible. The rhubarb and seakale in the forcing-house must be daily supplied with good cold water syringings, and be secured against light. 4, proceed with gooseberry pruning, and train espalier and wall trees.

MARCH.

THE FLOWER-GARDEN.—Take your memorandum-book and go over this department and number and note what you intend to fill each bed with. Carefully study the subject, and calculate upon the number of plants each bed will take to fill it, so as to insure perfectly full beds before half the season is gone. How the beds are to be filled should be decided in all cases this month, and then proceed to propagate accordingly; and if annuals of a half-hardy and hardy nature are to share in the display, these must be sown where they are to flower, many of them at once. Perennials must be planted, taken up, divided, and replanted. All kinds of trees and shrubs must be finally planted, and all pruning finished. Late-planted shrubs should be watered a few times; the lawn must be well rolled and swept, and a slight sowing of soot may be made over it if poor. Dress each bed or border with the peculiar kind of soil, leaf-mould, or dung best suited to the plant that is to occupy it. The spring flowers and those that are advancing apace may require some water at this time ; be careful to avoid washing down the surface of such beds ; water early in the morning, and holding the rose of the water-pot as close to the surface of the ground as convenient, let the water fall as softly as possible, and when the bed is dry slightly prick the surface over with a fine-pronged fork before watering again. Give some liquid manure to those coming into flower.

The Frames.—The auriculas will be advancing to flower,— give some liquid manure. Sow German and English ten-week stocks, auricula, carnation, antirrhinum, asters, choice phlox, dianthus, anemone, campanulas, delphiniums, poly-anthus, potentillas, pansies, &c., in seed-pans in the cold frames. All kinds of half-hardy bedding stuff must be pro-pagated briskly in the frames engaged with heat. Balsams, coxcombs, petunias, *Humea elegans*, thunbergias, egg-plant, mimosa, *Primula sinensis*, lobelias, ice-plant, marigold, gail-lardia, portulacca, zinnias, and all sorts of tender and half-hardy annuals may be sown and introduced into this department, where 65° or 70° are maintained. (See direc-tions for sowing.) Be careful to protect the seed-pans from the sun's full rays, and use the dew-pot with tepid water.

The Greenhouse.—This department will now be in full display, with cinerarias, camellias, azaleas, and many of the plants from the forcing department. Shift the geraniums, calceolarias, mesembryanthemums, and whatever stands in need of a larger pot, and propagate freely those that are wanting. Some early cuttings of geranium may be struck for strong and early plants and for specimens, stopping them as they advance in growth, and not allowing them to flower. Give liberal waterings during the mornings, plenty of good air, and close early. Look to the insect enemies, and avoid cold cutting winds. Shade with tiffany or some thin light canvas during hot sunny days.

The Forcing-house.—This is a trying time for delicate plant-structures,—cold nights, and often a rapid and fluctuating day-heat, in consequence of the sun's power, which raises the temperature of this department 20° or 30° in an hour or two. Slack the fire the first thing in the morning when the day is likely to be a sunny one. A rise of 10° or 15° during the day is of no consequence ; in fact, it is natural. Open the top of the house only, when cold winds exist. The propagation of all kinds of plants must go on briskly. The cucumber and vine houses will require frequent syringing with tepid clean water, careful ventilation, vigilant watching of the insect enemies, and vigorous means applied at this time of the year to prevent them increasing. Shade the cucumber-house and pit during bright sunny days with coarse gauze or fine netting. Give liquid manure to those plants in flower and coming into flower. Sow exotic shrub and flower seeds, and propagate gesnerias, gloxinias, and achimenes by seed, by leaves, and by offsets.

THE KITCHEN-GARDEN.—This is a most important month with the gardener. 1 and 2. Finish all pruning and training, fork the asparagus beds over, rake them down, and make new beds ; sow seed, and continue to introduce plants for forcing. The early batches of seakale may have their coverings removed, and rhubarb may be watered for the first time with liquid manure. Sow seakale, and make new plantations ; sow peas, and plant out those sown in December and January, likewise beans ; sow cabbage, and plant those sown in the autumn ; sow lettuce, and plant out those sown in September ; sow brocoli, and plant out cauliflower : sow onion, and pant out the autumn sowing ; sow a little Dutch turnip and turnip radish ; sow celery, and prick out those sown in February ; sow drumhead savoy and Brussels sprouts ; sow the London leek and the main crop of parsnips ; sow early horn carrot on a warm border ;

sow round spinach once a fortnight from 3 and 4 through the summer; plant shallots and garlick, and the early frame ash-leaved and fluke kidney potatoes. 3 and 4, sow ridge cucumber, melon, tomato, basil, and ice-plant on heat; sow carraway, dill, thyme, savory, summer and winter, chicory, borage, and all kinds of potherbs on fine light soil, and transplant the same ; give some liquid manure to the winter spinach and the early lettuce.

APRIL.

THE FLOWER-GARDEN.—Last month's operations in this department may be repeated and continued during the month, and every precaution should be taken to prevent lack of perfect display through the summer.

The Frames.—The same may be said of this department as was remarked for March; shading, air, and water must be attended to.

The Greenhouse.—Continue the same operations, precautions, and applications necessary to prevent the progress of the enemy, and for the advancement of beauty, as were noted last month under this head.

The Forcing-house.—The observations made for last month under this head hold good in April also. Cucumbers and grapes will require a good amount of stimulant in the form of vapour, careful ventilation, and feeding, with a timely application of the insecticide, remembering that "prevention is better than cure." During ' and 3 the sowing of all kinds of exotic tree, shrub, and flower seeds belonging to this department should be finished.

THE KITCHEN-GARDEN.—No time must be lost in finishing the work of sowing the main crops of brocolis, kales, savoys, carrots, parsnips, leeks, onions, cabbages for autumn use ; also cabbage, lettuce, parsley, beet, beans, and marrow peas—Champion of England, six feet; British Queen, seven to nine feet, a fine pea; Woodford Green Marrow, five feet, a small pea, of a beautiful green when cooked, fine flavour, a great bearer. Sow also green Windsor beans and some early dwarf French in pots, or at the foot of a south wall; sow also celery, and plant a little out from the first sowings. 3, 4, keep the melon vines thinned out, and sow seed for successional crops; also ridge, cucumber, gourds, and marrows.

MAY.

THE FLOWER-GARDEN.—3 and 4, commence bedding out some of the hardiest of the plants, such as scarlet geraniums, verbenas, calceolarias, nierembergia, and then follow on with those more tender, taking the precaution to harden all half-hardy plants off before bedding them out, by first removing them from the smallest amount of heat to a cold frame for a fortnight at the least. In bedding out plants advantage should be taken of the soil when it is half dry, so that it will admit of inserting the ball as it comes from the pot, without the earth falling into the hole made to receive it; this is best done with the hand, unless in the case of larger plants. The surface of the bed should be made fine and light to the depth of five or six inches, to admit of easy insertion. Plant the German ten-week Stocks out before they get carroty-rooted. The annuals sown in the beds in March should be thinned, if necessary —that is, they should not be too thick—say from two to three inches asunder, according to sort.

The Frames.—Cold frames are the most useful things a garden can possess for raising some of the choicer hardy perennials by seed, as well as annuals of a less hardy nature, and for hardening off tender ones. Shade newly pricked out seedlings in seed pans, give air to established seedlings, water carefully, and close an hour before sunset. Admit air freely night and day to those less tender bedding plants in these frames, preparatory to bedding out.

The Greenhouse.—Many of the inmates of this department will have made room for Calceolarias, Geraniums, Leschen-aultzia, Tropæolum, Fuchsias, &c., when they can be grown out—that is, more producing fine specimens. Often turn such as require to be grown symmetrically ; tie up neatly to sticks such as require it. The Greenhouse, or Conservatory as some call it, should present a neat and gay appearance. Give air freely by day ; close an hour before sunset, water freely in the morning, and fume the house at night on the least sign of the enemy. Remove from the house all the Cinerarias out of flower, and set under a north wall.

THE KITCHEN-GARDEN.—Sow more Peas and Windsor Beans—Green Windsor and Green Long-pods. Sow Dwarf Kidney and Scarlet Runner Beans ; sow the main crop of Crimson Beet and Carrot ; sow Drumhead Cabbage Lettuce, and Silver-skin Onion, thick, for pickling ; sow Turnip, and Turnip Radish ; sow during 3 and 4 some Asiatic Cauli-flower, and plant out Savoy ; make one more sowing of celery, and trench out the plants sown in February ; sow Gherkin seed, and ridge out the Cucumbers, Gourds, and Marrows ; give the Asparagus some liquid manure,—the Rhubarb also ; and well water the strawberries setting fruit, and follow up closely the nipping off the runners. Sow Spinach every two or three weeks, and small Salad once a week. Sow early Colewort in 4. Plant out Capsicum and Tomato at the foot of a south wall.

JUNE.

THE FLOWER-GARDEN.—1 and 2. Finish quickly all bedding out to be done. Take up any early bulbs that are matured, which is known by the leaf becoming yellow, and fill these beds with bedding stuff, as the *Phlox Drummondii*, petunia, verbena, &c. Commence pegging these down, and stop the leaders, to induce a rapid filling of the bed. Everything should present a neat and finished appearance by the middle of the month. Some newly set plants may require water; one or two soakings will be better than half a dozen sprinklings. The lawn will require mowing, sweeping, and rolling every fortnight. Lawns should not be cut down into the heart of the grass, as this exposes the root too much to the influence of the sun, and frequently causes bald spots and thinness of sward. Clip box edgings during the month.

The Frames.—Continue to prick out seedlings, and sow cineraria and calceolaria ; the former in the cold frame, and the latter on a slight heat. Pot off the *Primula sinensis*, and encourage the *Campanula pyramidalis* and the *Humea elegans*. These three will do better in shallow cold frames than they will anywhere else through the summer. Put in some cuttings of pompone chrysanthemum for miniature plants.

The Greenhouse will be gay with geraniums and calceolarias, which will still require attention as regards shading, feeding, and defending from the attacks of aphides. Admit all the air possible above and below ; keep the house cool ; this will prolong the flowering season of the inmates. Turn all the camellias, azaleas, and orange plants out, and set them in some sheltered spot for the summer ; the orange full in the sun, and the camellias under a north wall. Feed the orange trees every week with manure water ; shift those specimen plants requiring it ; stop, and feed them.

THE KITCHEN-GARDEN.—1. Sow dwarf beans and scarlet runners, turnips, the main batch of double parsley, colewort cabbage, more peas, and some Paris cos and drumhead cabbage lettuce. 2 and 3. Sow some early cabbage, and plant out that sown in the spring ; likewise the Brussels sprout, savoy, kale, autumn brocoli, and celery. Hoe and thin the crops of carrot, turnip, onion, summer lettuce, &c., and feed the strawberries swelling off and in fruit ; follow up closely the work of nipping off strawberry runners. Discontinue cutting asparagus to the same extent, now that peas are in. Thin the wall-fruit, and nail the young wood in.

JULY.

THE FLOWER-GARDEN.—Pegging down and occasional watering, mowing, and keeping everything in a neat and healthy appearance is all that is to be done here during this month, except budding roses, which should go on.

The Frames.—The instructions given respecting last month may be repeated this, except that little or no sowing of seeds will be necessary.

The Greenhouse.—The same may be said of this department as was remarked last month, as far as display and the preliminary observations and cautions necessary for the prolongation of floral beauty go. Good gardening consists not so much in doing everything mechanically well at the time, as in thoughtful anticipation and pre-arrangement. Some tact may be necessary soon to keep up the required display in the greenhouse department, therefore make provision in due time. The Achimenes, Leschenaultzia, Liliums, Chimney Campanulas, Tropæolums, Kalosanthus, Shrubby Calceolaria, Scarlet Geranium, Fuchsias, Tea Roses, Petunias, Mesembryanthemums, and some annuals will supply the place of the Pelargoniums and Calceolarias, and keep the house gay till the autumn.

THE KITCHEN-GARDEN.—This is rather a quiet month for the garden ; chiefly what has to be done is the sowing of dwarf beans, a few of the early peas for a late autumn crop, some cabbage for the earliest spring crop—such as the West Ham, East Ham, Shilling's Queen, or Atkins's Matchless. This last is an exceeding good sort for small gardens, being very dwarf, early, and of excellent quality. Sow any of these during 2 and 3. The Hams and Queen will produce very early cabbages, and the Matchless will form late coleworts, or earlier cabbage still, if it does not run to seed. Hoe and thin the crops of carrot, onion, parsnip, turnip, &c., and plant celery, brocoli, kale, savoy, endive, &c. Keep the hoe going among all crops to keep drought out of the ground, if dry weather continues; and if wet and good growing weather, the hoe must be going to keep the weeds down.

AUGUST.

THE FLOWER-GARDEN.—This month in some respects may be said to resemble the early spring; the foundation for the ensuing season must be laid during this month by propagating according to necessity, and by cutting down some plants, and thoroughly ripening the wood of all. This applies both to those plunged in pots, and to those intended to be preserved. But the permanent inmates of the flower-garden must be carefully attended to 1 and 2, such as the layering of carnations and picotees, and the piping of the same, as well as pinks. 2 and 3. Make cuttings of phloxes, verbenas, scarlet geraniums, petunias, Nierembergia, lobelia, pentstemon, gazania, alonsoa, mesembryanthemum, &c. The dividing of auricula, polyanthus, and primrose roots, and re-potting and planting should be done during this month, that they may get re-established before winter. 1 and 2. Proceed briskly with rose-budding, 2 and 3. Sow Nemophila insignis on some warm spot; likewise candytuft and Virginian stock for early flowering should they survive the winter.

The Frames.—The primulas, cineraria, calceolaria, &c., must be carefully propagated to preserve sorts; and seedlings must be shifted from the smaller to a size larger pots, and kept in a frame facing the north during this and the preceding month. Cold frames are the most useful things for this kind of work. The propagation of shrubby calceolarias by cuttings may commence; likewise that of China tea-roses by cuttings. The mignonette for winter flowering must be sown from 2 to 3. Sow some ten-week and intermediate stocks 1 to 2 for potting, three in a six-inch pot for forcing by and bye, and for turning out in early spring. Be nice in the choice of seed for this purpose. (See the Cultivation of the Stock.) The geraniums that have done flowering some time, and those that are later, should be cut back to a bud or two. Cut as close to the pot and as symmetrically as possible, to form handsome, bushy plants. Put the plants back into five or six-inch pots, using good loam and leaf-mould, shaking all the old soil out first, and place them in the cold frame facing the south from 1 to 2.

The Greenhouse.—Continue to feed the pots of Achimenes, Mesembryanthemum, Tropæolum, Thunbergias (a pretty creeper), Fuchsias, Begonia fuchsiodes, Hoya carnosa, Liliums, and whatever there is likely to continue in flower for some time. Turn out those that cease flowering and that will bear it, and replace them with others in flower. Air may be admitted day and night during this and last month. The kalosanthus may be cut back close as soon as out of flower, and subjected to heat, and the cuttings struck, and cuttings of Leschenaultzia, Pimelea, Plumbago Capensis, &c., struck, and some Schizanthus retusus and Grandiflorus oculatus seed sown. These will make most lovely objects in summer. The balsams and cockscombs will require good feeding with liquid manure.

The Forcing-house will require attention in ripening the fruit. The new parts of the flowering plants will need cautious watering, and the house must be kept free from damps and chills. Give water in the early morning. Drive off the damp by fire-heat during dull days: close early during the weeks of 3 and 4. Cut back any plants that require it.

THE KITCHEN-GARDEN requires steady forethought and prompt action in a few most important items during this month, the omission of which will tell sadly upon good gardening in this department. Close attention must be given to seedling Cos Lettuce, Cauliflower plants, Ham Cabbage, autumn-sown Onions for transplanting the following March and April, a good bed of prickly Spinach, Land-cress, some Cucumbers for bearing at Christmas, and plenty of Mushrooms, all of which must be provided this month; therefore sow from two to three of all these, and propagate the Cucumber by cuttings;—Cuthill's Black-spine and Lord Kenyon's Favourite, White-spine, are two good ones for winter: I prefer Cuthill's; it is a most abundant bearer. Propagate by cuttings, or seed on heat, and get the plants on as fast as possible. Make good mushroom-beds, or fill some plots and boxes with short dung and horse-droppings fresh from the stable, and spawn (see *Culture*). 1, 2. Plant out the June-sown cabbage for Coleworts, trench out Celery, and earth up that planted in June, plant out Endive, sow some olive-shaped Radish, plant out the last batch of Brocoli, plant out strong Strawberry-plants, and continue to nip off all the runners.

SEPTEMBER.

THE FLOWER-GARDEN.—The garden requires but little attention at this time, beyond looking on, removing some shabby occupants, keeping things as neat as possible, gathering any choice seed, and preserving it in paper bags, and striking cuttings of Calceolaria, Petunia, Heliotrope,

Salvia, and Verbena; continue to peg Chrysanthemums down in beds, and neatly nail those in that are growing against fences, walls, &c. Bedding plants that have done flowering, &c., may be removed at once, and their places supplied with dwarf plants of late-struck Chrysanthemum, Tea Roses, Hydrangea, Guernsey and Belladonna Lilies, Autumnal Crocus, and various shrubs; Carnation and pink pipings and layers may be planted out, and Hollyhocks propagated by cuttings of the stems eight or ten inches long, and by the offsets. 2 and 3. Sow hardy annuals; plant early bulbs, such as Crocus, Snowdrops; and take up and pot any favourites of the Geranium, Fuchsia, Calceolaria, Senecio, &c., before frost gets hold of them.

The Frames.—The cuttings in this department, on heat, will require daily attention. Newly inserted cuttings will require shading during the mid-day sun, and uncovering as soon as the full influence of the sun is passed off. Air must be admitted to those which have already struck root, and those that are fully rooted should be potted off into small pots—small and large sixties being generally large enough. The Cinerarias should be shifted into six or eight inch pots, and the Pelargoniums into five-inch pots. Herbaceous Calceolarias should be potted into forty-eights and large sixties to pass the winter in. Cinerarias must be put into pots proportionate to the object in view, and kept either out of doors, as long as there is no danger of frost, or in cold frames, as these do much better in a cool temperature than in a heated one ; frequently syringe them. The seedling Calceolarias must be kept in a sharp-angled cold frame, and carefully watered ; no syringing. This is the very best time in the whole year to strike shrubby Calceolarias. The stage Auriculas and Primulas must be shifted into their flowering-pots, and the Neapolitan Violets potted from the nursery-bed into six-inch pots, or bedded into a frame during 3 and

4. The pots of mignonette must be continued in cold frames, thinned out to three plants in a pot, and carefully watered ; close the frame early in the evening ; give abundant air during the day, and get them on strong. Shift Tea-scented China Roses on their own roots into their flowering-pots, *i. e.*, five or six inch, and make cuttings of the same. 3 and 4. Pot some early flowering bulbs, such as Cyclamen, Scillas, Lily of the Valley, Hyacinths, Crocuses, Snowdrops, and early tulips.

The Greenhouse will still continue gay with Lilies, Fuchsias, Coxcombs, late Balsams, Begonias, Shrubby Calceolarias, Scarlet Geraniums, and the *Campanula pyramidalis*, which feed, Tea Roses, Guernsey and Belladonna Lilies, and early dwarf pompone Chrysanthemums, and some of that singular plant, *Tigrida pavonia* and *conchiflora*, a bulbous plant (see "Culture"). As the Achimenes begin to fail in flowering, the liquid manure must be discontinued, and less water must be given. This observation holds good with reference to all the plants that have nearly done flowering. Keep the house cool, dry, and airy.

The Forcing-house must be kept quiet, dry, and with a nice circulating low fire-heat, to ripen the new parts and to keep off chills during the cold nights and dull days. This is all that is required here, except in cases of late cucumber and melon growing, and bringing early plants on : then an active growing heat will be necessary.

THE KITCHEN-GARDEN.—1 and 2. Plant out the June-sown Colewort and early Spring Cabbage, some early Lettuce and late Celery, and continue to plant Strawberry-plants and nip off all the runners ; hoe turnips and earth up celery. Dig potatoes, and lay out in the sun those that are for seed, so as to harden and induce to earliness. Blanch Endive, and pull Onions, and lay them out to dry. 3, 4. Thin prickly Spinach out to six or eight inches asunder, and plant Cauliflower plants into frames at the foot of a south wall, or under hand-lights, and some in pots for forcing. Make mushroom-beds, and fill boxes and pots with droppings, and spawn them for the cellar or to be forced in the cool end of the forcing-pit or house under the pit. Gather seed and fruit carefully; also pick and carefully select young French beans for preserving. Make hot-beds for winter Cucumbers, and gather Gherkins, Silver-skin Onions, and Nasturtiums, for pickling. Cut Red Cabbage and pull crimson Beet for pickling. Make another sowing of the Olive Radish, plant Rhubarb and Seakale roots, and make cuttings of Gooseberry (this will save a year). Cut potherbs for drying, if not done last month.

OCTOBER.

The Flower-Garden.—It is desirable to keep up a continual display, as far as possible, in this department. The ordinary course is not to wait for mere remnants of summer beauties, but proceed to pull up those flowers that are fading. Clear the beds, dress them with a good coat of loam and pit or road sand in equal parts, and fork the ground over spade-deep, well mixing and breaking the soil fine; then commence filling them with bulbs according to taste (see " The Dutch Garden "). Plant out Pinks, Picotees, Carnations, Hepaticas, Polyanthus, Roses, Phloxes, Shrubs, and Box edging. Continue to propagate whatever is desirable by cuttings; there are few old plants worth saving.

The Frames will require the same care as they did last month. 2 and 3. Finish potting off Calceolaria, Cineraria, and all bedding plants. The pots of mignonette must be removed to the warm house, and the early Cinerarias to the ordinary greenhouse; frequently syringe them with clean water, and look sharp after insects.

The Greenhouse may be filled with the Cinerarias Primulas, Geraniums. The Camellias must be brought in, as well as the Epacris and Oranges. The bedding plants in general must be placed in their winter quarters this month. The pots and baskets of Achimenes must be dried off thoroughly by exposing them to the full influence of the sun, and then stored away in some warm, dry, airy room, or somewhere in the forcing-house free from drips. The same instruction applies to the Gesnerias. The *Tropæolum Jarrattii* must be dried off and stored away in silver sand in a cool room. The greenhouse should be either painted or lime-washed previous to housing the plants, and fumed with strong sulphur, first removing every plant out of it for a night. House the plants, admitting all the air possible by day, and thus gradually adapting the plants to the house. Moderate fires will be necessary in damp weather during the day, and low fire-heat at night to ward off frost and chills. Avoid overcrowding and preserve bright light by clean glass.

The Forcing-house.—Last month's observations are applicable also to this month. The Mignonette, Double Ten Week Stocks, Double Walls, Early Tea Roses, Lily of the Valley, Perpetual Clove, Cyclamen, Tuberous Sweet-scented Geranium, and a few Camellias, Epacris, and early Azaleas may be introduced toward the end of the month.

THE KITCHEN-GARDEN.—1 and 2. Plant out Spring Cabbage, Cos Lettuce, and prick out Cauliflower. Thin and hoe late Turnips and Spinach ; make one more sowing of the Olive Radish on a warm border ; earth up Celery, and tie up Endive; plant Rhubarb (2, 3), and take up a few strong roots for forcing ; plant Gooseberries and Raspberries ; take up Carrots, Beet, and late Potatoes; top-dress Strawberries; cover a few strong crowns of early Seakale with pots, and two parts leaves and one part hot dung, well mixed.   Introduce some good lumps of fresh charcoal into the Cucumber-bed frame, and cover up one hour before sunset.   Frame full-grown Endive, using cold frames for this.

NOVEMBER.

THE KITCHEN-GARDEN.—1 and 2. Commence forcing Seakale and Rhubarb in earnest, and finish earthing up Celery.   Sow a few early Radish in a frame on a slight heat, and give all the air possible to Cauliflowers in frames. Sow small salad in seed-pans, and set on heat.   Make a sowing of early Peas and Beans on warm borders.   Commence planting new gardens, also fruit-trees of all classes, as speedily as possible.   Un-nail wall trees, prune Raspberries, and dig the ground between the rows with a three-pronged potato-fork, having previously dunged it and tied the canes up.   Augment the heat, and maintain from seventy to seventy-five degrees in the cucumber house, pit, or frame, and carefully cover at night with dry hay, and then with mats ; hang on a few bags of fine muslin filled with camphor on the walls of the house, pit, or frame ; and use the charcoal freely.   Always use tepid water, and give air cautiously.   A half-ounce of sweet nitre put into a pint of hot water, dissolved, and then diluted with eight quarts of tepid soft water, and made to go over thirty square yards of the surface, will be found exceedingly good for cucumber-growing, and be a preventive against insects.   Measure the surface of your bed, and apply as many half-pints as there are square yards therein once a month or six weeks. It is a fine stimulant, but must not be given too strong. 2 to 4. Cut the runaway Asparagus down close to the surface, and cover the beds with five or six inches of good rotten dung, leaves, and sand ; take up some five or six year old plants, trim them, and place them in 65 or 70 degrees of bottom heat, bedding them in six or eight inches of sandy earth, covering the crowns three inches. Top-dress with maiden loam and some rotten dung between the straw-berry rows (see " Culture ").

The Frames.—The Auriculas, Carnations, and choice Picotees, Pansies, Campanulas, and Roses, should be economically arranged for the winter, and the Calceolarias placed in a moderately deep frame or pit on cinder-ash. Little water and abundance of air must be given through the winter months. Guard against mice in due time, and poison them ; and trap slugs.

The Forcing-house.—Last month's remarks are applicable to this. Some September-potted bulbs may be introduced, and the Mignonette fed.

The Greenhouse.—The Cinerarias will require *daily* at-tention to guard them against insects, which are very ready to infest them. Syringe with a light instrument ; this is the only way by which good, healthy, and well-grown specimens can be obtained. Careful watering of the Primulas, but with very little given to the fancy Geraniums, will be neces-sary at this time. The free admission of good air, closing early, and guarding against frosty nights by a slow fire, are the chief things to be observed.

THE FLOWER-GARDEN.—The planting of Dutch bulbs in the room of the bedding plants, and in the ribbon beds of the Italian garden, and the professional Dutch or amateur gardens, may be proceeded with early in the month, during fine dry weather (see " The Dutch Garden "). Proceed as rapidly as convenient in laying turf, making gravel walks, planting box edging, and all kinds of deciduous shrubs and roses. Take up all the roses worked on the Dog-rose that have thrown up suckers from the root ; cut them clean out at the root, trim the roots, and replant them at once. Get the flower-garden into good finished order for the winter, as early as possible, before hard frost, snow, and continued rains set in. Tender Tea China Roses should be so arranged that protection may be conveniently afforded to them during severe frost. Cuttings of hardy sorts may be inserted on a warm border and under hand-lights.

DECEMBER.

THE KITCHEN-GARDEN. The observations for last month are also applicable for December, except that covering celery trenches with fern, old hay, or long stable litter may be necessary in the event of severe frost ; and the pruning espalier and wall trees may be commenced, vacant ground single and double trenched, land drained, and all kinds of fruit-trees speedily planted ; grape-vines should be pruned during the month, and early frame and ash-leaved kidney potatoes planted on a warm border on a bed made with fresh-gathered leaves, and one-third stable dung to slightly ferment it, and then covered with a frame. Sow Wood's early frame radish on the top of each plantation of potatoes, cover the lights with old hay and mats, and the sowing in the open border with a foot of ferns, or oat straw, and uncovering daily as soon as the radishes are up. Make up a good stout hotbed for cucumbers and early melons, use one-half leaves and one-half stable dung, fresh from the dung pit, well mix, build a good four-feet bed, well bedded; there will be no danger of such a bed burning, as the leaves will prevent it. Plant potato, onion, and sow beans and peas. Force asparagus, seakale, and rhubarb, and give liquid manure to the asparagus and rhubarb coming on. Get the seed list of your seedsman, and give your orders early.

The Frames for auriculas, carnations, and picotees, will merely require air and a slight protection during severe cold. The calceolarias and plants of this class must be provided with coverings.

The Forcing-house may have more subjects introduced into it by way of roses, various bulbs, flowering shrubs, and pinks, stocks, walls, and carnations, all of which must be well established in the pot, that is, must have become rooted in their pots.

The Greenhouse.—The cinerarias and primulas will be steadily progressing, the rest will be quiet, and should be clean and healthy. Guard against frost, back the fires of these structures well up at night ; Welsh coal will be found the most lasting of all fuels. About five or six o'clock pull out the dampers, rake the furnace well to clear it, and half fill the furnace with moderate-sized fuel. Close the furnace door, and set it going full speed at eight or nine o'clock. Bank it well up by filling the furnace full, throwing it chiefly to the far end, pack it well in, push the damper in halfway if it is likely to be a fair night, and if a sharp cold one, give it full draught ; the fire will last till six or seven o'clock next morning. By this management I never suffered from the effects of frost, although my houses were exposed to most cutting east winds.

THE FLOWER-GARDEN.—The last month's directions are practicable here, except that bulb-planting will be done at the latest time, and some of the earlier planted ones may want slight protection, which may be afforded by mats strained over poles laid in crutches, hoops, &c. Prune climbing and standard roses ; dig flower borders, lay turf, roll the lawn and gravel walks while wet, and do all planting before frost sets in. Manure the lawn with some good old rotten dung and fine maiden loam in a pulverized state, so as to have it washed in quickly by the rains : if the grass is poor, give a slight sowing over in the spring with soot.

PRIZE GROWING.—THE STRAWBERRY.

ANY method that will produce the greatest weight and number of either fruit or vegetables in the shortest time, and in a given space, will be the best all the world over.

The secret of doing this is, doubtless, no new thing ; but it is strange the best way of doing it is not followed by all who have the privilege of doing so. From the fact of its not being new, it cannot be a secret, and yet we may go into ninety-nine gardens out of a hundred, and find one only where Strawberry-growing is carried out to perfection, notwithstanding the reasonableness of the method, and the evidence of its being the only true method in its abundant success.

I am so convinced of its absolute necessity, both for economy and profit, that I advise every one, both amateur and professional, to practise it closely, whether he cultivates ten or ten thousand Strawberry plants, whether he grows them in this country or any other ; and it is an established fact that more fruit in weight and number can be grown in a given space by the method given below than by any other ; and this arises from two causes, viz., the reserved power of the plant, and the concentration of its virtue upon the issue in the shape of fruit instead of leaves and runners, by unrelinquished efforts to keep down all runners and weeds. This method of growing the Strawberry is not confined to sort or soil, for it is favourable rather to the worst soil and sorts. For instance, select the poorest sort you can find, and plant them on the most unfavourable soil ; and also take the best sort you can find, and plant these on the best soil you have, and let both be planted at the same time ; treat the former as below, or on the new method (as I will call it), following it up strictly, and let the latter take their own course,—that is, let the runners grow, as is usual on the old method, till autumn, and then mow the foliage off, dress the bed, &c., and you will find that the worst sort on the worst soil gives the most fruit, and the plants will continue in good bearing condition for a much longer period· But I conceive that the reason why it is not universally adopted, and why it does not answer with many, is that it is too tedious to be constantly careful to nip off every runner as soon as it is more than two or three inches long, and so neglect doing it; and others think the land appears to be only partially occupied, from the insignificant appearance of the top, and so much bare surface of land; but let such remember that the top of the Strawberry plant is no criterion of the root, for the Strawberry is a long and a strong feeder, and unless the precaution is taken to provide for this, by planting at an adequate distance from plant to plant, and maintaining this distance clear and bare by keeping down the weeds and runners, a failure will ensue, and the method be condemned for the trouble it causes without the expected result. First, then, select an open space for the plantation in the best part of the garden, and plant in rows two feet by eighteen inches apart, and never less than eighteen by eighteen inches; let the land be trenched eighteen inches deep in July, turning in a good quantity of old rotten dung and maiden loam; and as early as convenient in August feed in the plants. Fruit will be obtained from these early planted ones the very next season, but if the planting is deferred till the autumn a season will be lost. Plant in showery weather, if possible, with a thick-ended hand-dibber. Let the roots down straight into the soil, and close tightly about the new plant; water if necessary, and as soon as any runners appear nip them off, and keep the land shallow-hoed. No manure will be required the first season; and in the second and third seasons these plants will be in their full strength, and yield a rich crop of fruit if attention is paid to them. Some think they should be destroyed after the third season ; but I have found that they will last good for six or seven years by due attention to top-dressing (tor no other is needed) once a year, during November, with lime and maiden loam of a good nature,—such as can be dug from a rich pasture or common, and laid on the surface barely covering the crowns, and never injuring them by treading upon them, nor trimming off the leaves till March, and watering them abundantly during the setting of the fruit with clean water, and once a week during the swelling and ripening of the fruit with liquid manure, which may consist of any of the favourite sorts suitable ; the best being made of two or three ounces of guano to one gallon of water, poured on the ground without a rose to the water-pot, keeping the spout as low as possible, to prevent it falling upon the ripe fruit, and so probably spoiling its flavour. The autumnal dressing of loam may have some good old rotten dung added, if the soil is poor, and be pricked in two or three inches into the surface with a three-pronged fork. *Early* fruit may be had of Cuthill's " Black Prince," " Sir Harry," and " British Queen," by planting a row at the foot of a south wall, in nine-inch pots in the orchard-house, setting them in a cold frame, giving all the air possible during the flower, and keeping closer as soon as the fruit is set, and giving abundance of water. Late fruit may be had by planting under a north wall. In watering strawberries it is good policy to avoid watering overhead,—that is, over the ripe fruit ; for the water reduces the richness of flavour, and causes an insipidity. To produce good plants for forcing, the runners must be laid on the surface of three-inch pots filled up to the top, and made solid with maiden loam, and laying a stone upon them to prevent them being blown off during windy weather, and kept moist till rooted. As soon as fairly rooted these may be disunited and removed to any convenient spot, and kept moist, and shifted into nine-inch pots; using good stiff maiden loam and dung, filling the pot very firm and up to the very top, keeping the heart of the young plant just above the soil. Set these pots in an open and sunny spot, nipping off every runner as soon as they appear, encouraging the plants to form bold buds till November; then turn them on their sides to prevent supersaturation, and to give a little rest to the plants before you commence exciting them. These will not require much water till they are in bloom, then water freely, using both water and heat freely as soon as the fruit is set, and give manure water once a week. Fine and abundant fruit may be had in pots this way, and early.

FLORISTS' FLOWERS.

IT is not easy to define a perfect flower in words, and even if I could do so, I should not be understood except by those who have attained to the same knowledge by observation. There are two ways of doing that, viz., by visiting those places where they are exhibited, or growing them on your own premises; the latter is the more economical and certain of the two. A florist's flower is one capable of two things at the least, viz., propagation by seed and by cuttings or offsets, although it must be understood that not every plant capable of doing this is a florist's flower. The auricula, polyanthus, carnation, picotee, and pink; phlox, petunia, verbena, and geranium; cineraria, calceolaria, fuchsia, and anemone; the tulip, ranunculus, and lily; rose, hydrangea, and peony; narcissus, iris, and pansy; chrysanthemum, gladiolus, and hyacinth; the rhododendron and dahlia; amaryllis, anagallis. hollyhock, and achimenes;

gloxinia and primula; pentstemon, campanulas, delphiniums, and antirrhinums, &c.—most of these are florist's
flowers. The principal object of growing florist's flowers for
producing new sorts is to improve upon the existing sorts,
either in colour, character, or quality. No name should be
given to plants but what indicates quality; some of the
worst rubbish, " mere weeds," are circulated with popular
names attached. A plant should not be cast off before it
has flowered a second time; first flowers are frequently deficient. Speculators in "florist's flowers" desiring to raise
new varieties, or who wish them for any other purpose.
should either get their seed from confidential growers of the
identical sort, or purchase none but good sorts of growers
who warrant them. Cheapness should never be preferred
to good quality.

THE PERFECTION OF A PLANT

Is one well grown without stringent conditions; still there
are rules by which to proceed for bringing a plant to perfection. Climbing plants would possess a natural beauty
peculiar to themselves by allowing them to grow at will; but
this kind of gardening is practically inconvenient. Plants
should really be grown any way that will produce the most
beauty coupled with economy, and that requires the least
amount of room, but it frequently requires skill to apply art
to induce nature to display its beauties.

Nature should, in a great degree, be retained in its own
form; thus a climber, a trailer, an erect and sub-erect plant
should be grown as such. In the case of pot-work these
should be carried out to perfection, and is best done by
following up closely the hints here laid down.

The perfection of a flower consists in its having its due
proportions of symmetry, of character, decision of colour,

and full substance. These are the primary conditions of a good flower, and the want of either will prove fatal to a florist's flower, although the flower may largely possess some of the qualifications. There are other minor qualities required, such as the habit of the plant, trussing, &c., which, if deficient, will in some cases condemn the variety; these are the auricula, polyanthus, &c.

CUT FLOWERS

MAY be preserved longer by dropping into the water in which they are placed five grains of saltpetre, and by keeping in the water a good lump of charcoal; either of these means will act beneficially to cut flowers. Five or six drops of a saturated solution of ammonia dropped into a pint of water in which the flowers are kept is also beneficial. The flowers, whatever they are, should be cut clean, *i. e.*, the stem should be cut to a solid part, unfractured, with a fine-edged penknife, budding or trimming knife, as though it were expected to strike root.

A FEW NOTES ON MANURES.

EVERY man may make his own manure by adding to every pound of bones twelve ounces of sulphuric acid and twelve ounces of water; when the bones are dissolved add three pounds of charcoal dust, and mix all together. The acid will cost 4d. or 6d., and the charcoal a mere trifle—one half-penny perhaps. It may be mixed with dry wood ashes by six times the bulk, *i. e.*, six pounds of ashes to one pound of dissolved bones; thus a strong and exceedingly good manure may be made on the premises, at a cost of less than one penny per pound, and may be put on the ground five or six pounds per rod for heavy crops.

Throw gypsum into the cesspool every two or three months; this will fix the ammonia, the chief fertilizing property. This is a strong manure for cabbages, onions, brocoli, beet, &c., and may be put on at the rate of from two to three pounds per rod and dug in.

Soot is a very powerful manure applied at the rate of one pound to the rod; it abounds in ammonia, and consequently possesses stimulating power in a remarkable degree. Too much soot per rod will drive vegetation beyond what is desirable; three ounces of soot and six of guano possess more stimulating, energizing ammonia than any proportionate quantity of any other manure extant, and is the only manure that acts so immediately direct and so well upon rhubarb. (See Rhubarb Culture.) Soot forms an exceedingly rapid stimulator for peas, lettuce, carrots, spinach, and most crops in a liquid state at the rate of half an ounce to two quarts of water, given so as to soak down to the feeders —spongioles. Always give soot whilst the plant is in an active state. Most persons make soot enough to manure a whole garden for the year.

Chloride of lime is a powerful air-absorber, and may be advantageously applied to light land in spring. It suspends the ammoniacal vapours, and consequently forms a useful medium for the regulation of this volatile constituent of other manures; take some of it, dry, into a stable where horses are kept and urine abounds; the effect will soon be seen; it will in a few minutes absorb enough ammoniacal vapour to render it palpably moist, and this will go on till the chloride becomes liquid. A lesson may be learnt from this for porous, poor dry land, as it retains moisture and matter of no small moment during summer. This manure, sown carefully over turnips, will prove an antidote for the fly; it may also be mixed with wood ashes, and sown thinly.

The most rapid fertilizers are those that contain the most ammonia. The most durable are those whose ammonia is fixed.

THE BEST APPLICATION OF MANURE

Is by liquid, in the first instance, soon after germination; and secondly, at the time of the development of the fruit or flowers. There is a twofold advantage connected with the giving of manure in a liquid form to crops and flowers; being in a liquid state it is just in the necessary condition for the plant to absorb forthwith, hence an immediate benefit; ground also becoming saturated by the aqueous manure, all the tender fibres do a portion of the work of feeding the terrestrial parts as well as the whole plant at once, whilst in all probability a portion of underground plant, the spongioles, never come in contact with the manure when applied in a dry state; and if they do, it very much depends upon whether there is sufficient moisture to cause a sufficient solution of the manure for the digestion or absorption of the nutriment. Hence a frequent failure in dry seasons when manure is applied in a dry state. Another advantage is, that the whole of the ground (as far as it reaches) becomes manured in a less degree of strength by the saturation with the liquid; and, held in this compound form, it is capable of application to more than one crop, more particularly those manures that are less volatile than others, such as night-soil and gypsum, bone manure and gypsum, urine and chloride of lime, &c.

GUANO

In its pure state appears to contain the largest amount of stimulating power of any manure, that is, it has the more energetic property of ammonia in one form or another; hence it is found to be more rapid in its effect upon vegetation than any of its class, and I have, in my experience, proved this; but I do not think this is a recommendation, from the fact that its effects are soon exhausted.

HOW TO TAKE IMPRESSIONS OF PLANTS.

This is a most useful and interesting plan for producing *fac-similes* of parts of plants, and forms a method by which any, however remote the idea of drawing, may copy the object desired, and a book of nature's beauties may be thus preserved by all; hence it becomes one of the most useful adjuncts to the traveller, furnishing *fac-similes* far surpassing a sketch, however perfect; and it not only equals, but surpasses the finest photography, as it defines the most minute parts not attainable by that beautiful process. The impression is inverted, *i. e.*, the deepest shadows are the whites of the print, and the tints that should be high lights are blackest or the most coloured; this is unavoidable, but can, if necessary, be perfected by a soft black-lead pencil. But the principal object gained by this process is, to make any leaf or plant indelible with accuracy, economy, and despatch. Thus a book of nature may be made for a few shillings that would cost hundreds of pounds to engrave.

First, then, a large folio blank book should be made, which for convenience should not be less than eighteen by twelve inches, consisting of leaves of fine white cartridge paper; then a second book of about the same size as a yearly volume of the *Band of Hope* or *British Workman*, for laying in, for a few hours previously to the operation, the leaves to be printed. Having these two volumes ready, next take a sheet of about the same size of thin white printing paper, lay this sheet down on a newspaper on a table, oil it evenly over on one side with cold drawn linseed oil, and with a piece of clean flannel or sponge fairly

saturate the paper, wiping all the superfluous oil off.   Then
hang it up by a pin in the corner in some closet or room,
or in a large box, free from dust, for a day.   If done in the
morning it will be ready in the evening.   The leaves to be
pressed may be collected during the same day, and laid
in the folio *British Workman*, &c.   In the evening take
the oiled paper, and having a cotton candle or an oil lamp
with a good-sized wick, hold the oiled paper with both
hands over the flame, so close as to deaden it,—this will
cause a smoke which will completely blacken the paper:
by gently and continuously moving it till it is perfectly
blacked on one side, lay the sheet down, the black side
uppermost, on two or three folds of even newspaper, or
some slightly elastic bed, then open the folio volume containing the plates to be printed, and lay the type upon the
black paper, carefully maintaining its natural feature.   Take
a clean sheet of the same kind of paper and lay on the
leaf; hold the top sheet and the leaf firm with one or two
fingers, while you gently and evenly rub all over the portions
of the leaf underneath the sheet, taking care not to shift the
type-leaf during the operation of rubbing it down.   Sufficient
pressure must be given in this operation to induce the
leaf to take up a good proportion of the black; a few
minutes will do this.   Now take the leaf carefully off the
sheet, and very carefully lay it on a page of the blank
folio, and take a perfectly clean sheet of white thin paper
and proceed just the same as when the leaf was being
coloured on the black sheet.   Rub moderately hard to
get a good deep impression, which will be in a few minutes,
then lift the paper off, then the leaf, and it will be completed; proceed in this way till all the coloured paper
has been worked out, when another sheet must be prepared,
and so on, till a volume of beautiful leaf-type impressions
is thus produced, which may be coloured to nature.

The operation can be performed in colours to suit the tints of nature by using Prussian blue and yellow ochre, Naples, or any bright yellow. Any tint of green, desirable, may be made by these, or even by a bright yellow and blue : linseed oil and these colours mixed to the consistency of paint, and laid evenly and thinly on the paper with a fine painter's brush. A nature-printed book may be easily made, and young gardeners should acquire the useful art of pencilling and painting favourite flowers, as it would be a useful and an interesting occupation for their leisure hours during winter evenings.

GLOSSARIAL INDEX

AND

TECHNICAL TERMS.

ACRE. An acre of land contains 160 square poles of thirty square yards each.

ACIDS are a counterbalance for alkalies, and enter largely into vegetation.

AFFINITY, a term used to denote the relation existing between plants and parts of plants ; hence all that belong to the same class and order have an affinity ; thus, all the genus of Brassica,—Cabbage and Turnip, Kales and Brocolis, the Laurel and Cherry, the Pear and Thorn, the Pea and Bean, &c., have an affinity.

ALPINE PLANTS, a term applied to plants that grow naturally on high grounds, the chief of which come from the Alps.

AMATEUR, a pleasure rather than a professional gardener.

AMERICAN BLIGHT, small insects which appear on fruit-trees during the spring of the year.

AMMONIA, a very vaporous alkali ; difficult to fix, exceedingly energetic in its influence upon plants and vegetation in general, which are much benefited by its presence.

ANNUAL denotes the duration of the existence of a plant ; a true annual is one that cannot be propagated except by sowing seeds yearly.

ANTHERS, the heads of the stamens, like pins' heads in some flowers, and in others long, like the Lily. These possess a powder whose property it is to affect the flower so as to produce perfect seed, and by which varieties are produced.

ANGLE. On this depends the power of light ; the same angle that will do best for summer purposes (as a frame or house) for the growing Cucumbers, &c., will not answer well for the winter.

APHIS, a troublesome fly of a small size and poisonous nature.

AQUATIC, a term used to denote all plants growing naturally in water, and those that will not do without it. The *Victoria regia* is the most beautiful and noble of all aquatics, and the Pitcher-Plant the most curious.

ARTIFICIAL HEAT, indispensable in this country for the perfection of exotic flowers and fruits. That which approaches the nearest to the natural climate of the plant is doubtless the best.

ARUM, a curious genus of plants, some of which possess as it were a flower without petals, which are produced in a coloured sheath in some cases and in green in others.

ARCADE, a succession of arches, which may be rapidly formed of climbing roses.

ASH TREE, one of the worst kinds of forest deciduous trees that can be on tillage land, being a gross feeder.

ATMOSPHERE consists of hydrogen, oxygen, and nitrogen or azote. Water is composed of oxygen, hydrogen, and other bodies, and is the life of plants as well as of animated nature. Oxygen is the vitalizing element of the air we breathe, and also of plants, oxidizing or thickening the juices as they become exposed to its influence. Nitrogen is of itself a destructive element, but being only a component part with the other two gases, is counteracted in its influence and made to serve the progressive work of vegetation.

ARAUCARIA, a singular plant of the pine class, and should be possessed by all having a moderate lawn.

AWNING, a thin shade, which may be made of coarse net, fine net, coarse and fine gauze, thin and thick calico.

AXIS, the point from which the roots and stem proceed, and from which the branches and roots start, the top root and the stem, &c.

BARK, the outer coat of the plant for the prevention of the air acting upon the fluids while it passes from the ground to the branches of the plant or tree. The absence of this covering causes the destruction of the plant, or if the bark is injured the free circulation of the sap is stopped, and disease follows.

BARILLA, an inferior kind of carbonate of soda, destructive to insect life.

BAST, the bark of the Lime tree, imported from Russia in mats ; a useful covering for frames and various purposes.

BALM, a most useful hardy perennial plant for making cooling drinks in summer.

BASKETS, for suspension, may be of great utility.

BLACK MILDEW, a disagreeable fungus, appearing on plants, paper, linen, calico, &c. ; destructive in its influence, and poisonous to living nature.

BLANCH, to bleach, whiten. This is done by perfectly excluding the oxidizing component part of the air.

BUDS. Of these there are three distinct kinds, viz., underground buds, as in the case of bulbs and that of the roots of trees, from which proceed the leaf, stem, fibrils, and feeders ; aërial buds, comprising two sorts, one for the production of leaves and branches, and another kind for the production of flowers and fruit.

BIENNIAL STOCKS. A word used to denote the duration of a plant. A true biennial flowers but once, and then dies, consequently it must, to have it every year, be sown on each returning season. The Brompton, Queen, and Giant Stocks are true biennials.

BOILER. The best boiler is that which will heat the largest amount of water with the least fuel, trouble, and expense. Boilers for heating horticultural buildings, churches, &c., fixed underground, and subject to perpetual damp, should be made of the best galvanized wrought iron or copper, and, as some water destroys iron boilers much sooner than others, such boilers should be supplied with rain water.

BOTTOM HEAT. An indispensable for the well-being of many exotics for the establishment of their roots prior to the production of either fruit or flowers. Bottom heat should never exceed 75° or 80°, 70° being generally enough for most forcing purposes.

BOTANY. Systematic botany is a classification of plants according to their natural affinity ; descriptive botany refers to the hardiness and duration, habit of growth, and the uses of the plant ; and the third section of botany relates to the knowledge of the physical property of plants, and embraces all that is known of the construction and functionary powers of inspiration, of respiration, assimilation of the vapours, and of the fluids. Each of the branches of botany is useful and most interesting, but the descriptive conveys information of the nature and character of plants indispensable to the gardener, whilst a knowledge of systematic is essential to ascertain to what class a plant belongs. The Linnæan system is the least intelligible, on account of the numerous species each class contains, and because of such classes embracing plants of quite an opposite genus. De Candolle's, called the natural system, is the most useful, as one member conveys the character of the flower sufficiently to form a correct idea of what the plant is, or at least its affinity, although it cannot be seen in flower. The natural system will doubtless bear some modifications.

BOUQUETS, bunches of flowers. The best way to form bouquets of a large size for table purposes and for keeping long, is to get some fine clean sand and put it into a double table vase, then thoroughly soak it with soft water ; cut the ends off the flower-stems with a sharp knife in a slanting direction, then insert the longest stems an inch and a half or two inches deep into the sand, and then the next longest ;

then the pendulous and ferns and dwarf cut flowers on the outside, introducing some fine clean moss on the face of the sand between the stems to hold them up.   Hand-bouquets should be tied in with fine clean moss.   Flowers kept in soft water should have a small piéce of nitre dropped into it, or a bit of fresh charcoal now and then, and the water changed every two days.

CARBONATE OF IRON.   Iron converted into rust by the action of the carbonic acid gas of the atmosphere.

CAMPHOR.   The gum of a tree possessing the extraordinary property of disinfection and preservation, soluble by degrees by the air, but insoluble in water.

CANVAS AWNINGS.   Shades made of fine net, coarse netting, fine gauze, coarse gauze, &c.

CANKER, in the vegetable kingdom, is altogether a different thing from canker in the mineral kingdom.   The one is caused frequently by a bruise, and by the weak constitution of the plant, which, coming in contact with some uncongenial subterranean substance or fluid that it cannot digest, produces the effect observed in the hard wood of the Apple, Plum, Cherry, &c.   This is what is called "gangrene," and is said to be produced by some atmospheric influences.

CAUSTIC LIME, unslacked lime.   This property is produced by applying fire to a soft kind of stone, found in different parts of the country. Devonshire is famous for it.   It is this caustic or burning property that makes it so valuable for the destruction of insect life, and produces fertility in the ground.   When this property is exhausted or passed off (which is very rapid), it becomes of the same value as chalk to the soil, and is exceedingly beneficial to corn crops.

CALYX, that part of the flower next the stem and the corolla.   The outer covering of the flower, which is coloured in some cases, as that of the fuchsia, but generally of a green, as in the rose.

CARBONIC ACID GAS.—Carbon in combination with oxygen, and serves in the formation of the vegetable fabric.

CLASS, a division of the vegetable kingdom.   The whole vegetable kingdom is divided into classes ; the system of Linnæus contains twenty-four, that of Jussieu three, and that of De Candolle contains several hundred classes or orders.   There are also numerous minor classes and sub-classes.   Roses, for instance, comprise several sub-classes ; as Provence, French, Bourbon, China moss, Scotch, &c., &c. Geraniums also comprise several sub-classes, and the bulbous flowers contain many classes and sub-classes, and so on.

CLIMATE.—The chief object in gardening should be to approximate as

nearly as possible to the mother climate of the plant; hence the necessity of being a geographer as well as a gardener.

CONTAMINATED AIR in horticulture is caused by uncleanness and bad ventilation, dampness from bad drainage, and is productive of mildew and insect pests.

CONIFERA, the natural order for the whole fir tribes.

CONES, the fruit of the firs which contain the seed.

CONSERVATORY, the show-room of flowers. Should be always near the house.

CROSSED, a word indicating an artificial change of character; for instance, a rose hybridized with the pollen from one of quite an opposite class is in process of being crossed, and the seedlings from this would probably partake of both parents; but if the anthers of the one that is to bear the seed were cut out before the discharge of the pollen, and the pollen then brought from quite an opposite kind, the seedlings would not be likely to partake of the character of the seed-bearer so much as of the other. Still this would be a cross. When the seedlings are not affected by the process of fertilization there is no cross; new, rare, and beautiful things are produced by crossing, both in fruits and flowers. The object is to produce the beauty or quality of the one with the desired character in another of the same genus.

DECIDUOUS.—Trees and shrubs that lose their leaves during the autumn; a provision of nature, but chiefly the effect of climate. Foliage acts as lungs to the plant, and deteriorates, and is ultimately altogether inactive by the influence of the cold nights of autumn—an effect similar to that of a person taking a cold on the chest, and ending in consumption.

DECOMPOSED.—All things that are perfectly decayed, destroyed from the original state by age, fermentation, and the influence of the air.

DEGENERATE, to go back to the wild state, to become single from double; thus, apples, pears, and plums will go back to the wild state from seed, and roses often go back to semi-double and to single flowers, and almost everything has a tendency to become worse.

DESIGN, to plan, to invent a good design for a well-arranged arboretum, a rosary, a flower-garden, a rockery, a picturesque park, &c.; this requires a considerable amount of genius, judgment, and foresight.

DEW-POT, a most useful description of water-pot called an irrigator, and should be possessed by all in the habit of raising seedlings.

DEVELOPED denotes a full-grown and full-blown subject, whether it be

a rose or a cabbage.   There is something curious about the development of some flowers.   The Œnothera only opens its flowers in the
evening, and the Mesembryanthemums in the morning ; the former
in the absence of the sun, the latter in its presence only.   Others open
but once, and that in the evening ; others in the morning.   *Vide*
the Tigrida and Convolvulus, Ipomeas, &c.

DIBBER, an instrument for planting cabbage plants, &c., and for
potatoes.

EVERGREENS, plants that never lose all their leaves at one time.   It is
a remarkable fact that, while the same agency that produces leaves in
or on deciduous plants, cause the fall of leaves in the evergreen class
of plants.   The fall of the leaf of the deciduous class is produced by
the same cause.   The fall of the old worn-out leaves of the evergreen
class is in summer and during the active state of the plant ; that of
the deciduous class is in autumn, or in the inactive state of the plant :
both are caused by the breathing pores of the leaf becoming im-
paired and worthless.   The cause of plants being evergreen is owing
to the persistent character of the cuticle of the leaf, and its having
less stomata, and the parenchyma abounding with oily matter : these
qualities render them proof against the same influences that destroy
the leaf of the deciduous class.

EXOTIC.—All plants of foreign growth.

FERNS, the most lovely class of plants extant without flowers, with one
exception, viz., Osmunda regalis.   All ferns bear their seed on the
under side of the leaf except the one above.

FELICITE, a term applied to give a high tone to a flower.

FERTILIZE, to make productive.   The natural air and water are fertilizers ; so are the manures and the pollen of flowers acting beneficially upon the stigma.

FUNGI.—The whole genus of mushrooms.   Toadstools, truffles, and
mildews are included in this term, of which there are many species
and numerous varieties.

FUMIGATING BELLOWS.—A tin box like a half-pound coffee canister,
with a screw fastened on one end and a half-inch opening on the
other.   The nose of the common bellows made to fix in the nut will
answer very well for the same purpose.

GENERA, the plural of genus.   All the Roses of every class are one
genus.   All the Cabbages, Brocoli, and Turnips belong to one genus,
and the whole tribe of heaths are a genus ; and so are all the
Dianthuses, although they may differ in appearance.

GREEN GAUZE, a coarse netting useful to protect fertilized flowers, and for the prevention of bee operation on those kinds of flowers that are necessary for the preservation of the genuine stock.

GISHURST COMPOUND, a very useful soft soap-like substance composed of soap and acids, for the destruction of insect life (in boxes).

GUANO, a most energetic manure, that requires caution in using, as too much of this forces the crop or plant too much.

HALF STANDARDS. Roses are about two or two and a half feet high ; apples, pears, plums, &c., about three to four feet high.

HARD-WOODED CUTTINGS. Cuttings from hard-wooded plants, such as some of the heaths, Epacris, Leucodendron, Myrtle, Camellia, Azalea, Laurestine, Acacia, Orange, &c., &c., some of which are difficult to strike, and all hard-wooded plants are at all times slow to strike.

HEATING is the chief feature of all horticultural buildings. The largest amount of heated air with the smallest amount of fuel are the two principal objects for all purposes of forcing.

HERBACEOUS, a term used to denote one of the three great divisions of plants. All plants that have stems that die down in the winter. Biennials, plants that flower once and then die, and annuals that must be sown every season. The nemophila is an annual. The Canterbury bell a true biennial, and the Lupinus polyphyllus a true perennial.

HARD WATER.—Water impregnated with acid salts, which render it unfit for watering plants. When water is hard it should be exposed to the sun's influence for at least 24 hours before using it on plants.

HOTBED.—For good effect, and where no apparatus is constructed, nothing is better than a bed made of one-half leaves raked up during December, and one-half fresh stable dung well mixed together, and permanently bedded and made firm four feet high while the leaves are wet.

HORIZONTAL TRAINING.—Train trees horizontally instead of upright, or converging from one point fan-shaped, which is the best, as it partially checks the too free tendency of the sap to run to the extremities.

HORTICULTURAL MANURES.—A name given to some manures that are pretended to be especially adapted for gardening, but all manures are equally good by regulating the quantity according to the constitution of the subject and the strength of the manure.

HYBRIDIZING.—Introducing the pollen of one flower to another from a different species or variety.

LATERALS.—Those shoots that spring right and left of the leader.

LEAVES are the clothing of plants, and serve as lungs to the body, as by these the plant throws off the refuse superabundant moisture, and inhales the oxygen gas from the atmosphere; leaves are composed of two kinds, as two great divisions, viz., simple and compound, *e. g.*, the Ash, Acacia, Chestnut, &c., are compound, and the Oak, Holly, Laurel, &c., are simple leaves.

LEAF-MOULD. Decayed leaves, of which Oak, Hornbeam, and Beech are the best constituents.

LIGHT. The chief agent that promotes the perfect development, the maturity of the parts, the character, the colour, and the fruits of the vegetable kingdom; the absence of this proves detrimental to most plants, and its entire absence is fatal to vegetable life.

MAIDEN LOAM. Soil that has not borne a cultivated crop.

MUNDIC. A beautiful brassy-coloured mineral found in Devonshire, and Cornwall tin and copper mines; is poisonous to plants, on this account the peats of Dartmoor are unsuitable for growing heaths.

NATURAL ORDERS. Under this head the whole vegetable kingdom is arranged. This system supersedes all others, inasmuch as every genus has its type, this type prefigures the whole family, and is in most cases a sufficient guide for a correct knowledge of the rest of the members of the same family. This arrangement was introduced by De Candolle, and modified by Hooker, Dr. Lindley, Don, and others. We now possess several hundred heads, as Ranunculaceæ, Convolvulaceæ, Rosaceæ, Campanulaceæ, &c., &c.

OXYGEN, a gas, forming a component part of the air, that gives life and power to vegetation, whilst it destroys minerals.

PETALS, the parts that compose the flower. See Rose Geranium. When a flower is composed of more than one single row of petals, as in the case of a Rose, Geranium, Stock, &c., it is nothing more nor less than the stamens converted into petals : this is done by additional vigour being imparted by high culture to the parent.

PERENNIAL, a term used to denote the constitution or duration of a plant. The hardy Phloxes, Delphiniums, and Chrysanthemums are examples.

RESTING SEASON. The time varies considerably in the vegetable world. Bulbs rest during the summer and other plants during winter. This should be well understood by all who grow plants.

RESPIRATION. A term used to express the idea of breathing, although this is not exactly the case, but a simple discharging of superfluous water in imperceptible vapour.

ROD, five and a half yards of land square ; thirty square yards of nine superficial feet.

ROOTS, called subterranean branches ; but their office is widely different. The branches are the consumers of the food the roots absorb from the ground, and are the first in action ; the branches are the last.

SAP, the life of the plant, derived from the moisture of the ground ; taken in by the spongioles at the extremity of the roots, drawn up into the branches by the sun's influence, converted into a thick juice by the influence of the atmosphere, when it consolidates, and forms another layer of wood, denoted by the outer circle observed on cutting a branch or stem of a tree in two at right angles. The sap does not, as some remark, ascend and descend after it has been circulated over the area of the whole tree ; for if so, a cavity would be formed in the channel every season, which cannot be found. The watery humour is thrown off by the leaves, the saccharine remains and consolidates.

SCALE, THE.—An insect that infests hard-wooded plants more generally, such as the Orange.

SCALE in feet, inches, or eighths of an inch; thus one foot is reckoned for a yard or a rod, one inch for a foot, one eighth for an inch, and so on.

SAWDUST.—Useful for plunging.

SCILLA.—A lovely class of early flowering bulbs, of which blue is the prevailing colour.

SET THE BLOSSOM.—To impart additional power to the flower for the production of seed by the introduction of the pollen from the flowers called male flowers that contain it to the seed-bearing flowers ; the fruit is also probably benefited by it.

SEEDLINGS.—Plants in their early stages ; plants raised from seed.

SHRUB.—A plant that never assumes the character of a tree like the Oak, the Ash, the Lime, the Acacia, &c. The Rhododendron, Laurestine, Portugal Laurel, Andromeda, and Holly, may be called true shrubs.

SHANK OFF.—A phrase used to describe the death of a plant when it rots at the surface of the earth.

SPONGIOLES.—The extremity of the root, furnished with a sponge-like receptacle for supplying the whole plant with strained fluid.

SPECIES, a member of the whole genus ; for instance, the pansy is a species of *Viola*, although it is not a violet. *Viola* is the genus.

STOPPING.—Descriptive of pruning by the thumb and finger.

STRIKING LIGHTS.—A class of hand-glass capable of the perfect exclusion of the external air.

STEM, the chief channel of the plant, and the support of the branches.

The stem of standard fruit and ornamental trees should be looked after while young, and induced to grow clean and straight.

STIGMA, the organ immediately on the top of the style, which forms the receptacle for the pollen.

SUBSOIL, the soil immediately under that in which the crop grows. This, if at all good for anything, should be broken up.

SUPERSATURATE.—To overdo the plant by too much watering, and not sufficient drainage to carry it away.

SYSTEM.—There are in horticulture the artificial and natural systems. The artificial is that adopted by man ; the natural is that provided by our Creator, and this will not admit of any modification or addition.

TAP ROOT.—The root that starts in 'a direct line downward from the stem. This (except walnut) should in fruit-trees be cut early.

TAN, a useful article for gentle heat in which to strike cuttings.

TUBERS.—A class of underground roots capable of sustaining themselves out of the ground for a considerable time, as the Potato, Dahlia, &c.

WATER.—A plant will live in pure water when it will pine away and die in water that has become foul by stagnation.

WOODLOUSE.—An annoying insect that commits its depredations during night by gnawing the bark off some plants and fruits, and by destroying mushrooms.

THE END.

J. AND W. RIDER, PRINTERS, LONDON.

NEW AND UNADULTERATED SEEDS

FOR THE

𝔎itchen-𝔊arden, 𝔉lower-𝔊arden, and 𝔉arm.

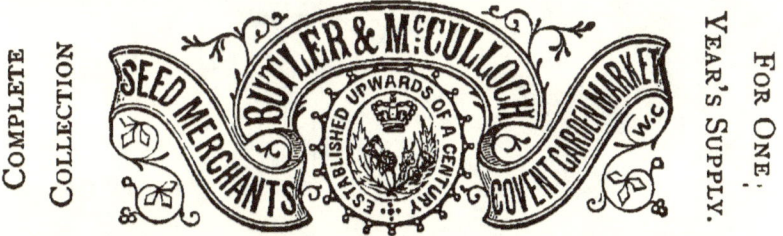

COMPLETE COLLECTION

FOR ONE YEAR'S SUPPLY.

Prize Medals at Great Exhibitions, 1851 and 1862.

COLLECTIONS OF FLOWER SEEDS,

FOR PRESENT SOWING.

Hardy Annuals,	100 varieties	...	20/-	Hardy Perennials,	15 varieties	...	3/9	
„ „	50 „	...	10/-	Everlasting Flowers 15	„	...	3/9	
„ „	25 „	...	5/-	„ „ 10	„	...	2/6	
„ „	12 „	...	2/6	Ornamental Grasses 12	„	...	2/6	
Bedding Annuals,	100 „	...	30/-	„ „ 6	„	...	1/6	
„ „	50 „	...	15/-	Carnations, very choice 12 „	3/- & 5/-			
„ „	25 „	...	7/6	Picotees „	12 „	3/- & 5/-		
„ „	12 „	...	4/-	Stocks, Imported German Seed,				
Hardy Perennials,	100 „	...	25/-		2/-, 2/6, & 3/6			
„ „	50 „	...	12/6	Asters „	„ 2/-, 2/6, & 3/6			
„ „	25 „	...	6/6					

COMPLETE COLLECTION OF VEGETABLE SEEDS

FOR ONE YEAR'S SUPPLY,

63/-, 42/-, 30/-, 21/-, and 10/6.

SEEDS FOR EXPORTATION.

Carefully selected and securely packed for India, China, New Zealand, Australia, Japan, &c.; and from B. & McC.'s extensive experience in this branch of their business, good results may always be depended upon.

CATALOGUES POST-FREE.

BUTLER, McCULLOCH, & CO.,

27, SOUTH ROW, COVENT GARDEN MARKET

(Opposite Southampton Street).

ESTABLISHED UPWARDS OF A CENTURY.

GREENHOUSES

FROM THE

Finsbury Steam Joinery Works,

121, BUNHILL ROW, LONDON.

W. H. LASCELLES, Proprietor.

LISTS SENT ON APPLICATION.

Prices for houses made of the best red deal, the sashes two inches thick, glazed with 16-oz. good sheet glass, delivered and fixed within thirty miles of London, painted four coats in best oil colour, including locks, gutter, down pipe, and gearing for opening the ventilators at one time, no heating, staging, nor brickwork included:—

20 ft. × 12 ft.	40 ft. × 16 ft.	60 ft. × 20 ft.	100 ft. × 24 ft.
£40 0 0	£79 0 0	£132 0 0	£238 10 0

GARDEN LIGHTS AND BOXES.

6 ft. × 4 ft. lights, 2 in. thick, unglazed . . . . 5/- each.
     ,,   ,,   glazed, 16 oz. good sheet glass 11/- ,,
Portable box containing one 6 ft. × 4 feet light, painted four
  coats ready for use . . . . 30/- ,,
Portable box containing two ditto . . . . . 55/- ,,

Estimates given for Conservatories or Greenhouses to any design.

E. H. KRELAGE & SONS,

NURSERYMEN, SEEDSMEN, AND FLORISTS,

HAARLEM, HOLLAND.

ESTABLISHED 1810.

GOLDEN MEDAL FOR HYACINTHS, Paris, 1867, and about 300 other prizes at the various shows of the Continent, among which are a great number of FIRST PRIZES at the International Shows of BIEBRICH, AMSTERDAM, GHENT, PETERSBURG, and HAMBURGH, and SIX GOLDEN and many other medals for TULIPS.

BULBS, SEEDS, PLANTS, SHRUBS, TREES,

AND MISCELLANEOUS

Horticultural and Agricultural Articles of every description,

WHOLESALE AND RETAIL.

CATALOGUES PUBLISHED IN ENGLISH, FRENCH, GERMAN, AND DUTCH.

Now ready, an International Catalogue of TULIPS (No. 60), containing prices of nearly 2,000 varieties (notes in English, French, and German), 36 pages, 8vo. This Catalogue will be addressed without any charge if solicited by prepaid letters, addressed directly to—

E. H. KRELAGE AND SON, HAARLEM, HOLLAND.

NETTING

FOR

Fruit Trees, Seed Beds, Ripe Strawberries, &c.

TANNED NETTING for protecting the above from Frost, Blight, Birds, &c., 2 yards wide, 3d. per yard ; per 100 yards, 26s. ; 4 yards wide, 6d. per yard, or 50 yards, 20s.

NEW TANNED NETTING, suited for any of the above purposes, or as a Fence for Fowls, 2 yards wide, 6d. per yard ; 4 yards wide, 1s. per yard ; ¾-inch mesh, 4 yards wide, 1s. 6d. per yard. TIFFANY can be had in any quantity of

EATON & DELLER, 6 & 7, CROOKED LANE, LONDON BRIDGE, E.C.

GLASS FOR GARDEN PURPOSES.
JAMES PHILLIPS & CO.

BEG TO SUBMIT THEIR REDUCED PRICES AS FOLLOWS :—

PROPAGATING · GLASSES.

2 in. in diam.—each 0/3½		13 in. in diam.—each 2/0
3 ,, ,, 0/4½		14 ,, ,, 2/6
4 ,, ,, 0/5½		15 ,, ,, 3/0
5 ,, ,, 0/6½		16 ,, ,, 3/6
6 ,, ,, 0/8		17 ,, ,, 4/0
7 ,, ,, 0/10	10 in. in diam.—each 1/4	18 ,, ,, 5/0
8 ,, ,, 1/0	11 ,, ,, ,, 1/6	19 ,, ,, 6/0
9 ,, ,, 1/2	12 ,, ,, ,, 1/9	20 ,, ,, 7/0

BEE GLASSES, with ventilating hole through knob.

4 in. in diameter, ea. 0/6	7 in. in diameter, ea. 1/1	10 in. in diameter, ea. 2/0
5 ,, ,, ,, 0/8	8 ,, ,, ,, 1/4	11 ,, ,, ,, 2/6
6 ,, ,, ,, 0/10	9 ,, ,, ,, 1/8	12 ,, ,, ,, 3/0

CUCUMBER GLASSES.

24 in. long ...... ,, 2/0	18 in. long ...... each 1/6	14 in. long ...... ,, 1/2
22 ,, ... ,, 1/10	16 ,, ,, ... ,, 1/4	12 ,, ,, ... ,, 1/0
20 ,, ... ,, 1/8		

WASP TRAPS, 3s. 6d. per Dozen.

HAND GLASSES, with Open Tops.

12 inches .... each 6/6		20 inches ...... each 10/6
14 ,, ... ,, 7/6		22 ,, ... ,, 11/6
16 ,, ... ,, 8/6		24 ,, ... ,, 12/6
18 ,, ... ,, 9/6		

GLASS FOR ORCHARD-HOUSES.

As supplied by them to Mr. RIVERS, to the Royal Horticultural Society, and to most of the Nobility, Clergy, and Gentlemen of the United Kingdom.

Each Box contains 100 feet. The prices only apply to the sizes stated. Squares 20 by 12, 20 by 13, 20 by 14, 20 by 15, and 20 by 16.

16 oz. to the foot.	21 oz. to the foot.
Fourth quality 15/0 Seconds 18/6	Fourth quality 19/6 Seconds 26/0
Third quality 16/0 English 20/0	Third quality 22/0 English 27/0

The above prices include the boxes, which are not returnable.

HORTICULTURAL GLASS.

Stock sizes, 16 oz., in 100 feet boxes, boxes included. These prices only apply to the sizes stated.

11 by 9	12 by 9	13 by 9	14 by 9 }	4ths.	3rds.	2nds.
12 by 10	13 by 10	14 by 10	15 by 10 }	13/6	15/6	17/0
13 by 11	14 by 11	...	...			
14 by 12	15 by 12	15 by 11	16 by 11 }			
18 by 12	19 by 12	16 by 12	17 by 12 }			
16 by 13	17 by 13	20 by 12	20 by 15 }-	15/0	16/0	18/6
16 by 14	20 by 13	18 by 13	... }	16 to 17 oz. to the foot.		
	17 by 14	18 by 14	20 by 16 }			
	20 by 14					

To parties wishing for a stronger kind of Sheet Glass than 21 oz., we can recommend our Horticultural 26 oz., packed in cases, 200 feet each, of the uniform size 30 by 20—price 3¾d. per foot.

SMALL SHEET SQUARES (in 100 feet boxes).

6 by 4 ... 6½ by 4½ ... 7 by 5 ... 7½ by 5½ } 12s. 6d.   10 by 8 } 13s. 6d.
8 by 6 ... 8½ by 6½ ... 9 by 7 ... 9½ by 7½ }   10½ by 8½ }

Boxes 2s. each, returnable at full price.

London Agents for HARTLEY'S IMPROVED PATENT ROUGH PLATE.
LINSEED OIL, Genuine WHITE LEAD, CARSON'S PAINTS.
Paints of various colours ground ready for use.

SHEET and ROUGH PLATE GLASS, SLATES of all sizes, BRITISH PLATE, PATENT PLATE, ROLLED PLATE, CROWN, SHEET, HORTICULTURAL, ORNAMENTAL, COLOURED, and every description of GLASS, of the best manufacture, at the lowest terms. Lists of Prices and Estimates forwarded on application to

JAMES PHILLIPS & CO.,
HORTICULTURAL GLASS MERCHANTS,
179 & 180, BISHOPSGATE STREET WITHOUT, LONDON, E.C.

Just published, crown 8vo., cloth, bevelled boards, 3s. 6d.,

PRACTICAL SERMONS,

CHIEFLY ON

THE SECOND ADVENT OF OUR LORD JESUS CHRIST.

By J. FAWCETT BEDDY, M.A.,
Late Vicar of St. Thomas's, Monmouth.

Small 8vo., attractively bound, gilt edges, 3s. 6d.,

WHAT ARE THE STARS?

A TREATISE ON ASTRONOMY.

For the Young.

By M. E. STOREY LYLE.

WITH ONE HUNDRED ENGRAVINGS.

A few copies only remain of this work, but a New Edition is in course of preparation.

LONDON: G. T. GOODWIN, 8, PATERNOSTER ROW.

www.ingramcontent.com/pod-product-compliance
Lightning Source LLC
Chambersburg PA
CBHW020939030726

47496CB00005B/1266